Thank you!

www. Pantapride.org

WITNESS

A CIVIL WAR THROUGH THE EYES OF A CHILD

Quanuquanei A. Karmue

SUGAR HILL
PUBLISHING

Photo Credits
Quanuquanei A. Karmue
Bong, County, Liberia, Dec 2008

SUGAR HILL
PUBLISHING

WITNESS: A CIVIL WAR THROUGH THE EYES OF A CHILD

ISBN: 978-0-9600329-4-5 (Hardcover)
ISBN: 9780960032914 (Paperback)
ISBN: 978-0-9600329-0-7 (ebook)

Designed by Karmue Media

Printed in Canada
This book was made possible with funding from NLightenment Media LLC
& Karmue Media LLC

To God!

Nothing I have ever done would be possible without His love and grace...

...you cannot change what you refuse to confront»»

To Mama
With gratitude...

And to the two million children who have been killed by conflict over the last decade; six million children who have been made homeless; 12 million children who have been injured or disabled; and the 300,000 child soldiers operating in 30 different conflicts across the globe.

Acknowledgement & Author's Note

Ever since I was a little boy, the microscopic fabric of my existence has been knitted and guarded with tremendous favor from the Almighty God. I have always been surrounded within a community of concerned Earth Angels who have served as life's guarding posts—signal markers along my diverse and complex life journey. My journey would have been brief if I did not have a hero of a mother, one that is a true Warrior Queen, an ambassador of courage and bravery. She is the epicenter of hope and transformation in our family.

Alongside every successful Queen is a King, my father: Fungbeh D. Karmue. He has been a rock and tremendous inspiration. Through his example, he shows how a man should live a good and Godly life.

I would also like to acknowledge my beautiful life-partner, my soulmate and bff—my wife Wendy Ekai Karmue. The blessings of the love I have for my mother trained me to care for strong women. My love and blessings grew when God brought this amazing woman into my life. She's the wind beneath my wings, a true partner who accommodates and supports my life-sized dreams.

And my four siblings, Nyempu Karmue-Hall, Kormahyah Karmue, Kulubah Karmue-Gbaa and Fungbeh B. Karmue: thank you for holding the circle of love and family unity strong! We have been through so much together.

When I started the journey to write the Witness Series, I knew the books had to serve a higher purpose than just recounting what I experienced and saw during the Liberian Civil War. I believe there is a tremendous level of responsibility and opportunity in telling this story from my eight-year-old perspective. I hope that it can serve a purpose far greater than I could ever imagine. Through this book and the ones to follow, I want to create a monumental memorial of the tragedies of the Liberian Civil War. I also want to put a face and identity to the millions of children and families who are the victims of the Liberian War and similar ones in other countries. I dedicate this book to all the refugees and the immigrants who themselves have also had to migrate from their beloved homelands. I want to bring light to what it takes to take refuge and build new lives in other countries because of war and atrocities in your own.

In order for my journey to be both fruitful and successful, I started the WITNESS Experience (WE). I invited one hundred distinguished individuals to participate in creating the book and building a wave of influence around it. The WE readers were tasked to read the draft manuscript and provide intricate feedback. There is value in the collective voices of people and from them, I learned a lot. I am using the knowledge to ensure the book becomes part of a meaningful experience that drives people to improve the world.

I would like to send a special acknowledgment to the WE readers. These readers accepted the responsibility to help support and guard WITNESS to completion. A special appreciation goes out to the Bancroft WE readers who have become more than just WE readers. After being part of the WITNESS Experience, they decided that reading WITNESS was not enough. This group of motivated students become trendsetters and establish the Save More Kids Ambassador Club at Bancroft School in Worcester, Massachusetts. They will be the first group that will visit Liberia through the WITNESS Experience Tourism Program. This is for readers who would like to take the experience right to Liberia.

Acknowledgement & Author's Note

On the journey of life, even Batman has a Robin. I would like to recognize my friend Crytal Andrus-Morissette for her tremendous support and for introducing me to my Robin, Jackie Brown. Jackie grabbed my draft manuscript and could not let go. Her belief in this story and the process has led to many sleepless nights of work and her faith-led contributions to the process.

I would also like to acknowledge Edwina Kumba McGill who has been relentless in her support for Save More Kids and the publication of this book. Edwina is a motivating spirit, a great advisor, and a strong advocate for the success of Witness and Save More Kids.

Many people have dreams that evaporate like moisture in the air. I know that not many people's dreams are nurtured into reality because, most-often, this requires funding. I want to acknowledge Dr. Keith Johnson and Kevin Johnson with NLightenment Media for not only believing that this story needs to be known but also for funding this effort. We aim to transform the world together.

Finally, I would like to recognize and acknowledge *you.* That's right, YOU, the reader who has dared to become a witness by reading this book. Thank you for picking up this copy of *Witness: A Civil War Through the Eyes of a Child.* Like the Bancroft Save More Kids Ambassadors, becoming a WITNESS is the first and most crucial step. After you read this book, the challenge for you is to take the experience on the road. Come with SaveMoreKids.org to see how, together, we can transform an entire nation: Liberia. Join the WE community online and continue the discussion. You can find us WitnessLiberia.com and @WitnessExperience on social media.

Content

PART III: *Terror. Survival. Death. Miracles*

PART IV: *Desperate. Abandoned. Faith. Freedom*

EPILOGUE: Troublemaker

ABOUT THE AUTHOR

PROLOGUE
Life in Paradise?

Bodies jostle and bump as my buddies try to distract me from shooting the ball. Dribble, dribble, dribble, shoot: the ball hits the backboard and sinks through rim. The ripped net is dripping grey strings.

"Yes!" I shout, smiling as I rush to take the ball from Zian, who has his back to me. Zian dribbles then pivots, circles, and blocks everyone from the ball. I rush, sweating and my shoes skid on the court's rough asphalt. The wind howls through the dilapidated three-story brick buildings surrounding the basketball court. I can see the puffs of my breath in the air.

"Fallou, *va!*" yells Zian, directing Fallou with his head. Fallou runs and we chase after. The ball sails over our heads and Fallou catches it.

"*Bon lancer!*" Fallou calls back, dribbling toward the net.

We speak all languages on this court today: French, English, even American.

"*Kpaah*, pass, pass!" I shout. I notice I am happy. "Here, bro!"

It is getting late. I have to leave soon, or my family will get worried. My sister will come looking for me. But I am on my game, and we so rarely get the court. Usually it's occupied by black Americans who don't let us join.

I see André on the sideline. He's a kid in my class who everyone calls Dray. He's with Conrad and three others I don't know. The first thing I notice are their cool red shoes. Jordans. I know not to even bother asking my father for those. Papa is already working two jobs to care for us all, and saving to move us away from this neighborhood. "You never know what will roll up on you in these corners," Papa reminds us on the rare times between jobs when we see him. We are under strict orders to stay put: in the house by six o'clock sharp with doors locked.

Dray is taller than me and he can palm the ball like a real NBA player. I hope he saw me get that hoop. He is always making fun of my accent in class, calling me names, making the whole class laugh with him. Sometimes, it is impossible not to hit back. Too often, lately. I have been fighting with him and with others. Papa would be so angry if he knew. But I never show him the notes my principal sends home.

I get the ball from Moses and take the shot where I stand. I miss.

Dray laughs. "Looka that African nigga! Us against yous." He is already on the court. His friends are stripping off their winter jackets to join him. I can see my friends are uneasy.

"Okay," I say as Zian grimly bounces the ball toward me. This time my shot goes straight through the rim. We celebrate, Moses pats my back, and we rush to our spots, emboldened. I see Conrad foul Zian hard, but Zian gets right back up in front of Conrad as Dray passes the ball. Zian is the shortest kid among us, but he's quick and strong. Sometimes we call him Midget Z, which he hates. Zian jumps and his outstretched arm intercepts Dray's pass. The ball is knocked in my direction. I race to secure it, and once again I shoot it right through the rim.

"You guys think you all that?" shouts Dray. "Dumb asses can't even speak English."

Dray maneuvers toward the net, Zian guarding him close. Dray is trying to fake him out, but once again Zian knocks the ball out of his hands. But when Zian goes to pass it, it goes out of bounds. Conrad gets it, and goes for a three pointer. He misses the basket, its our ball. We all run for it and I bump into Dray.

"Little nigga, who you think you messing with?" Dray whips out a gun, grey-black dulled metal. He raises it at me, inches from my forehead. I can feel the distance between it and my skin, as if a magnet is drawing it to me. My breath stops. I look straight past the gun and into Dray's eyes. I do not move.

"Quanei!" I hear Nyempu call. I hear the scuff of running, but I do not move. "Quanei!" she calls again.

I slowly back away to gather my knapsack, coat, and math book, never taking my eyes off Dray. My friends have scattered.

"African booty scratcher," he says smirking. He lowers the gun back to wherever it came from and skip-walks toward Conrad and the others. They take every ball, including ours, and disappear between the shadows of the high-rises, toward the high school.

I turn and walk to Nyempu, my sister. I am not sure how much she saw. She does not ask and I say nothing. We just walk quietly, dragging our feet, immersed in the sound of distant sirens, a sound so familiar it hardly registers unless loud enough to suggest trouble is too close. Together we walk the path lined with packed grey snow, through old two- and three-story brick tenements, each yardless and separated by dark, narrow passageways, musty and plastered with ugly dull graffiti I try not to look at. Old Sanchez Liquor Store is behind us as we head between the urine-splashed alleyway that will take us to building number 47, then up the stairs to Apartment 307.

In the dimness of my room, I think back to the room I shared with my brothers as I grew up. I think of how different it was to run around on grassed fields rather than the paved fields around me. If my eight-year-old self could see the paradise he imagined was America, he would not believe it. I think of that naive me as I lie down on my bed and rub the bruise on my forehead.. That eight-year-old-me with fancy new things, without worries, who could barge through neighbors' doors and re-

ceive welcoming smiles. That boy who would lie on his back beside friends he knew as well as his own heart, looking up at stars
too multifarious to count, knowing they were all his. The me of
high-walled immaculate schools—respected, not yet judged a troublemaker at a gang-filled inner-city school.

We had paradise once, far away. But it disappeared—poof.
Or more like a rat-a-tat-tat of automatic gunfire. Paradise disappeared into the metallic smell of blood, the nauseating funk of decaying bodies we numbly passed, walking barefoot mile after mile
seeking the next safe place, our stomachs nearly accustomed to the
ache of hunger.

My own life makes it possible to believe in horrors, having
lived through things that would make fake tough guys like Dray and
Conrad pee their pants. Survival replaced paradise. Now it's all
that's left, even here.

The America we dreamed of was not in Rhode Island, that is for
sure. But I still see it on television and in movies. Then I think Dray's
taunts and I want to hit everyone. My father says, study and you can
change anything. But I'm not sure. When he says this, I look away.
In my gut, I feel embarrassed for him.

In my bedroom, I change into my indoor clothes and sit on
my bed, blocking out the street noises and the I can barely hear the
TV in the next room. I doodle absently on a piece of lined paper.
When I look down, I see I have drawn the face of my mother.
I purposely add a coconut tree behind her, then another, just like
the ones I remember lining the streets of our village. Will paradise
ever come back for us? For me?

WITNESS

A CIVIL WAR THROUGH THE EYES OF A CHILD

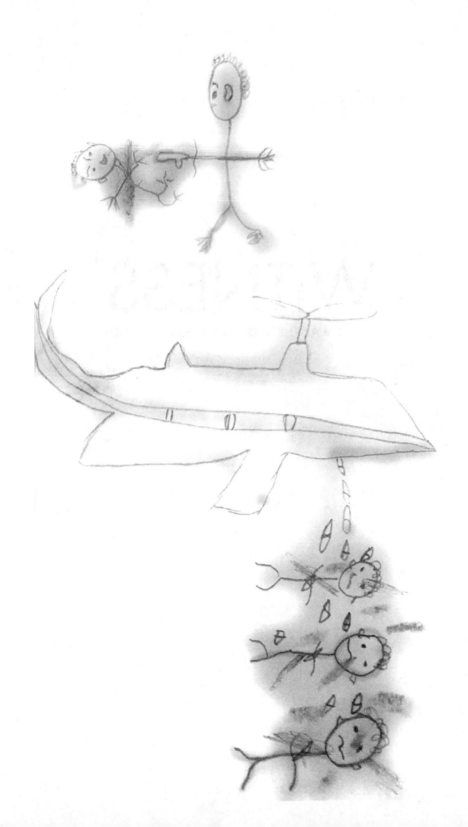

Part One

Light. Community. Confusion. Bloodshed.

*These are the things that I have witnessed
And this is how it all began*

*Art credited to Liberian children, survivors of war now living at Christ's Children
Orphanage Home on Sugar Hill, Liberia-September, 2010
WITNESS: IN PARTNERSHIP WITH SAVE MORE KIDS, INC*

1

Life in Paradise

Before December 1989

I am eight-years old. Mine is a world of sun-bathed African hills. Gorgeous palm trees sway freely over lazy afternoons, the wind carrying hushed adult gossip and children giggling from house to house. In this life, each home I enter is filled with joy, family, and love. Each home is kept peaceful by the discipline of honor. This is life in serene Sugar Hill in 1989. I am Quanuquanei Karmue, son of Fungbeh Alfred and Neyor Karmue. Quanei for short.

Our family is originally from Gharmue, a village in the tropical country of Liberia, on the west coast of Africa, rimmed by the North Atlantic Ocean. Mama says that my great-great Grandma Gbenjih was a beautiful and powerful queen who founded Gharmue Village. Its lush farmlands were passed down to us, generation after generation. Kormah, Nyempu, and Austin were born in Gharmue. Nyempu, my eldest sister, is ten. She learned to follow our tribal traditions, and knows that you never give an elder a glass of water without a saucer under it. She knows some of the secrets of the moon. Kormah may have learned the traditions I hear so much about, but he still needs lots of help with the discipline and honor bit. Maybe all he needs is more whippings from Papa. Austin is the third oldest. We share a room; he's pretty cool.

I was born in the new house that my parents built after Mama finished her studies. When I was born, Mama had already become a nurse in Phebe Hospital in Gbarnga City, and my parents had opened their first pharmacy. Before there was any of us, Mama said she and Papa passed this hill, 20 minute drive from the hospital. Papa told her, "One day I'm going to build a house up there." Mama replied, "There? In the middle of nowhere?" Papa nodded. Papa always does what he promises. They named the place Sugar Hill because, before it was ours, this land was once a sugarcane plantation. Also, Sugar Hill sounds like a nice place to live. And it is.

Of course, we are not the only family in Sugar Hill, which is one big family. Kids call all men "Uncle" and women "Auntie" even when they aren't your real ones. Though we had plenty of real ones. Grandpa Fungbeh had over fifty kids, or so I am told. Some of our real aunties and uncles live with us because they don't have homes of their own. With all the relatives plus honorary aunties and uncles, everyone knows everyone in Sugar Hill. You can't get away with anything. I still don't get why Kormah does what he does because it all gets back to Papa, and then Papa takes off his belt or makes Kormah get a switch from the tree.

I'm the quiet one, or so they think. You have to be quiet to hear all the secrets, the things adults say when they think no one is listening. Since Nyempu is the oldest, she watches out for us and sometimes helps Mama around the house. Nyempu helps with the smaller ones, like Kulubah, who is five years old, and Fungbeh, the baby. Papa calls Kulubah his "little Chuckubee." Fungbeh is barely two and gets all the attention now. Together, we are six kids, Mama and Papa, and about 20 relatives living together in our two-house hilltop compound.

My best friend, Boye, also lives in Sugar Hill and together we explore the world. From morning to night, we run from house to house, playing tag and hide-and-seek. When we aren't playing, we are spending our allowance on milk candy from an old lady who makes it fresh each week. When the sun goes down, there is no playing outside or inside, as it is so dark you can't see your own hand in front of your face. Until the sun comes up again, the only safe way to move around at night is with a lantern or candle. Sometimes at night, the grown-ups light a campfire and sit around talking about everything in the world. Whenever this happens, Kormah, Austin, Boye, and I lie in the grass just a few feet away, listening and looking up at the stars.

Most of the children here go to Sugar Hill Episcopal School, the public school in the community, but my siblings and I go to St. Martin's, a prestigious private school two miles up the road from home. It is the best school in Gbarnga City. Papa and Mama both work hard to send us all there—Mama as a nurse and Papa in agriculture at a company called BCADP. Papa says he and Mama want us to have the best education so that we can grow up and live the best lives. It seems that everyone in Sugar Hill knows how hard Papa works, even our teachers. They often tell us how they expect more of us because we are Mr. Karmue's children. Our uncles and aunts are always telling us the same thing, that we should appreciate how hard Mama and Papa work for us to have the "best life." Once, I asked Mama what all this meant and she told me a story of the history of the Liberian people.

Mama told me how many, many years ago, white Americans came to Liberia to steal people and make them slaves in America. Later, because they feared revolts from these slaves, the Americans allowed some Liberians to return home. Mama and Papa call these returned people "Americo-Liberians" and Mama explained that Americo-Liberians were believed to be better than regular Liberians. The Americo-Liberians believed it and so did regular Liberians. Regular Liberians tried to be as much like the Americo-Liberians as possible.

Some people, like Mama and Papa's parents, sent their children to live with America-Liberians, in hopes that they could get a better education. But along with their improved Western way of life, America-Liberians also brought with them the abusive mindset of slave owners. They often treated Liberian children like slaves. Mama and Papa had a terrible time living with America-Liberians. When they had their own money, Mama and Papa did not send us away. They were determined to provide us with a great education and a great life while keeping our family together—no matter what. Pride in their upbringing and in the rich heritage of the Gharmue Village caused them to have great respect for their own people and they longed to create communities where everyone had a chance to succeed. This was part of the reason my father built not one, but two brick houses atop Sugar Hill.

Most thought Papa was crazy to build brick houses when clay was thought to be more than good enough. But Papa felt the brick houses favored by the America-Liberians were better, more Western, more modern. He built the second house to make sure everyone had space, including house cleaners and help staff—some of whom were our relatives, too poor to live on their own.

I could see that my parents were unique creatures in our area. In a culture where people are accustomed to doing just enough to get by, Mama and Papa have always pushed harder to break the mold of what was possible and to create magnificent lives for us. After hearing stories of how they grew up, I could understand why Mama and Papa work so hard for us and everyone around us. They want us to do bigger things and live lives of greatness. They want us to be like Americans.

The Wealth of Liberia is Real
Scan the QR-Code or navigate to the link and click on Ch.1 to watch
a short video about the wealth and beauty of Liberia.

www.resources.witnessliberia.com

2

Catching Light

Opening my eyes in the morning is always the hardest thing for me. My head feels like a boulder as I try to sit up, my arms and legs are heavy as logs. But I manage to slide out of bed and set my feet on the cold cement floor. This usually zaps me fully awake and in no time, I am skipping across the cool floor and out of my room.

As I walk toward the bathroom, I hear Mama and Papa talking. The warmth of their low voices draws me toward them—silently, so they don't stop talking. Of all her children, Mama says I am the most curious. We all agree that Nyempu is the most responsible and sensible, Kormah is the naughty one, and Austin, smack dab in the middle of all our personalities, is the kindest. I don't often misbehave, but I am curious about everything and everyone. Kulubah and Fungbeh are too young to be real people. They are cute with chubby cheeks and when Fungbeh is older I will teach him all the tricks I know.

This morning I find myself inching closer to Mama and Papa's door. Because it's still early and the others are sleeping,

I can hear clearly. I love Papa's voice. Its deep tone carries so much power, even when he's speaking quietly. To me, he is the strongest, smartest man in the world. Outside my parent's room, I think I hear Papa say he is going to go buy light and bring it to the house. My heart races a little and my ears perk up. I scrunch my nose as I try to understand. Did Papa say that he is going to buy light? Why would someone buy light when we have light, outside, from God? Mama told me that all light—even the big and powerful sun—comes from God. I am listening now, not moving, barely breathing, straining to hear what either will say next. Finally, I peek around the corner into their room. I can see Fungbeh sleeping, and I know Mama and Papa are speaking in hushed voices to not wake him up. This talk of "bringing light to Sugar Hill" makes no sense. I know that light comes from God and we already have it—I can see light coming into the house through the windows. So where is Papa getting the other light, I wonder. Finally, I can't take it anymore and push open their already cracked door to make my presence known.

"Good morning, Mama and Papa," I say, interrupting. I can see Mama smiling at me, her eyes running over me in my favorite pajamas. Even in the early morning, Mama is the most beautiful woman I know. Her almond shaped eyes and pretty brown skin seem to glitter in the new light. The gap between her teeth is her special beauty, I think. Both Mama and Papa are used to my curious way of bursting into morning conversations, so my eavesdropping is no surprise to them.

"Good morning, Quanei," Mama smiles at me. The mixture of her sweet perfume and my father's earthly smell make me feel wrapped in love.

I blurt out, "Did Papa say he is going to buy light?" I look back and forth between them. Mama is smiling, Papa is sleepily running his hand over his face to see if Mama will take the chance to answer me first. Mama nods Papa back to me.

"No, son—I mean, yes, son," Papa says. "But Mama and Papa will have to buy the light to bring to the house."

Papa is the smartest man I know, so I don't say anything for a moment to try to give my brain time to catch up with his.

"So," I say, creeping further into their room. "You are going get light? For us? From God? Because that is where light comes from, Papa."

"Yes, son," Papa tells me. "And no."

"You have to buy the light from God," I press. "Well, where does He sell it? Have you talked to Him?"

Mama chuckles and smiles at me with a little mischief in her eye, letting me know that she is staying out of the conversation.

"No son," Papa says. "You get the lights from a company called LEC and they bring the lights to the house."

I climb up on their bed. What Papa said doesn't make anything clearer. "But I thought you said we get light from God," I continue. "Does LEC get lights from God?" This is what I need to know.

"Lize!" Dad calls to Mama using her nickname. He gives her a quick pleading look.

"Son," Mama says, "we are getting electricity so that we can turn on the globes on the ceilings." She points to the light fixtures above us. "You see, all the globes around the house are like little moons or lamps. Once LEC brings the electricity, they will light up and you will see better at night."

Who is LEC? I wonder. And do they know God? Do they work with Him? Talk to Him? Are they talking to God for Papa?

"Son," Papa says in his reassuring voice. "Don't worry. You will see. Now," he says in his time to get things done voice, "I have to use the bathroom. You have to get ready for school. It's too early for all of your questions, Quanei."

"Oh, Alfred," Mama says, pulling me into her arms. "Don't give him a hard time. Quanei is our curious baby. He wants to know everything, and this is good."

Mama chuckles again when Papa's head wobbles as he crawls out of bed, then stomps his way to the hall bathroom. As I watch him go, I am suddenly filled with wonder and excitement—and with many questions that I immediately ask Mama. Mama takes a moment and explains it to me again and soon pride mixed with awe wells up inside me. I realize that although I have no idea how, my own father, the greatest man I know, is somehow going to get light from God and bring it to Sugar Hill.

As soon as I get back to my room, I share this exciting news with Kormah and Austin. We discuss Papa bringing this light while getting ready for school. We get so caught up in our conversation that Mama has to tell us several times to stay on task or else we will be late for school. When we are all finally ready, Kormah, Austin, Nyempu, and I head outside.

"C'mon Quanei," Kormah says. I am always a little behind them. They are taller and bigger than me, but when I hurry, I can keep up.

"I'm coming!" I say, as I catch up and we start down the hill.

The fresh morning air fills our lungs and the ground crunches beneath our feet as we walk the dusty gravel road to school. We hear families getting ready in their homes and roosters crowing. The smell of fresh mangos makes my mouth water. Though I've already had breakfast, I crave something sweet like sugar donuts or milk candy. In our green and white St. Martin's uniforms, we are eager to tell our school friends about the light my father is getting for our house. Boye does not go to my school so I will have to tell him about the light later.

My brother keeps my attention as we walk. Kormah is giving us a list of who he will tell about the light. I picture him boasting to a crowd, talking fast and loud. Kormah's way of doing things often gets him in trouble. He always manages to annoy our teachers. Papa, never taking Kormah's misbehaving lightly, whips him good, but Kormah is always back in trouble the very next day. I hope the excitement of the light doesn't cause Kormah to get out of hand because this is starting off to be a very good day.

St. Martin's sits hidden behind by a brick wall surrounding the entire campus. You must enter through a big metal gate, which

I imagine as the mouth of a big dragon. We all hurry because no one ever wants to be late at St. Martin's. The day starts with a big assembly where we say the Liberian pledge of allegiance and salute the flag, and everyone can see if you walk in late. St. Martin's is very strict and lateness brings shame and punishment.

This is my first year at St. Martin's. I started elementary school at Sugar Hill Episcopal, but I received a double promotion—moving up a grade twice within one year. There is an American missionary family, the Robinsons, who make St. Martin's even more special and prestigious simply because they chose us. Of all the children at St. Martin's, I would say my siblings and I are the most like the Robinsons. Mama and Papa have raised us with a lot of American influence. We speak proper English at home and out and about, but sometimes with family or other Liberians, we speak our native dialect. I have seen Mama and Papa do this many times. When Papa is doing business, he sounds proper; yet in the next moment he sounds like a countryman in conversation with a friend. Mama is the same way, and we kids have picked up their ability to change our speech.

I have never been to America. No one I know has been there. But everyone in Liberia has grand thoughts about what America must be like. Our country's capital, Monrovia, is the biggest place I have ever seen. I imagine America is as special as heaven. I imagine America must be like a million Monrovias put together. Although no one says it, everyone sees the Robinsons as royalty because they are from America. They show up every day in their shiny car, and sometimes as I watch them drive off, I wonder what kind of spectacular life they must have, and what kind of life they once had in America.

I may not be as big and important as the Americans at St. Martin's, but I still know what is expected of me: to work hard, pay attention, and stay out of trouble. Today this is especially difficult because I am so excited about Papa's light. I don't get a chance to tell Boye about the light until that evening when he and I are playing in the field near our compound. The fireflies are just starting to creep out. Boye and I are trying to catch them when I tell him.

"Boye," I say, as we are closing in on the little creatures. "Papa says that people named LEC are bringing light to our compound next week." We are creeping around near the sweet flowering bushes that fence our compound.

"I know," Boye says. He focuses on a firefly that has just landed on leaf.

My eyes grow huge. "Well, that's the thing," I tell him, "I don't understand—even the fireflies bring us light at night. Why do we—"

"Shhh, shhh," Boye interrupts, waving his hands for me to be quiet as he tiptoes into position to grab a firefly.

"Ah, oh! I got it, Quanei!" he cheers. His eyes lock on mine in amazement.

"Aye yah, kpaah! Let me see, yah?" I come closer as Boye keeps his fingertip tight against his palm, trapping the firefly inside.

"Kpaah, let me see. Did you kill it?" I ask when I notice the firefly has stopped glowing.

Boye leans in closer to make sure. He grips his fingers tightly, the black skin of his hands blending in with the darkness. All of a sudden, a sliver of light comes through his dark skin, illuminating the blood vessels in his palm.

"Look, man! It's flashing again, kpaah," Boye laughs.

I lift my head and notice a million fireflies across the dark sky, and imagine all of them clumped in a single ball, creating one giant sphere of light. Maybe that would be enough to light up all of Sugar Hill.

"I know about your Papa and the light, Quanei," Boye tells me. "Uncle Karmue came to my house and I heard him talking to my Pa about it."

"Why do we need light anyways, Boye?" I say. "Look at this. We have all this light out here." I smile at the fireflies lighting up the sky. "But Mama says this new light will be very good for all of us."

Boye plops down on the grass and lets out a sigh. He turns to look at me. "Well, when your Pa came to my house the other day, I think he was telling my Ma and Pa about the same thing. But my Pa said that we not used to light so he not getting light to our house."

I plop down beside Boye and think about this for a moment. I have heard something like this at my house among Mama, Papa, my aunts and uncles. Sometimes, I hear them say that people on Sugar Hill are "backwards thinking." No matter how stubborn or backwards they may be, I can't imagine anyone not wanting to have the kind of light Mama and Papa described.

"I been thinking about how real light will look like, Quanei," Boye says, interrupting my thoughts. "But I guess we will just have to wait and see."

We lie on our backs on the damp courtyard grass, staring up as the stars begin to appear like diamonds.

"Quanei, you think your light will be better than this?" Boye asks.

"I don't know," I tell him. "But I wonder if the Night-Night things will still talk to us when Papa brings the light."

The Night-Night things are what Boye and I call the creatures that come out at night, the ones that we can hear but not see. When the sun drops behind St. John's River and daylight vanishes, when everyone in our compound is asleep, I lie awake in my dark room looking at the moonlight through my screen window. I listen with all my might to the mysterious world of the Night-Night things. I listen to their invisible universe that comes alive in darkness while others sleep.

"Maybe the Night-Night things will come to see the light too," Boye says. "Maybe they know about it and will come out to see it. We will just have to wait and see."

That night I can't sleep, so I sneak into the hallway and overhear my parents discussing light again. I enter their room and plop on their bed. Mama takes this as an opportunity to tell me that when the men come and set up the lights, we are going to invite everyone in Sugar Hill to see.

"So, we are going to have a light party here?" I grin as her warm eyes meet mine.

"Well, I guess you can call it that," Mama says. "Everyone is going to want to see it, so yes, we are having a light party tomorrow. We hope when they see it, they will be convinced to get their own lights."

"Tomorrow!"

"Yes, Quanei," she laughs. "LEC is coming to bring the light tomorrow and we are going to have a light party."

"Tomorrow!" I exclaim again.

It was almost too exciting to think about. So much pride and excitement swell up inside me that I think I may just flip over backwards. Instead, I get up and dance in circles right in the middle of my parent's room.

After school the next day, Kormah, Austin, Nyempu and I can hardly hold in our excitement walking home. They have all been telling their friends about the light party and it seems as if everyone at school and throughout Sugar Hill knows about the light now. When we get home, Mama tells us to change our clothes quickly and go play. And to be sure to stay out of the way of the men who will be working on the light.

I find Elijah and Tito and tell them that I'm planning on having a light party on the hill at my house because Papa is bringing us our very own light. My friends get excited too. They also tell me that Papa visited their parents about getting light. And just like Boye's father, their parents also insisted that they "don't need no light."

"It's okay," I tell them happily. "You can come to my house every night to see the light if you want to. We can stay up all night and look at it."

Later that evening, it seems as if every child in Sugar Hill is sitting in the grass watching our house, waiting for the light to come on. As the sun finally begins to fall, we start to get weary and agitated. It is taking too long and, after a while, my eyelids begin to get heavy. I slowly drift off into a nap. I must have been asleep a while because when I wake up, I hear voices—familiar ones in the distance. It sounds like Uncle Wallace, Uncle Paye, Auntie Mary, Mr. Jackson, Mama, and Papa. Still sleepy, I peek open my eyes and lift my head to see what is going on. My eyes open fully to see a glimmer of light running across the grass in front of me.

Is it still nighttime or is it morning? I wonder as I follow the gleam toward the house. And then I see it. Light. All around and inside my house. I sit up in disbelief. Sleep leaves my body like a thief running for his life. I am wide awake and my heart is racing.

"Kormah! Elijah! Kpaah, the light on!" I exclaim.

"Yeh!" Elijah says.

"The light on?" I ask again in disbelief.

"The light on!" Kormah answers, hopping up.

"Yah, the light on!"

I prop myself on my elbows in the grass, in awe. It is night but our whole compound looks like daytime. There is light everywhere.

I get up with everyone else and start running toward the glow. Sand and dust kick up on the path as my feet carry me as fast as I can go. As I make my way to the door, I see nothing but light. Light is everywhere, not just in the dim lantern I am used to, but a real light that is everywhere. This light is bright and white gold and just there. As I walk through my house, I whip my head around to find whatever giant lantern could provide this much light, but all I see is a bulb hanging from the ceiling. I am mesmerized. My siblings and most of our friends are here too, standing with their faces and white teeth lit by the single bulb, admiring the light in disbelief. The house is filled with people and excitement.

All of Sugar Hill seems to be at our compound tonight. Everybody has come to see the light on top of the hill. I want to hug Papa and Mama for bringing our new light. I slip around the crowd of grownups' legs to find Papa. He is surrounded by people. I wrap my skinny arms around as much of his hips as I can hug. Papa lifts me atop his shoulders, just like he did when he walked me to elementary school at the bottom of Sugar Hill. I let out a laugh, happy and proud to be atop his shoulders and atop Sugar Hill in this moment. Up here, I can see the top of every head. I can see everyone at our light party. Up here, I am so close to the light.

I can see how far back the light has pushed the black pillow of night, all the way past the flowering bushes and against the shadows of the plum trees. Across the courtyard, I see shadows moving fast like giant birds. At first, I am frightened, not knowing what could be flying in the black sky so near our home. I quickly motion to Papa to let me down from his shoulders. Then I run to get closer to these shadows, trying to see where they are coming from. My eyes follow the shadows into the sky, but they are too quick and I cannot see what is making them They must be the Night-Night things! I am even more frightened so I run and get Boye and Elijah. I point to the sky and whisper, "Kpaah, looka dat thing flying there." I try to point out the flying object in the shadows. They stand watching and looking around to see where it is coming from.

"Oh!" said Boye.

"Kpaah, you think dey are da Night-Night things making da noise at night?" I ask him.

Boye looks at me with wide eyes, a little frightened. "Yeah, I tink dey can be look'n at us from the sky too."

The light had brought the Night-Night things right to our house, to our Light Party, where all of Sugar Hill is laughing with joy. The whole compound is glowing, and the glow is upon everyone's face—a luminance that feels like it could drive any bad thing a million miles away.

Electracity Awareness in Africa

Night-Night Things Art

Use the QR-Code or the link to navigate to Ch.2 for a chance to own your own Night-Night Things Art and contribute to bringing lights to villages in Africa.

www.resources.witnessliberia.com

3

The Ride of a Lifetime

S oon after we get light at our house, other families begin to get lights in theirs. Once Papa brings the poles to the community, all they have to do is pay to wire their house and buy the bulbs. Soon, light becomes contagious. It isn't long before electric lines run like webs from light poles to our neighbors' small mud and brick houses. Little by little, everyone receives light on Sugar Hill. Even though Papa has made the biggest sacrifice, he doesn't mind because his dream is to make Sugar Hill and the surrounding area an abundant community.

Whereas just a few weeks ago, all this light had been considered impossible, now it is just a matter of doing. It amazes me how people's beliefs can change just by witnessing. One day something is impossible. Then you see it and boom—suddenly you can do it too. It is magic to me, how one person can wholly change others' beliefs and actions just by painting them a new picture. This is what Papa has done for our community.

I wonder what makes Mama and Papa so special that they can see things others cannot. I wonder what else out there we are simply unable to see right now. Who is in charge of looking for these new things or knowing what is possible? I think about all this and discuss it with Boye while we lie gazing at the stars. He doesn't know the answers either and that's okay for now. I'm sure with time I will know. When I ask Mama my questions, she says the thing Papa has is called "vision." She explains that vision is when you imagine how you want things for your life and for your family, and then you go to work to get it. Before bed, I ask God to give me vision so I can also know everything that is possible to achieve.

My father once tried to get his Sugar Hill neighbors to build a road. He told us stories about how he went door to door, just like for the light, trying to get everyone to build a road through our community. "We don't need a road, Mr. Karmue," they would say. "Why do we need a road, Mr. Karmue? We don't have cars." This has been the mentality of the people in Sugar Hill then, and my father is fixing that.

The first time I see the car, my siblings and I have just arrived home from school. I is about a year after we got the light. I am now nine years old. From the top of the hill, we see it, big and yellow, in front of the house. We are used to seeing cars, although we don't know anyone who owns one. Some of the white American missionary children at St. Martin's come to school in cars. Also, some of Papa's business friends have cars. We all look at the yellow car as we make our way into the house and then to our rooms to change. I wonder who has come here to see Mama for medicine or do business with Papa as I unbutton my school clothes and start my homework. After a while, I'm startled by my father's bellowing.

"Nyempu, Kormah, Austin, Quanei, Kulubah! Come here!"

I freeze. I know that tone. This is how Papa calls us when he is really mad. Oh no. I try to think of what I could have done. It is probably Kormah, and now he is getting us all in trouble! When Papa call us like this, his voice fills the whole house and comes right up to my face, no matter where I am. I look at Austin and he looks at me, and we start to move toward the door together. I just hope we don't get a whipping.

We all go to the living room where Mama and Papa are standing, straight-faced, watching us file in. We stand before them, silent as mice, waiting for them to say something.

"Come outside," Papa says sharply. "All of you. Now." He heads to the door without another word.

Is he going to whip us all outside? My legs can hardly move as I force myself forward, following everyone outside. I look at Nyempu, trying to figure what is going on. Outside, we line up facing our parents. The big yellow car is still there, but right now that is the last thing on my mind. I look at Kormah. He looks scared too.

"Now," my father says. "I need to tell you. . ." He pauses. Even the wind seems to wait for him to speak. Then he lifts his hands in a big sweeping gesture toward the car and breaks into a grin. "This is our car!"

Our stiff silence erupts into roaring. I am screaming. I am jumping in disbelief, my eyes trying to take in Papa, the car, and Mama all at once. Kormah is shrieking, Nyempu is shrieking, Kulubah is shrieking, and Papa and Mama are laughing. In seconds, I am running down the hill, legs flying through the grass then onto the village's one dusty gravel road.

"Boye!" I am trying to scream so loud he will hear me from wherever he is. My brothers and sisters are all screaming and running too. My heart is pounding with so much excitement I can barely breathe. "We have a car! We have a car!"

By this point, we have attracted so much attention that people are peering outside. I get to Boye's house and push the door wide open. He appears before me looking excited and confused.

"Boye!" My excitement increases at the sight of his face.

"You have to come see! Now we have—" I am breathing hard and talking so fast he is even more confused.

"What is it, Quanei?" he asks, just as excited as me.

"Come!" I pull him outside. We run up the hill and the car comes into view.

"Oh, kpaah, is that your car?"

A happy laugh escapes me. "Yes!"

My brothers and sisters are back with their friends too. Others have come to admire our new addition. The excitement in the air is like buzzing bees all around. Everyone is oohing and aahing at the car. Boye's eyes are racing over the whole car, trying to take it in. I'm doing the same. Everything about the car seems so shiny and clean. The yellow sun is beaming down, making it gleam like a bolt of lightning sitting right in our yard. I slide my hands along the car. The metal is smooth and hot against my palm. I slide my hand up to the bright red taillight sitting perfectly in its little corner. The black wheels sturdily hold up the big machine. I am in awe. The fact that we, the Karmues, now have a car is almost too much for me to take in. I am used to our doing and having things others do not, but a car is for people who are really big and important. And this car is ours. People from all over the community come up, touching the car and asking questions. I look up at Papa and Mama. Once again, they are my heroes.

At night, after the people have gone and the commotion has calmed, I lie in bed, hardly able to sleep for thinking about the car. Papa has told us that tomorrow he will take us to school in the car. I'm thinking of how amazing it will be for us to ride in the car tomorrow. We have a car. I want so badly to tiptoe to a window and look at the car. I imagine it sitting there by itself, all shiny and nice, and I can hardly wait until we can ride in it.

The next morning, we cannot contain ourselves, rushing get ready for school and choosing where we want to sit.

"It's time to go!" Papa calls.

We rip through the house and out the front door like a pack of hyenas. I feel we are the luckiest people in the world. The car is still there and we scramble in, the smell of the new black leather seats filling the air as soon as we open the door. We all push and pull. Austin's hand is on my back. He is stronger than me and gets in first. Nyempu runs around and gets in on the other side. "Oooh, I get to sit by the window!" she says.

"Aye, no, I sit in the front!" Kormah snaps. "I'm dah oldest one here anyways."

"No, you're not!" Nyempu shouts back.

"Yea, I am!" Kormah argues, even though he knows he's not the oldest.

"No, you are not!" Nyempu says firmly.

"Yes, I am!" Kormah stretches his eyes wide and gets close to Nyempu's face.

"No, you're not!" This time Kormah knows he's gotten under Nyempu's skin.

"Okay, that's enough!" Papa's strong voice stops them.

"This is how it is going to be," Papa says. "Quanei, you are in the middle. Nyempu and Austin, you at each of the doors, Kormah, sit between Austin and Quanei. And no more fighting!"

I get into the middle, feeling excitement all around me. Papa walks around inspecting the car. He gets in, sticks the key in the ignition, and the car roars to life like a lion. Yes, our shiny yellow car is our personal lion roaring through the streets, carrying our family on its strong back. I look through the window at Sugar Hill and feel like a king. I notice all the shiny important-looking knobs on the dashboard. In this car, I feel like we can fly. I feel like I can do anything.

The car rolls and bumps, and I notice Papa switching gears and steering. I am so impressed with him. Driving a car must be hard work for serious people. My sisters and brothers are chattering away as I turn my head and watch the trees, fields, and houses gliding past now. This is nothing like when we walk to school, when everything just stands still around us. We are zipping forward, and it looks like everything else is too. I try to keep up as we move faster and faster. In no time, the grand campus of St. Martin's come into view. I catch Papa's eye in the rearview mirror. I can tell he is happy to be dropping us off at school today, and at how much fun we are having. As we pull up, Papa does a full circle around the big fountain. I can see people staring at us.

We are all so proud of our new car and it shows as we get out. We hold our heads up high, our eyes are gleaming as we run inside. All day people ask about our car and we are happy to tell them it is ours. Usually, I try not to talk and fidget so much in class, but I am so happy that I can't contain myself. Even the risk of getting in trouble at a school as strict as St. Martin's cannot ruin this day.

Scan this code with a QR reader or use the link below to follow selected chapters for a more purposeful Witness Experience

www.resources.witnessliberia.com

4

Building Our Legacy

After Papa buys our car, life in Sugar Hill gets bigger and better. While we go to school during the year and play during the summer, Mama and Papa work hard. Mama becomes well known in the neigborhood treating people's ailment in our home after her nursing shifts. I watch nearby, fascinated. Mama always knows what everyone needs, whether for a severe headache or malaria. She even teaches Papa how to give shots so he can help when things got really busy. I love being with Mama, watching her make people better. Mama is so graceful that watching her work is like watching a magic show—her tools, tricks, clicks, lotions, potions, and miraculous pills making people well.

When Papa sees how many people come to the house to get treated by Mama, he decides that it would be better if she could sell medicine to the people herself, instead of sending them all the way to Phebe Hospital. So, Papa builds Mama her very own pharmacy right at the bottom of Sugar Hill.

Papa takes regular trips by himself to Monrovia, but now that we have a car, we can all go too. We are going today and we are all too excited to keep still. We talk of all we will do when we get to the big city.

"Mama says we can get ice cream in Monrovia," I tell Austin.

"Yes, kpaah," he says. "And we are going to get new shoes, too!"

The car starts, and we are on our way. Mama and Papa have already told us that Monrovia is far away, that we'll be in the car for three hours, but I don't care. I am just excited to be in the car with everyone. Since I am sitting in the middle, I can see everything ahead and watch what Papa is doing. The two-lane highway is dotted with yellow lines in the middle. We are behind a red station wagon whose driver has noticed Papa closing in on his bumper. I see the other driver adjust his rearview mirror. There is another car in the distance coming toward us. Kormah sees it too. I can feel Kormah is anxious to say something. We are moving faster than the car in front and eventually will need to pass.

"Papa, race him!" Kormah calls. "Go around! Go around!" He pumps his fist in the air, wanting Papa to play chicken with the oncoming driver.

"Go around?" Papa asks, looking at us in the review.

Before he even finishes talking, Mama interrupts: "No, no! Alfred, you wait until the other car passes!"

"Go around, Papa!" Kormah urges.

"Yea! Go around!" Austin adds. Nyempu and I join in and now we are all chanting "Go around, go around." In the mirror, I can see the gleam of mischief in Papa's eyes.

"Going around!" Papa announces and presses the car hard. The car launches forward as Papa starts to go around the other driver.

"No!' Mama cries. "Alfred, wait!"

Our car pulls forward and suddenly we are racing like in Arabian Nights, faster, and faster, then flying like a bird. Mama is protesting but Papa is laughing and we are cheering him on. Papa passes the car with a swoosh, just in time to miss the other car speeding directly at us. We are squealing with excitement.

"Yay, Papa!" I exclaim.

"That was good?" he asks, noticing Mama's disapproval. For some reason, her expression makes the game all the more fun, and when the next car comes, Papa races to pass again, with us cheering him on from the back. To see Papa joking with Mama makes me warm and happy inside. As we ride to Monrovia, I am happy as any boy could ever be. Papa, Mama, my brothers and sisters all together and daring to cheat death. Little did we know that disaster was preparing to meet us as quickly as those oncoming cars.

5

Rumors and Whispers

Early December, 1989

Life in Sugar Hill keeps getting better and better. Our family is happy, our family's businesses is growing, and so is our community. Mama and Papa continue to work hard and now have several pharmacies to run. Although I don't know exactly what Papa does all day, I do know it must be special and important because he always goes to Monrovia and other big towns for his business trips.

One Friday, Boye and I go out to catch frogs and chase birds near a swamp at the bottom of the hill behind Mr. Jackson's house. I have seen our dog catch a bird, but they are too fast for me or Boye. I can get close to the little ones, but just when I am ready to pounce, they fly off. I decide that if Boye and I work together, maybe we'll catch a bird or a frog today.

I watch Boye closing in on a tiny bird when the warm tones of grown up voices reach me. Their sounds are heated, as if debating something. I look at Boye and see that our bird has flown off. Boye chases after it, but I follow the voices, which lead me near Old Man Jackson's house. I see Old Man Jackson on his porch with three neighbors, but none of them can see me. I am thrilled to be spying on grown people, it makes me feel like I have secret powers. I creep closer to hear what they are saying.

"I promise you!" Old Man Jackson exclaims. "War is coming to Liberia, ooh."

When I hear the word "war" I am intrigued. I have heard many whispers about our government, war, and rebels, but it is not something Mama or Papa let us discuss. They don't allow such talk in the house. I take a few more steps forward to hear Old Man Jackson better.

"Charles Taylor has become a powerful man," he continues. "Look at what he has done already, starting this revolution. I am hearing stories about his rebels coming into Liberian towns from behind Nimba, recruiting people to take over the government— just like President Doe took over in 1980!"

"Papay, old man, that is crazy," replies one of the neighbors. I take a peek. It is Uncle Peter Ezra, a man, around Papa's age. "I have heard all about this Charles Taylor. He calls himself a freedom fighter, fighting against a corrupt government. But they cannot take over the government. All of this so-called war talk is pointless! Doe has the backing of the Americans. These rebels will never come into power."

"Do you really think that the Americans want President Doe to stay in power?" Old Man Jackson asks. "Just think about it, okay? President Doe staged a coup to take over Liberia in 1980 and had the full support of the American government. Doe allows the American's to do their business here and lets them do whatever foreign trading they need. Then, all of a sudden Doe gets greedy and decides to change the game on the Americans and his own people.

"Now, pay attention to this: Charles Taylor used to be Doe's second in command, but then he breaks away from Doe. You know why? Because he sees what a greedy man Doe has become. Taylor goes to America and gets arrested for whatever crimes they come up with. Then, just as soon as Doe cuts the Americans out of all these foreign deals, Charles Taylor miraculously escapes the American prison and just magically shows up back in Liberia? And he has enough money and guns to take down Doe and replace him? Do you really think that is a coincidence? Do you really think that the Americans do not know what is going on? Why do you think they have not yet intervened to help Doe if we are their ally and sister country?"

"Old Man Jackson, you have lost your mind," Uncle Peter Ezra. "That is a conspiracy theory. Charles Taylor and his rebels are just greedy men who want power. Trust me, President Doe has power behind him with America."

"Well, how do you explain Charles Taylor just showing up here like that? If you don't believe me, just watch what happens. I guarantee you that as time goes on, even if our country is falling apart, the Americans will find a way to make sure that their businesses go untouched! They will probably find a way to make deals with the rebels for protection or something, so they can keep bringing their money in while we all die!"

A woman speaks up. "I believe Old Man Jackson. The rebels are slowly taking over. They are going to bring war to Liberia! We are already at war. People are being killed on the border every day."

"Oooh she is right, my people," Old Man Jackson says. "I have heard terrible stories about rebels killing people in villages near Nimba County, especially people working in the government and tribal people related to the president. People saying these rebels are bad pekens, ooh. They vex like nobody business. They will stop at nothing!"

"The president needs to go anyway because he's corrupt," someone says. "Look at how he came to power—through corruption! Look how he treats his people. This is why these rebels are creating this war. This why people follow Charles Taylor and he has become a great man in Nimba County. Because President Doe is corrupt and tormenting people in this country every day! He is the reason for the rebels. He is putting us all in danger."

Another neighbor jumps in. "How can he be putting us in danger if he is supported by America? They are a great country.

And they support Doe. Or at least they seem to support Doe. But now when I think about it all, I don't know whose side they are on."

"Americans are not being killed by angry rebels led by a smart and powerful Charles Taylor," says Old Man Johnson. "Charles Taylor has become a legend here. He is bold, and he does not care about Doe—only wants to kill him and take power. He is bold enough to broadcast messages on Doe's airwaves. Taylor commands an army of rebels more vicious than anything we know. I am telling you this is what America wants. They want someone like Charles Taylor who can take over. He and his rebel army have already taken over the weak areas in our country. My sister had to leave her home to escape the rebels the other day. They are growing in numbers and getting the small children to join them too. It is on the news every night."

"Then our government will squash them out!" cries Uncle Peter Ezra.

"How?" Old Man Jackson throws his hands toward the sky. "How can he squash them out when they are everyday people like us? They do not wear uniforms. They do not march in the streets. They are country people, you hear? Farmers—men and boys. They look like you and me. How can Doe know who is who? I hear girls are joining them too! This is why we are in trouble, my people."

I hear a twig snap behind me. I jump and cover my mouth at the same time. I don't want to give myself away. But the twig-snapper is just Boye.

"Come on, Quanei," he crouches down with me. He knows what I am doing but does not understand my love of the spy game. He is ready to go to our next adventure. "Let's go. Big people are so boring and my papa says Old Man Johnson is a fool and drinks too much palm wine". He tugs at my t-shirt and stands up. I pull him down quickly, relieved that the grown ups did not see him.

"Careful!" I snap. I am reluctant to leave, but I know Boye's twitching and loud whispers will get us in trouble.

We creep away. Soon we are running, racing, both of us are breathing heavily. One day I will beat Boye, I think as he pulls in front of me. I pump my arms faster and reach out to tap his shoulder.

"You're it!" I call, laughing and I spin in another direction. Now Boye is chasing me and all thoughts of guns, dangerous Does, and powerful Taylors vanish. I laugh and run into Boye's yard, running under clothes hanging on the line.

"Ka kpla te ma, nuta a pa wulleh!" *Stop that right now or someone will cry!* yells Boye's mother and we stop for a moment and look at each other. Boye touches my shoulder and off we run. I am "it" again.

6

America, America

The next day is a lazy Saturday. All morning we mill around the house, each doing our own thing. I am in my room playing jacks with Austin and Kormah when Mama and Papa call us into the living room. I can tell that we are not in trouble.

"Come on." Austin pushes himself up from the floor.

"I'm coming!" I say. I am the last to enter the living room.

"Come in, Quanei," Papa says, waving me along. "Have a seat, all of you."

Like little sheep, we happily make our way to the couch. The smell of milk candy has entered the room and I know that Ms. Mary is making a fresh batch. I lick my lips and plan to get some with Boye. I wiggle between Nyempu and Kormah. Mama and Papa sit across from us in two chairs, patient looks on their faces as we all settle in. Fungbeh sits on Mama's lap. Austin is the last to find his seat, and Nyempu pulls Kulubah into her lap with a quick, sweet squeeze before turning her full attention to Mama and Papa.

"Now that we have you all in one place," Papa says, "we have some news."

I look from Mama to Papa and back again wondering if it is another new car. Or a TV, or a trip to Monrovia again. Maybe we are getting another dog!

"Well, Lize?" Papa says with a smile on the edge of his lips. "Do you want to tell them?"

All of our heads shift in unison back to Mama. I want her to hurry and tell us.

"What is it, Mama?" Kormah blurts out.

"Well, children," Mama takes a deep breath and looks at all of us. "Your father. . ."

I am about to fall out of my seat. My eyes are fixed on Mama, who suddenly breaks out in a grin and spreads her arms wide. ". . . is going to America!"

I stare at Mama in shock. My eyes are as big as dinner saucers. I can't move. Papa smiles too, his deep dark eyes twinkling like stars.

"Really?" Nyempu asks, leaning forward with Kulubah. Nyempu's eyes are wide like mine and none of us have moved. My heart is pounding. It is as if someone has told us we are all angels directly from heaven, and all we can do is fight hard to take it in. I can feel happiness bubbling up as I try to know what I just heard. My stomach swarms with butterflies. I can barely breathe the air that dances all around us.

"What?" My voice is so small only I can hear it.

Papa can see we are all stunned. He lets out a quick laugh and grabs Mama's hand. "It's true! I am going on a business trip to America next week."

"Oh, my goodness, Papa!" Nyempu is the first to jump off the couch, tipping Kulubah off her lap. They both run to Papa. She throws her free arm around his neck as Kulubah clings onto Papa's right leg.

"Aye, PAPA!" Austin runs over too, hugging Papa on his other side.

Kormah high-fives me and does one of his MC Hammer dances. He cries, "We will be eating baked chicken, Quanei!"

I clasp my hands on either side of my face. Then it is true. Papa is going to America. I am so surprised I can barely stand it.

"Oh, Mama!" I say running to her. "I can't believe Papa is going to America!" I can hardly hear my own voice over the shrieks and squeals of everyone in the room.

"I know, Quanei," Mama says, squeezing me tight. "Yes, it is such great news."

"Yes, Mama, it is!"

I step back and look at her. Suddenly I'm breathing hard as if I have been running outside. "He is really going? To America? Papa?" I need to say the words over and over again to even receive them. Mama understands. She just smiles and nods her head.

Austin, Kormah, and I grab hands and start spinning fast so the room spins to match how we all feel.

"Papa is going to see the whole world from up there," Austin says. "America!"

None of us can contain our excitement. As we dance, I feel like I'm flying. Surely nothing is better than being in a family with a Papa who goes to America. I can hardly believe it, but at the same time, it feels right. Papa is an important businessman. Still, I never thought anyone I knew would ever go to America. I think of the Robinsons and realize that now we will be as great as they are. I don't know whether to stay here and jump up and down or go running through Sugar Hill screaming at the top of my lungs. I want to do everything all at once. My head fills with images of giant cities a thousand times better than Monrovia, where the sun glistens off the buildings like rays of gold. The people in America must be amazing and now Papa is going to be like them. In an instant, God has raised my own Papa and our family so high that we can touch the sky.

Once the excitement has calmed, I tug on Papa's arm with questions. We are all talking so fast I can barely understand what is coming out of my own mouth.

"When Papa? When are you going?"

"In just a few days, Quanei," he says. "Just a few days."

We have created such a commotion that our aunts and uncles have started to peek their heads in the door. In my heart, this day deserves a celebration that is bigger than a million light parties. I know America is real, but it has never occurred to me that it is a place that I or anyone I know can really go.

The rest of the evening is filled with talking about the amazing things America will bring us. That night I can hardly sleep. As I lie in the darkness, my mind is alive with visions of Papa walking around tall buildings in his best suit, looking sharp, riding in fancy cars that sparkle like sunlight on the ocean. I see him going in and out of giant palaces, talking with important people, doing his business and gathering great things to bring home to us.

We have been taught in history lessons that America is our sister country. Now that seems truer than ever. We are going to be like the Americans when Papa gets back. My friends in the city tease that the Karmue's have the nicest of everything, but now we are going to have the best. Clothes, shoes, the best of everything when Papa comes home. We are going to be like a whole new family. Or the same family, just better. I can't wait until school tomorrow because now I will be like the missionary children. Perhaps I will sit with them at lunch now. Talk with them. Invite them to our house, since we are now a part of America too.

I am getting sleepy but I am sure Austin and I will talk more about America tomorrow. I can't wait to tell Papa what I want him to bring me. I want him to go so bad that I imagine packing his things myself.

When I crack open my eyes the next morning, I still feel on top of the world. To be sure I had not been dreaming, I turn to Austin and Kormah, who are already talking about America.

"Is Papa really going to America?"

"Yes, Quanei! Yea!" They both respond with excitement.

Every day we talk and talk about America. I didn't know one person could talk about one thing so much. But I will never be tired of thinking or talking about America. One night,

Papa and Mama sit us down to tell us that he is leaving the next day. Mama is going to drive him to the airport while we are at school. We will see him in the morning, but when we get home, he will be gone. That is fine with me. I just want Papa to hurry and go to the most wonderful place in the world, though I do wish I could see him get out of the car and onto the airplane. I have never seen an airplane before, but I imagine it must be even better than our yellow car. Mama says they fly miles in the sky. I wonder if America is behind the stars or really close to heaven. This is how Papa will get to America and I beg him to tell me all about the airplane when he gets back.

Papa reminds all of us to behave, mind our mother, and do well in school while he is gone. We eagerly agree to be on our best behavior –– even Kormah. Had Papa been going anywhere else, I probably would have been sad. But we want our Papa to be a big businessman with his big briefcase, doing important things that would be good for our family. After all, Papa will be back in only two months to tell us all the wonderful things he has seen.

The next morning, we are all up early. I rush to get ready so I have time to see Papa before he leaves. When I go into his room, he is already dressed in his best suit. I think he is the best looking Papa in all of Liberia. There are three big suitcases on the bed. Two are closed. Mama is packing a few things into the last suitcase. I hug Papa. I have hugged him so many times in the past few days.

I am excited to tell all of my friends that my Papa really is going to America today. Nyempu, Kormah, Austin, and I are all buzzing in and out of our parents' room. When it's time to leave for school, we tell Papa goodbye and rush off to tell all of St. Martin's the good news.

"Papa is going to bring me American shoes," says Austin.

"If Papa is going to America then we must be like the rich people, right?" Kormah asks.

"Papa says he is going to bring me an American dress and shoes, plus pretty bows and other things for my hair," Nyempu says. "What do you think he will bring you?"

"Papa is going to fly over the ocean and land in America," I say, ignoring her question. I spread my arms and pretend to soar like a bird. "I wish I could see da airplane."

"Me too!" Austin agrees.

In school, I cannot concentrate. I know that Papa will get to America while I am at school. I try to focus, but I keep imagining Mama taking Papa to the airport in our big shiny car. I know Papa will be gone for two months. I know that something like this is a very, very big deal for our family. I know this trip means so many things I don't fully understand, but they will all be grand. All day I think about how our lives will be different now.

Scan this code with a QR reader or use the link below to follow selected chapters for a more purposeful Witness Experience

www.resources.witnessliberia.com

7

Change on the Horizon

Things in Sugar Hill do indeed change. Right after Papa leaves, I see our driver, Shi-Shi, leave with the car as he does every morning. Most days, he takes the car around the back of the compound to wash it, or gets gas in town. But a few hours later, I notice Mama walking through the compound asking our aunts and uncles when they last saw Shi-Shi. When I hear Mama's worried tone, I run outside to see that our car is still gone. My eyes grow wide as I take in the empty space. This is the longest the car has ever been gone without Mama or Papa in it. I wonder where Shi-Shi could be with our car. The look on Mama's face is starting to worry me. Uncle Thomas marches past me toward the main road and I know he is going to look for our car. This doesn't seem right. I run to tell Kormah and Austin what is happening.

"Aye, the car! It is gone!" I say. "It's true. Mama says Shi-Shi has run off with it and Uncle Thomas has gone to find it."

They stare at me for a moment before going to see for themselves. I follow behind.

"Oooh! Papa is going kill Shi-Shi for sure!" Kormah says.

"This is so bad," Austin says, peering out at where our car used to be. As the entire compound erupts with the news, I hope that Shi-Shi just brings our car back with a good explanation. The missing car keeps our attention all day. Every time I hear a door close, I stop and listen for any news. My heart keeps its own steady rhythm throughout the day, as if it too is waiting for an answer. Anytime I forget about the car, the quick steady beating of my heart reminds me that something is terribly wrong. By nightfall, it has become clear that the car is stolen and gone for good. Uncle Thomas returns and everyone gathers in the living room.

"I asked around," Uncle Thomas tells us. "Several people told me he was seen with the car, packing up and leaving town. It seems he has taken the car to try to help his family escape with all the rumors of rebels coming this way."

My ears perk up at the word rebels. I hear reports on the radio when the grownups are listening, and now I think about Old Man Jackson's words about the powerful Charles Taylor and his army of rebels. Was Shi-Shi so desperate to get away from the rebels? Does this mean we need to leave too?

Mama throws her arms up. "And why would Shi-Shi do something like this as soon his boss man leave?"

Mama is sitting on the couch with her mind on all things. I feel bad for her, that the car she and Papa worked so hard to bring to us is gone. The car Papa bought for us, our magnificent roaring lion and the pride of the community, is gone forever.

"How could he have done this?" Uncle George mutters. "Boss man gave him a job. A place to rest. And he steals from Alfred while his back is turned? Human being is so wicked. He takes this family's car to help his own family run away from the rebels. Shame on him!"

"I am so sorry, Ma Neyor," Aunt Cecilia says, sitting down next to her. "These rumors. This war. The fear is making people do some stupid things. Don't worry, Ma Neyor. Perhaps when Mr. Karmue comes back, we will get this all sorted out. Mr. Karmue will find him and get the car back, I'm sure."

"Not if I find him first," Uncle Thomas says as he storms out of the house.

I run over to hug Mama. Aunt Cecilia has said everything to Mama that I could ever want to say. I feel Mama's warm body against my face, and I slowly feel my heart steadying to its normal beat. Just being close to Mama makes everything calm down. Mama rubs a hand up and down my back and the butterflies go away too.

"It's okay, Mama," I tell her, even though I do not feel okay. I feel sad and hurt, but I don't want Mama to feel bad. "Auntie is right. Papa will get the car when he gets back, right?"

"I am not worried, baby," Mama says, patting my back. She turns to Aunt Cecilia. "We are fine. I am most upset because we will no longer have a car to help those in the community. Alfred would give people rides to their jobs. When the women go into labor, I can't drive them to hospital anymore. My God, what a selfish man." Mama shakes her head and lets out a deep breath. "But other than that, we are going to be just fine. We have gotten along fine without a car before and we will make do now."

I look up. "Until Papa gets back."

She gives me a small smile. "Yes, Quanei, when your father returns, all will be right again." She kisses my forehead. "Now, everyone, if you want to help me in some way, then help me get dinner done!"

I watch Mama and my aunt go into the kitchen. I decide that if Mama can have a good attitude, so can I. I decide that when Papa returns, he will make everything alright.

The next few days prove Mama right. We got along fine without our car. Mama and Aunt Cecilia walk to the market if we need something, and we walk to school. Maybe it is not so bad, life without a car. It's not like anyone else in Sugar Hill has one anyway. The only thing that changes is our trip to our home village of Gharmue. Without the car, we are no longer able to make such a long trip. This makes me sad because Gharmue, one of my favorite places in the world, is like our second home. Papa makes sure we visit Gharmue almost every weekend to keep us close to our family and our rich heritage. Visiting Gharmue is like returning to a special land of just my family. Our family owns lots of Gharmue land, which all feels like one giant farm. You could walk for hours from house to house seeing family, eating food, and playing with cousins. During the day, we run through the village lined with fresh food grown right on the land. Mama and Papa are always happy in Gharmue. Family members sing as they prepare big dinners. You can hear the sweet African melodies rise from the village like steam. Gharmue is where my father learned to be a respectable man and where my mother learned the cultural traditions of being a strong and powerful woman.

I do notice, though, that things have seemed to slow down in our house and all throughout Sugar Hill. Sometimes when there isn't much going on in the house, I stand in the doorway looking at the space where our car used to be. I stare as if the empty space itself were something to see. The longer Papa is gone, the more things change in Sugar Hill. I catch myself staring off in space for long periods of time. I don't know why or how long. It is as if I go into another world, and when I come back I don't even realize I was gone. Sometimes I see Mama staring too, mostly out the kitchen window with her arms crossed, for a long, long time. I wonder if she is doing the same thing as me. Or if she is thinking of Papa. Or if she is thinking anything at all. Sometimes at night, after the grownups listen to the news of the rebels and the war on the radio, I see Mama staring, miles away. Mama does this more and more now, and so do I.

One day, about a week after Shi-Shi and the car disappeared, I am in the middle of staring at nothing when I see a man in a uniform come walking up the hill towards our house. The hot sun is beating down on everything, and I squint against the light to see the man better. In seconds, I recognize his uniform. He is from Telecomm, the building where Papa goes to use the telephone and get his messages. No one has a telephone in my city, not even us. If you want someone to know something, you have to walk and tell them yourself or write them a letter. But if you are really important, you can go to Telecomm and make phone calls. I have only seen this done on television, but I know Papa does it often. I am excited, thinking the Telecomm man must be coming for Papa!

"Mama! Mama!" I call. "There is a Telecomm man!"

"What?" She comes out of the courtyard. "What did you say?"

"A Telecomm man!" I tell her. "He is coming here."

Mama rushes to the front door, gathering up her long skirt to keep from tripping as she walks quickly out of the door towards the front gate. I follow her. The man tells Mama that Papa has called from America and wants her to come to Telecomm to talk to him. I am so full of happiness that I want to shout and jump. Papa sending word to us from America is the best news I have heard in so long.

"Come and find me when you get there," the man instructs, passing a piece of paper to Mama.

Mama takes the paper, nods, and walks back towards the door.

"Mama!" I say jumping up and down. "Are you going to Telecomm? Did Papa say for you to come and talk on the phone?"

"Yes, Quanei." She is walking quickly through the house. "I have a message from your father. He is going to call. I have to walk to Telecomm to go and talk to him."

My eyes light up . "Oh, can I go, Mama?"

"No, Quanei, not today. It's quite a walk. You stay here."

She goes to her room, looking around for something. Mama always lets me go places with her. Why can't I go now?

"But Mama, I walk to school every day," I plead. Every bone in body feels that I will die if I don't go with Mama. "Mama, please can I go with you? Please?"

"No, Quanei," she says, gathering her things and bustling about. "You stay here with everyone and wait for me. Where is everyone?"

"But Mama, I beg you!"

I must convince Mama quickly, before the other kids find out what is going on. If there is a call from Papa, I want to hear it, but I will have no chance of going once they all find out and beg to go too. Mama will definitely say no to all of us.

"If you go, everyone else will want to go," she tells me. "All of you can't go."

"But none of them asked!" I am tugging on her arm. "Please, Mama, please," I say, begging with all my heart. "Everyone is not even in the house right now. Nyempu is out in the kitchen with Auntie Garmen. Auntie Cecilia is cutting potato greens for supper. Kulubah and Fungbeh are playing with Auntie Rebecca and Uncle George, plus Kormah and Austin are across playing with Junior, Boye, and Elijah. See, Mama? They will not even ask to come. Can I come? Please, Mama, I beg you, please!"

Mama stops in her tracks, her gaze set sharply on me as if she is thinking about the many words spilling out of me. She is silent for a moment. Only my excited breath and Mama's stare are in the room.

"Oh, Quanei!" Mama says. "You are something else. Okay, let's go."

Everything inside me relaxes suddenly. I am dry as a desert and Mama has poured cold water down my insides so I can breathe again. I leap up like a frog.

"Yes! Yes! Yes! Tink you, Mama! Tink you! Oh, Ma, you so good! I will be good!"

I run off to get my shoes. I am so excited to go to Telecomm. I hope that when I get there, I can ask Papa all about America.

8

A Touch of War—the Kiss of Death

Mama and I walk through Sugar Hill to Telecomm. She tells me to stay close and to look out for cars as we cross Ghanta Highway. I press closer and hold Mama's hand tight when we get closer to the road. While we walk, I ask Mama all sorts of questions. I ask if she knows when Ms. Mary, our candy lady, is coming back to Sugar Hill. I have noticed over the past few days that Ms. Mary has not been home.

"I do not know, Quanei," she says.

"Did she leave with her family like other people in Sugar Hill?" I prod. "I hear Uncle Thomas say people are leaving to go to safe places because a war is coming. Where are they running to, Mama? Is Sugar Hill in trouble?"

"People do what they want to do, Quanei. We will be fine and wait for Papa to come home. Don't worry, little boy."

We keep walking. I notice the street is busier today than I have ever seen it—even on the days we rode in the car. There are people walking in almost every direction, some rushing ahead of us and some running back toward Sugar Hill. Something has everyone in the city wound up. I turn to watch one man run past me as fast as he can, and I wonder where he's going so fast. A few people are shouting in the distance, something that I can't understand. Suddenly Mama stops in her tracks and grips my hand tightly. I look up to see what is happening. Mama is frowning at something up the road, but I cannot see what she sees. I can hear some sort of commotion ahead of us and now Mama is walking slowly and very carefully.

"What's happening, Mama?" I tug at her.

"I'm not sure yet," she says carefully, as we get closer. "Do not let go of my hand, you hear me?"

I nod and squeeze tightly, getting closer to Mama's legs. I don't know what is going on, but I know enough of Mama's voice to know that she is serious about me staying close.

The yelling and cars and commotion grow louder as we approach a group of people in the middle of the highway. My eyes dart under the hot sun. I see military trucks with soldiers inside moving slowly up the road. People in the street are yelling and pounding their fists against the giant trucks. My eyes grow wide at government soldiers standing on the back of the trucks, guns in hand. I freeze, suddenly afraid of everything before me. Maybe they have captured the rebels, I think. Maybe Mr. Jackson is wrong about the rebels taking over. I wonder how we will cross over to Telecomm with so many people, trucks, and soldiers blocking the highway.

The crowd is roaring like angry lions, pounding and shouting at the passing military trucks. The noise is much louder and stronger than any noise the Night-Night creatures ever make. "This is murder!" the crowd shouts. "These are children! Oh, Doe, why? Oh, Doe!" Women and men are shouting, and I am confused. Are children the rebels? Mr. Jackson said the rebels were recruiting children too.

The military trucks are as big as elephants, driving in a slow line, with stoney-faced soldiers on top looking down at the crowd. I can see sweat glistening off the people's angry faces. Some of the soldiers jump down to push the crowd away from the trucks.

"Move back! You hear me?" they shout in broken English.

One soldier speaks quickly and violently. "I say, move back now! Or else we will beat you to the ground like market dogs! Stupid people! Get back from here man, you stupid people!" He grabs a few protestors by their clothes and shoves them back.

As the soldiers push the mob, the backs of the giant trucks come into view and I see tiny brown faces peering at me. Little wet eyes filled with terror look directly at me. A yelp escapes my throat and I jump back, bumping into a stranger. Mama must be able to feel the fear running through my arms because she instantly pulls me closer to her body and tries to move us out of the way of the commotion. I stand closer to Mama, unable to tear my eyes away from the eyes in the back of the passing truck. There are children in the back of these trucks. Lots of them. They cannot be rebels. Many of them look my age, some even younger. Angry yelling and the smell of motor oil fill the air. I whip my head around to see that four more trucks filled more children coming my way. I feel my chest constrict as if my heart was stabbed with a sharp needle. Fresh fear runs down my spine.

"Aye, Doe! Oh! Don't kill these innocent children, ooh" the protestors continue to cry. "Innocent, ooh! The children are innocent, ooh, my people!"

The cries from the protestors pound through my eardrums and into my soul as tears well up in my eyes. I don't understand what is happening to these kids, why they are being carted away by President Doe's soldiers? Why would someone do this? I wonder as Mama squeezes my hand and pulls me even closer. As the trucks roll by, I can hear some of the children crying, full of fear and anguish, a sound haunts me to my bones. I want to go now but there is no way to leave. The road is blocked and there is chaos everywhere.

"Murder!" someone behinds us yells. "Doe is killing young people, ooh!"

Other people are getting in front of the trucks, waving with handkerchiefs, begging the soldiers not to take the children away.

"Look what Doe has done, my people!" someone cries. "The man is evil, ooh! Evil!"

A thick wave of sadness and despair fills the air as a woman runs behind the trucks, beating the metal, begging, crying, as if she was mother to all the children. From inside the trucks I can see tiny hands gripping tightly. I know this is wrong and I feel sick.

"Mama," I hear myself say. But I am not sure I am even speaking. I think it is the only thing I can say. I cling to her as the trucks pass. I feel so small looking at the children and the men with the big guns. I don't want the soldiers to take the children. I don't want anyone to be inside these trucks. I thought the Doe army was supposed to protect us from the rebels, not hurt children.

"Doe is going to burn!" someone cries. People continue to protest loudly hoping the soldiers will stop and let the children free. As I watch the trucks roll away, I know something terrible has happened. Then there is a break in the crowd and suddenly Mama is pulling me with her. I am gripping Mama's hand so tight mine is hurting, but I do not care. We slowly make our way through all the bodies then finally into the open street again.

"Quanei, walk." Her voice is unsteady, her face like etched stone. I can see Telecomm in front of us. The further we get from the noise, the better I feel. I cannot stop seeing the trucks and the little faces. I still feel as if I am still standing before them.

"Mama, what happened? Where are the children going?" I ask. I had never seen anything like that in Gbarnga City before.

She doesn't answer me. I see tears welling in her eyes. She clears her throat. "I do not know. Just stay with me. Let's talk to Papa."

When we reach Telecomm, I let out a breath. The trucks and the children are still with me, but I am in Telecomm, a place I have often thought of, and the biggest building I have ever seen. Inside people bustle about, talking on phones, taking notes.. There are people in suits with briefcases, mothers with children, all sorts of people. There is a steady buzz of important life.

For a moment, I forget about what just happened and I am excited to see a real telephone.

As Mama and I find the main desk, I see operators sitting side by side against a long wall. They are busy making and connecting calls. I am amazed at how they work the telephones so well. They look so professional and important. Inside, I cannot wait to talk to Papa.

Mama finds the same Telecomm man who came to our house. The man takes us to a desk and gives the woman behind it our information. The woman points to an area where people are standing. "Wait there," she says.

In the waiting area, Mama tells me Papa is going to call us at a certain time. She also tells me Papa won't have time to talk to me because calls are very expensive. Looking around at the people, I believe her. I'm happy to be there with Mama, even if I don't get to talk to Papa. After a while, the woman at the desk calls Mama's name and points us to a phone. We go to a booth and Mama picks up the line.

"Alfred? It's me," Mama says. She sounds relieved and scared at the same time. Her voice is shaking a little bit. I wonder if it is because of what we just saw. I am shaking a bit too. Although I cannot talk to Papa, I am happy to be with them both in this way. Mama and Papa jump into a very serious conversation. It takes everything within me not to tug her arm and beg her to let me speak to Papa. I wonder what he is saying on the other end. I wish I could hear. I stand on my tiptoes, trying to drown out the buzz of the room, hoping to pick up the sound of Papa's voice. For a while, Mama writes quickly, nodding and uttering short phrases back to Papa.

"So, this is the number where you are staying in Providence?" I hear Mama say. "This is where I can reach you?" Then she turns her back and says things I cannot hear.

I look at all the people talking, doing their important business. The hum of voices and the ring of telephones filling the room is strangely comforting. In this place, things are happening. Lives are turning, the world is moving. I see a man in a bright blue suit, balancing the phone between his ear and his shoulder, taking notes on a pad. I wonder what he is talking about and who he is. His face is serious, as if he is getting the important direction from God Himself.

"Okay, Alfred." I see Mama shift her weight and readjusting the phone to hear better. "I will. Yes, okay. Goodbye."

And just like that, it is over. Papa is gone. I stare blankly at Mama feeling a loss for something I never had. For a second Papa was with us, and now he isn't. Mama returns the phone to its cradle and nods to the woman behind the counter.

"Okay," she says, letting out a deep breath. She takes my head. "Let's go."

Mama is quiet, the same kind of quiet as when Boye and I lay on our backs and try to figure out the universe. I know what it is like to be thinking hard, so I don't interrupt her this time, even though I'm itching to ask her about what she and Papa talked about.

We step back into a world of chaos outside. News of the soldiers has apparently spread, and it is like someone has set fire to Gbarnga City. Mama and I make our way home against the crowd. Everyone is walking fast, talking, pointing this way and that, and very upset. I look to Mama for answers, but she is focused on getting through the sea of bodies. When we pass others, we hear them talk about the trucks, the children, the soldiers, and the rebels.

When Mama and I get back to Sugar Hill, our entire community is in an uproar, like a lion has been set loose in the city. Just a few hours ago, everything had been normal. Our neighbors are standing on each other's porches, pacing, talking in big groups and looking over their shoulders. There have always been rumors of war, but today, soldiers in the city confirm everyone's worst fears. There is a real war in Liberia. It's not in Sugar Hill or even in Gbarnga City or Bong County yet, but it is happening, and drawing closer. Before we reach our house, a neighbor rushes to meet us in the street.

"Ma Neyor," she calls. Her eyes are wide with fear and she is breathing quickly. "Are you going to open the pharmacy today?

I think me and my family are leaving Gbarnga today. My cousin was hurt by soldiers in Nimba County today. They came looking for rebels. They were sent by Doe! I need to send some medicine to him and his family."

She talks fast. Mama tells her to calm down, that she will meet her at the pharmacy in an hour.

"We must hurry," she tells Mama. "Did you hear what happened today? With the children? The war is here! They are coming!"

"Yes," Mama says. "I know."

"Ma Neyor, President Doe, he—" She stops and glances down at me. "It is bad. So, so bad, oooh. I will meet you in one hour." She shakes her head, her hand covering her mouth. She looks at Mama, then rushes off.

Everyone in Sugar Hill is now rushing somewhere. Some are closing their doors and windows. Others are standing huddling in front of houses, talking quickly, looking around as if waiting for giant rocks to fall from the sky. I can hear them talking.

"The children are dead!" I hear someone say. "Doe killed their parents when they entered that town looking for rebels and he killed them all and took their children to go bury them alive in Monrovia."

My breath stops. I feel an empty blackness swallowing me up inside. The whole world is drowned out and I have a terrible pit in my stomach. All I can think of are those kids in the trucks, staring back at me. I realize why the people in the street were so upset, why they cried and begged the soldiers to let the children go. I can still see the terror in their eyes. I realize those kids must have seen their parents killed. It is then that I understand why people are leaving. Something major has shifted in the world. President Doe is killing his own citizens and taking their children to be killed in the capital city. This must be why Ma Mary, the candy lady packed up and left Sugar Hill. This must be why our driver stole our car. Something is happening beyond the rumors. Something big enough to come and eat us alive. Worse than the Night-Night things.

I am glad to see we are nearing our house on the hill. Some of our aunts and uncles are outside.

Aunt Cecilia rushes over. "Oh, Ma Neyor, thank God you're back! It is terrible. President Doe. . ."

"I know," Mama says. "We saw."

"Oh, God. Oooh!"

My aunt covers her mouth her eyes grow big with shock. "Things have gotten out of control, Neyor," my aunt says as we make our way inside the house. "This is not right, oh!"

"I know," Mama says again. "I talked to Alfred. He says the war in Liberia is the news in America."

"My goodness," my aunt gasps. She stares at Mama for a moment, her eyes wide as chicken eggs. I wonder if she is even breathing. Finally, she blinks, never taking her gaze off Mama. "Then these rebels. This war. Is bigger than we knew. It is not just rumors and stories on the radio, Ma Neyor. It is real. It is here, oh!"

My aunt is afraid like everyone else in Sugar Hill. Now I am afraid too.

"I know, Cecilia," Mama says, slipping her arm around me. "Quanei and I saw quite a bit today."

Mama stoops down and look me in the eye. "Go on and play now. You have had a busy day." She rubs my shoulders. "But stay inside today. No running outside with Boye. Tell Austin and Kormah I said do not go outside the compound today, okay? You hear me?"

I nod obediently. I don't want to go outside anyway. I go to my room where my brothers and sisters are eagerly awaiting my return. They are abuzz like everyone else. They have heard the older people talking and all the commotion. They ask me questions about what I saw. I try to tell them as best as I can, but I feel tired and afraid, like I could lie down and sleep for hours. But I know I can't sleep. My mind is running.

For the rest of the day, our once quiet and lazy community is churning with voices, rumors, and dreadful news. President Doe ordered a massacre of Liberians from Nimba County. Everyone knows that Nimba County is the heart of the rebellion, so they would have been the first to suffer. When Charles Taylor came to Liberia, he recruited very popular leaders from the Mano and Gio tribes, and together, they began their rebellion by recruiting people from Nimba County. Now the President has killed his own citizens from Nimba just because he feared the rebel movement.

The entire day has been turned upside down. No one is concerned with our snacks or washing up or tutoring. It is like a Friday evening—unstructured, not because we are happy and carefree, but because everything is changing.

Make your own Milk Candy

Watch Nyempu's Milk Candy video and learn to make your own. Post photos
of you milk candy on Witness social group and you could win a free Witness shirt.

www.resources.witnessliberia.com

9

Terrible Night-Night Things

Late January 1990
Three Weeks After Papa Has Left for America

By morning, new rumors and rumblings have created a wave of terror that slowly and surely begin to swallow up our entire country. Nothing was this out of control when Papa was here. The car was not gone. The candy lady was not gone. There were no soldiers. Our neighbors and friends weren't packing up left and right, and no one was afraid.

As we eat breakfast, I listen to my aunts and uncles' worst fears. Some of our help staff and uncles pack up and tell Mama they have decided to leave the compound and go back to the village of Gharmue, or elsewhere. Some are even thinking about going as far as Guinea, across the border. I am a little sad to see them go, but so much is happening now, I don't even have time to be upset. It is like Mama told me, people have to do what they feel is best now. I think, surely when Papa comes back, he can get all this straightened out.

Later, in the small hours of the night, I can't sleep. I am thinking of the trucks, the children, the war, and how everything has changed so quickly. I hear a noise outside and step up on my bed to look out my window. I stare into the darkness as if I am a Night-Night thing, watching, listening. I see the small glow of a lamp and the outline of bodies moving. I wonder what they are doing, then realize they must more neighbors leaving Sugar Hill in the dark of night.

The next day, Mama tells us all we are not going to school. Instead, we are to stay home and remain close to the compound. She tells us that she must go to the pharmacy to help a few people. I ask Mama if I can come, and she agrees. "But we will not be long," she says. "So, don't go getting lost in the store. Stay close."

As Mama and I walk through Sugar Hill, I notice how still everything is. The air is suffocating. There are not many people outside, and those who are, scurry like squirrels. Even Mama is walking very fast and is jittery, looking all around as we walk . When we reach the pharmacy, Mama quickly locks the doors behind us.

"People who need help will knock." Mama flips the Open sign around. "Then I will let them in. In the meantime, help me set up, Quanei."

Soon, just as Mama predicted, there is a knock at the door. Those who come are asking for supplies, enough to last a few weeks. They are buying lots of things and putting them in bags as quick as they can. It is obvious they are getting out of town too. We do not stay at the pharmacy very long. Mama locks the doors tight.

As we walk back to the house, I look around for Boye or J.R., but I see no one. The street is nearly empty. Not even the palm trees are swaying. The whole world is holding its breath.

Three nights after the terrifying event with the soldiers and the trucks, my mother's sister, Auntie Korto, and her husband, Uncle Nenwon, from Nimba County, come to stay with us. They arrive in the night with their truck packed with belongings. I know this is not a normal visit. Still, I am excited to see my cousins, Siaka and Saye. Since the news of what happened with the soldiers, most of our staff and family have left. Now Auntie Korto's family are here and the house is filled with people again.

When dinnertime comes, the grownups eat in the dining room and us children sit at a table in our living room. We laugh and play and show our toys and talk about our school. At moments, we can hear the grownups talking about what has happened. I wonder what happened in Nimba for Auntie Korto and Uncle Nenwon to leave their home and come here. I wonder if the soldiers came to their town too. Even with a touch of fear in the air, it is fun having our other family here. None of us has to go to school, and although we are not allowed to leave the compound anymore, we still spend the day playing and running through the courtyard. It is almost as if life has returned to normal for now. I am sure when Papa returns, everything will once again be the same.

Our room is completely full now. Saye sleeps in my bed. One night, before I fall asleep, I lie awake listening to the Night-Night things. I wonder what they are saying. Are they, too, passing messages of war? Are they worried? Are they moving away like everybody else? I hope not, because when all of this war calms down, I want to be able to listen to their world again, just like I used to with Boye.

As I lie there listening, my ear catches the soft hum of voices. I am used to this sound now, as the grownups usually stay up late talking about grownup things. I am the only one awake in our room and I decide tonight will be a perfect time to eavesdrop. I glance at Saye sleeping, then slowly slide out of the bed without a sound. My feet hit the floor and, like a squirrel on a shaky branch, I take a few careful hops to the door. I turn back to see if I have disturbed anyone. I open the door slowly and silently, letting in a small sliver of light. I poke my head out to see if anyone is there, then squeeze through the small opening into the hall. The grown-up voices are louder now. Unbeknownst to them, I am in their world.

"I cannot believe what you are telling me," I hear Mama say.

"Neyor, it is much worse than you can ever imagine,"

Auntie Korto says. "If we had stayed we would be dead."

My heart leaps in my chest. I scoot a little closer to hear more.

"It was terrible," my uncle says. "People stopped showing up at work. The word had gotten out that the rebels were close, that they are killing anyone who works for Doe."

"That means us," my aunt puts in. "My husband works for the government. Anyone who is affiliated with Charles Taylor or his VP Commander would assume that Nenwon is loyal to Doe. I don't care who is the president. That Charles Taylor is far more powerful than Doe. He is making these rebels do terrible things."

"And that is why my neighbors and coworkers started to leave town," Uncle Nenwon says. "I only wish we had gotten out sooner so that the children didn't have to witness what happened in our community."

"What happened?" Mama asked. I see her sitting on the edge of her seat, holding Auntie Korto's arm. "You said the rebels came to your neighborhood. Tell me everything."

"First, you have to understand, these rebels are not like anything that you have ever seen," Uncle Nenwon says. "They are not trained soldiers, they are rabid killers." His voice is cold. "These rebels are young, Neyor. They are not even men. Their minds are completely gone."

"Gone?" Mama asks. "Gone how?"

"They have been turned from normal boys into something less than human and more vicious than the devil himself. The rebel leaders who started this war have gone to each and every town and are killing families, and making their children watch. Then, those same children, while they are grieving and afraid, are given guns and told that Doe did this. They tell these children that the only way to get revenge is to join. And if they don't join, they will die."

Uncle Nenwon lets out a sigh. "Then they destroy their humanity by making them take their grief, confusion, and rage, and use it to kill their own family. They give them guns and force them to shoot innocent people, convincing them that they are small soldiers killing for their freedom."

"They are turning them into monsters," Mama says.

"Worse," says Auntie Korto. "This is why no one can afford to die and leave their children behind. The rebel army will turn them into something worse than we have ever thought."

"I have seen it," Uncle Nenwon says. "I saw a truck of them pass by on the way here, and a boy I know was in it, holding a gun. I was afraid for my life. I thought they would stop us. But that same boy, who used to be shy and respectful, glared at me with a sick grin on his face and blood on his shirt. I knew that boy. Now he is one of them."

"And these are the people who came to Nimba?" Mama asks.

"Yes," Auntie Korto says. "We barely made it out, Neyor."

"Oh my God, Korto. What exactly happened?"

There is silence for a moment. When my aunt speaks, her voice is small and flat, as if her body is here but her mind far away.

"We were asleep when we heard shooting and shouting right outside the house. It felt like they were shooting right at our house. It was so loud. I jumped up and woke up Nenwon. The noise was coming directly from next door and it sounded like someone was raiding our neighborhood. There were screams, shouts, and noise. I could hear men barking orders. And there were these pop, pop, pop noises. Even though I was half asleep it was like, I knew. I knew it was the rebels and they were looking for us."

"Oh my God," Mama says.

"We jumped out of bed and ran to get the children. I hid them in the closet and Nenwon peeked out the window, to see what was happening."

"It was the rebels?" Mama asks. "You saw them?"

"Yes," Uncle Nenwon says quietly. "I saw them, teenage boys with AK-47s dragging a woman out of her house. She was screaming so loud. I could hear her husband shouting. And then there were gunshots. Then he was silent." Uncle Nenwon pauses for a moment before going on. "These boys, they took the woman to the side of the house and they raped her. Right there on the grass. And then shot her right in front of the house. I saw it, Neyor."

"Oh my God," Mama says again. I can hear her voice trembling from where I stand. My eyes are large and my heart is jumping, as if I am running from something. I have to cover my mouth tight so that I don't give myself away.

Uncle Nenwon's voice shakes. "The other rebels were walking up and down the streets with guns. Throwing rocks at houses. Yelling about death to Doe. I think they chose that house because the man worked on a commission with Doe and is always doing business in Monrovia. They questioned him all night before killing him."

"That was when we knew we had to leave," my aunt says. "I prayed to God that night. I told Him, if we just made it out alive, we would leave."

"We barely made it out with our lives," Uncle Nenwon says. "And now we are here. Thank you, Neyor, for opening your home to us. You have saved us."

"We know there are whispers about us being here," says my aunt. "Your neighbors are talking, wondering if we are part of the rebels or with Doe. Wondering what trouble we may be bringing here."

"Yes," Mama says. "You are the talk of our little hill." I can hear the smile in her voice. "But you are my sister and we are safe here. We are closer to Monrovia than you, near the government. The rebels will not be coming here soon. You are safe here. Alfred says that the war is on the news in America. Now that it has gotten out of control, the Americans will step in and help our government take care of this. They have to. They will not let this go on long, I don't think. They cannot allow people to continue to die. This is outrageous."

"Neyor, even if the war never comes this way, so much damage has already been done to our home and our society," Uncle Nenwon says. "You have not seen the eyes of a child killer. Innocent little boys are having guns put to their heads while watching their mothers get raped and killed and then being told by those same killers that it is their father's fault. Then they place guns to these boy's heads and tell them to be a man and protect themselves by killing their own father, or else die."

"In most cases, some of these children are shot right in the head in front of their siblings or friends if they refuse to follow orders. Often times this is enough to force fear in the minds of innocent children to be convinced to pull the trigger at the next command. Even if the Americans send help to our government and end this war tomorrow, the damage has already been done to these children. How can someone recover from something like that? How can they cope? How can they live? In a single second, their life is destroyed!" Uncle Nenwon sounds distraught as he makes his point.

"Charles Taylor is a smart man and knows that if you can convince a child to kill his own parents, you can destroy their soul and replace it with whatever you want, getting them to carry out whatever you need done. Even if it means getting themselves killed to help overthrow their own government."

I sit listening in the dark, taking in every word Uncle Nenwon says. Even though I am not sure what "rape" is, I know it must be terrible. I have heard so many scary things about Charles Taylor and what he is up to, but this felt more real than the rumors. It reminds me of when Boye and I play war. I always convince Austin to share his soldiers with me so that I can easily defeat Boye. As I listen to Uncle Nenwon speak, I realize that through violence, death, fear, and threats Charles Taylor has created his very own army of toy soldiers.

Finally, I have heard more than enough. I creep quietly back to my room, not because of the fun of a good sneak, but because I suddenly felt heavy all over. As I slip back into my room, my eyes fall on Austin and Kormah sleeping soundly and I feel a lump rise in my throat. I would die if they or I had to face these rebels and do what Uncle Nenwon just described. I fight hard to stop trembling as I get back into my bed.

10

Separation Anxiety

Sugar Hill has become eerily quiet, heavy with uncertainty, and slow. Still, Mama goes to the pharmacy and people come to the house for help. When they come, people bring stories of rebel conflicts, of soldiers ripping apart villages and towns in the name of their cause. Mama always looks upset to hear these accounts. As more of our staff leave to find safer places to wait out the uncertainty and danger, I wonder what our plan is. Are we still safe here in Sugar Hill? When Papa comes back, can he do something to make it all better? When will we see Papa again?

One day, after Mama finishes her work, she gathers us in her room while Auntie Cecilia prepares dinner. We all stand around her bed and I can tell from her serious look she has something big to share.

"Mama," I say. "What is it?"

"Be quiet, Quanei!" Kormah snaps at me. "Wait."

"Listen to me," Mama says, cutting off my reply. "The things that have been happening here, in Liberia—they are very serious. Things are changing quicker than Papa and I expected. So, your Papa has cut his trip in half and will be coming at the end of this month. Then we can decide on what to do."

As soon as I hear this I let out a big sigh of relief. Papa is coming home. Thank goodness. Now everything is going to be just fine.

"When is he coming?" Nyempu asks, her voice shaking. It sounds as she is about to cry, and I don't blame her.

"He is taking care of some final things for the business and then he is coming home. But first he needs some papers from me to finish what he needs to do. . . some very important papers that I must go travel to Monrovia and send them to him."

"You are going to travel?" I ask, my voice shaking too. "When? How, Mama? No!"

Mama runs a soothing hand down my back and looks at each of us. "I have to do this for Papa. I will be gone for few days, but I will be back."

"When will you come back?" Nyempu asks, already stepping up and taking charge.

"In just a few days," Mama repeats. "You all will stay here with your Auntie Korto, Uncle Nenwon, Uncle George, Thomas, Cecilia, Isaac, and the others. With so many, you are not alone."

"I want to go!" Kormah cries. "Take me, I am big enough!"

Mama shakes her head. "No, baby. You must stay here with family and you will mind each of them. And do what you're told until I come back. I am leaving very early in the morning."

And just like that our world takes yet another turn.

The morning comes much too soon, and we are all standing outside watching Mama leave. Mama hugs each of us, then walks down the hill, across the road to Monrovia Parking to meet the bus that will to take her on her trip. As we stand in the window, I realize that Mama is the only one out walking in our entire community. There is not a single other soul on the street.

As if life has not become strange enough, things only seem to get worse after Mama leaves. The entire compound walks on eggshells, and at night we have gone back to using kerosene lamps instead of the glowing electricity Papa worked so hard to bring. Now we only get electricity from 5pm to 8pm each day. The grownups are acting really strange too. They spend most of their time peering out windows and wringing their hands, as if they are waiting to be eaten by a lion.

The day after Mama leaves, Kormah, Austin, Saye, and Nyempu and I are all playing games in Nyempu's room when our cousin Siaka bursts into the room, her face bewildered. We all stop in our tracks. I can see she is very upset.

"Mama says we are leaving!" she says breathlessly, tears brimming in her eyes.

"What?" I jump up quickly. "What?"

"Mama says that it is no longer safe here in Gbarnga and that we have to pack our things and go."

Now it is Saye who jumps up. "What?"

No, no, no. This cannot be happening. Auntie and Uncle can't go. They are in charge. They are the ones taking care of us.

Nyempu looks as if she is figuring out a giant math problem. "When?"

"Today!" Siaka says. "Right now." She looks at Saye. "Mama says pack your things."

"No," Kormah says. He jumps up and leaves the room. We follow him and run outside to see her parents packing up their Jeep. I don't know what to make of what I am seeing. Where are they going? Are they taking us with them? For a moment, we all stand there just looking at them.

"Hey!" Kormah shouts, running to the Jeep. "What are you doing? Why are you leaving? You can't leave. Mama is not back yet. Mama says you are taking care of us."

Auntie Korto looks at us for a moment before simply saying, "We have to go. Now go inside." When we don't move, she gives us a stern look. "I said now!"

We do as we are told, bewildered as we watch Auntie Korto and Uncle Nenwon pack their things. They are rushing, moving quickly in and out of the house, telling their children to hurry, that it is not safe, that they must go.

"If it is not safe, then why are they leaving us? Who will take care of us?" I ask Nyempu and Austin and Kormah. "What are we going to do?"

Nyempu pulls me close and holds my hand like Mama does sometimes when I'm worried.

Auntie Korto stops her rushing around for a moment and says to Nyempu, "It is not like we are leaving you all alone." She looks around for a moment. "Go and tell your uncles and whoever is left in the other house to look out for you. They can do it. But me and my family, we have to go."

I stand in our living room in shock as Auntie Korto walks out the door, climbs into the Jeep with her family, and backs away. As dust gathers behind the tires, we watch the red taillights in the distance and I cannot help but think we are all alone. Mama is gone, Papa is gone, Auntie Korto and Uncle Nenwon are gone too. As soon as the car is out of view, Nyempu runs to the other side of the compound and returns with Uncle George, Uncle Thomas, Auntie Cecilia, Uncle Isaac, and Auntie Sarah. They are bombarded with the commotion of all us trying to tell them what happened.

Auntie Cecilia looks down the road. "They left you?" she asks incredulously. "She didn't say a word to us!"

"Because she is wrong!" Uncle Thomas says angrily. "How can a woman do this to her own sister's family? Neyor will never forgive her for this."

"C'mon, let's get you children something to eat."

"Don't worry children, we are still here," Auntie Cecilia says. "We will be here with you until your Mama returns."

I hear the grownup voices as if through a wall. All I can think is what is happening to us? Our aunts and uncles begin to usher us to another house in the compound where we will now stay.

"How Korto and 'nem just leave without even telling us?" shouts Uncle Thomas. "Human beings wicked, Oh! What good is surviving the war if you don't have no family?"

Everything is happening so fast it nearly knocks me over. I'm upset but I don't even care anymore that they left us. I just want Mama and Papa to come back home.

On the third day of Mama's absence, things quickly worsen when Papa's father comes to our house. I am surprised to see Grandpa Karmue because he hardly ever comes to see Papa. I do not even see him arrive, only hear his big bellowing voice filling our compound. Everyone else hears too and rushes to meet him. I run out and see him, his tall powerful frame at the main house where he is calling for my aunts and uncles. He is wearing a green shirt and black pants, almost like an army uniform, except he seems bigger and louder than any soldier I have ever seen. His voice shakes the entire compound. He stands in the doorway of our house, his face full of fury. It seems my Auntie Cecilia has been arguing with him.

"You cannot do this, Papa!" I hear her say. "I know there is war but, Papa, we cannot leave yet!"

"Everything has changed!" Grandpa barks at her. "Now, I have come for my family and I am taking all of my children out of here. Go get your things! The rebels are coming this way. It is not safe here anymore."

My eyes grow wide when I hear him say that the rebels are near. My heart beats fast and hard and I wonder if we are going to be overtaken by war that very day.

"But, Papa!" Auntie Cecilia pleads. "We can't leave. Ma Neyor is not back! The children have been left with us."

"My children that are here are coming with me!" He growls. "This town is not safe anymore and I am getting my family out of here."

Grandpa pushes past Auntie Cecilia and marches through the house and out the door to the other compound, looking for the others.

I am getting scared. I don't want Grandpa to be so upset and angry. I watch him go room to room, telling Uncle Isaac and all our remaining aunts and uncles that they are leaving. Auntie Cecilia continues to plead but Grandpa ignores her and continues gathering my aunts and uncles who have lived with us all this time.

"Austin!" I hear him bellow. "Austin, where are you? We are leaving."

I snap my head up and stare at him. Austin? Why is Grandpa taking Austin? He is our brother.

"Let him stay," my aunt says, still following behind Grandpa. "He can stay with me. Papa, Austin is my brother and has been with Ma Neyor and Mr. Karmue from the time he was a toddler—all this time. They are his family, Papa, he can stay. He can stay!"

Grandpa whirls around and faces my aunt. "I don't care who he has been living with! He is my son and he is leaving with me. You are my daughter and you are leaving with me."

I stand in the hallway with a giant hole growing in my chest and stopping my breath. What is Grandpa saying? Austin is his son? It is no secret that Grandpa has more children than most people can count, but Austin is my brother. He lives with me. He sleeps in my room.

"No," she protests. "I will not leave these children alone."

"Thomas and George are here, Neyor's own brothers. They will look after them."

"Papa, Thomas and George are just children—they are teenagers! Thomas is only a few years older than Nyempu. I am not leaving Ma Neyor's children here like this. Leave me and Austin here. We are not coming with you."

"Foolish girl!" Grandpa says to Aunt Cecilia. "Do you forget I once served in the Liberian military? Do you think I am going to sit here and let my children be found by Charles Taylor's army?"

Aunt Cecilia sticks her chin out in defiance. Grandpa gives her a look of disgust. "Fine! You stay here and die if you want. But my son is coming with me."

With that, Grandpa pushes past her and marches into the hallway. He comes back with Austin by the hand. Uncle Isaac has already packed his suitcase.

"Austin? Austin!" I run and fling my arms around him. I hold him so tightly I think my arms might break right off. But I don't care. Hot tears sting my eyes as I squeeze them shut. I don't understand all of what is happening, but I do know that I don't want Austin to go.

"We must go." Grandpa pushes me and I fall to the floor.

Nyempu scoops me up, her eyes fixed hard on Grandpa's, her jaw set in anger. Kormah is standing silently at the front door. We watch Grandpa push Austin out the door. We watch their small convoy leave Sugar Hill with the now familiar dust picking up behind the truck. I notice that I am not the only one with tears streaming down my cheeks as we watch more of our family leave.

"C'mon," Aunt Cecilia tells us. "Let's go get you children something to eat."

As night falls, we eat our meal of pepper soup and rice in silence. The compound which once housed almost thirty people is nearly empty now. Only my brothers and sisters, Aunt Cecilia, Uncle Thomas, Uncle George, and I remain. As we eat, I catch the worried looks our uncles exchange. For the first time, I realize they really aren't that much older than us. I used to think everyone bigger than me was a grownup, but tonight I can see that they are not. They are wondering the same thing as me. Are we in trouble? Is it safe? What do we do next?

When we finish eating, Nyempu and Kormah clear the table and wash the dishes. Later, Kormah and I go to our room and gaze at Austin's perfectly made bed. I don't know how long we stand there, but while we take in his absence, a noise outside catches our attention. It sounds like a rumbling machine on the hill. I look at Kormah and we both bolt into the living room to see what is coming.

"It's a van!" Kormah shouts, as Nyempu and I rush to see.

"Come away from the window, all of you," says Auntie Cecilia, pushing us back us as she squints to get a better view. "Oh, thank God," she breathes. "It is Ma Neyor!"

We all shout as Kormah wrestles the front door open. We run outside with our emotions pushing us forward. Uncle Thomas and Uncle George come rushing behind us. The van rolls to a stop, Mama steps out, and we fall into her.

"Look at all of you!" Mama says, embracing us all. "Oh, I have missed you!" Mama kisses each of us and suddenly I don't feel as if the entire world is crashing down. She quickly gathers her things from the van and waves goodbye to the driver. We all talk at her and pull her inside. Inside, Mama looks around. "Wait. Where is everyone?" Her eyes dart around to each of us and then she looks up at Aunt Cecilia. "And where is Austin?"

Auntie Cecilia tells her that Auntie Korto left us alone in the main house and that Grandpa came and raided the compound. Then she tells her that Grandpa took Austin back to Gharmue to leave for Guinea with the rest of his children. Mama is still. I can see the rise and fall of her chest. I notice the tired lines around her eyes. I see her shoulders and neck are tight from her long journey.

"I see," Mama says. Then she gathers us all in her arms for a long time and we all hang on to her for dear life. I breathe in the smell of her clothes and feel her warm body against mine. Mama is warming my entire soul and I never want to let her go.

"Children," she says as she is holding us. "We must rest very well tonight."

I pull back to look at her. "Why, Mama?"

"Because tomorrow we are all leaving."

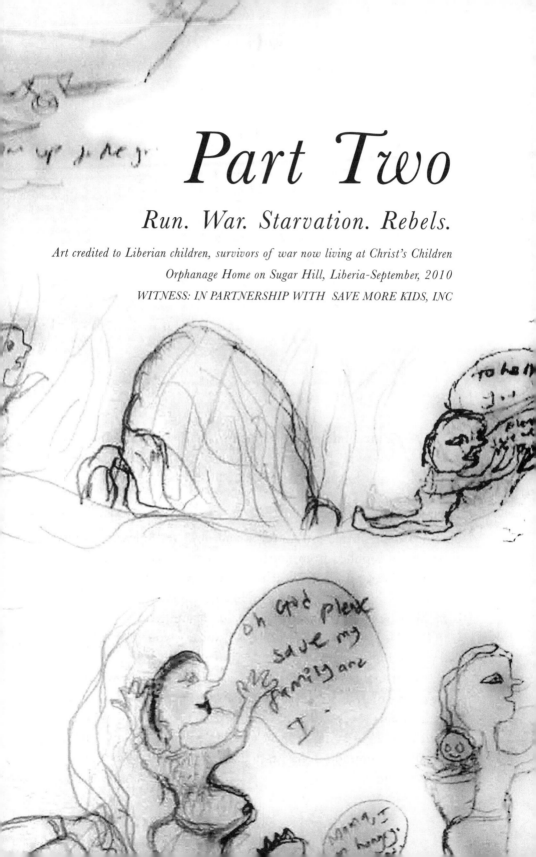

Part Two

Run. War. Starvation. Rebels.

Art credited to Liberian children, survivors of war now living at Christ's Children
Orphanage Home on Sugar Hill, Liberia-September, 2010
WITNESS: IN PARTNERSHIP WITH SAVE MORE KIDS, INC

11

Leaving Home

Late February 1990

We are all dead silent, looking up at Mama. "Tomorrow, we will be leaving to go to Monrovia. It will be safer for us there. It is time for us to leave Sugar Hill," Mama says.

I can hear Aunt Cecilia saying something, but I am silent. My brain is frozen. Mama just got back and now we are leaving? Our entire world is pulled from under my feet and right out the front door, just like sand on the beach that slips away with every wave. The wave of this war has come, and like those grains of the sand, it is washing away every bit of what used to be our lives.

"Ma Neyor," Auntie Cecilia says. "What is your plan? Where will you and the children go?"

"We are going to Monrovia, to Gaye Town Church. We know some people there. We need to go someplace safer while we wait for Alfred." Mama turns to us. "Kids, your papa is coming home from America and he is going to meet us there, at Gaye Town Church. Since all this commotion has started, I think it is best we wait for him in Monrovia."

I look at Mama and for a moment the sick feeling is lifted. I think everything is going to be okay. Thank God Papa is coming home. I know that when he gets here, all will be right again. Mama has told me this so many times.

"Oh, thank God," Uncle Thomas says. His voice is full of relief too. "We must go and meet Boss Man then."

"And we will be safe in Monrovia. It is the capital city and the government is in charge there. Liberia will protect its citizens from the craziness that the rebels are bringing." Mama is talking quickly and urgently, like she does when something is really important. "Brother Wesley from Gaye Town Church has already agreed to take us in until Alfred gets back from America. I have paid a man with a bus to take us to there. I am also going to get some of my sisters and Alfred's sister and take them with us, so we can all be there waiting for him together. There is not much time, so everyone must get some rest tonight. Sugar Hill is not safe anymore." She turns to Aunt Cecilia. "It is time for us to go."

"Very well," Aunt Cecilia says. "Now that you are back, I will go to Gharmue and cross over to Guinea to meet up with Papa. I did not want to leave the children alone when he came to get me. But now that you're here, I will be on my way to Guinea."

"You sure? Cecilia, you don't want to come with us to Monrovia?" Mama asks.

"No, Ma, let me go meet the old people in the village. I think I will be safe there with them."

"Okay," Mama says. "We will drop you off there tomorrow. As soon Alfred comes, we will find a way to reach you again." Mama gives Auntie Cecilia a long hug.

While Mama goes over more details of our plan, I wonder what she has seen during her trip to make her so eager to leave home. Before she left, she was happy to stay and wait for Papa, but now she is saying that we must leave too. Whatever is happening outside of Sugar Hill must be serious. I feel very grown up as I know more than Nyempu and Kormah: the rebels must be taking over more and more and maybe we could be next.

Mama kneels and draws all of us close. "My babies," she says. "We must get plenty of good sleep tonight, you hear?"

We all nod obediently and Mama kisses each of us on the head before sending us to our rooms to get ready for bed. The rumors of war are true and have created a great tidal wave that not even we can escape without moving to higher ground. Apparently, that is what we are all doing now.

That night, while everyone is preparing for bed, I slip into Mama's room where she's busy shuffling things about.

"What is it, Quanei?" she says when she sees to me. "Why aren't you getting ready for bed, baby?"

"I can't."

"Why not?"

I cross my arms tight across my chest and frown. "I am too mad to sleep, Mama."

"Mad?" Mama frowns back. "At whom?"

"I am mad at Auntie Korto for leaving us here all alone. You told me to stay with her and that she was going to look out for us, but she left us here and Nyempu was upset and I was scared!"

"Oh baby," Mama says, grabbing my hand and pulling me to the bed. We sit down and Mama takes my other hand too. "Do not be mad with your Auntie Korto."

My eyes are wide with disbelief. "But she left us! And she is our family! You and Papa said that family is the most important thing, and she left us like we are not her—like we are no one." I drop my head. "And then Grandpa came and took Austin. And he was mean too and I am just so mad!"

Mama slips her arm around me. "I know, little boy. I am sad Austin is gone, too."

"Then why aren't you mad at Auntie Korto?"

"Because, sweetie, it's just like when me and Papa send all of you kids off to school every day. We tell you the best way to behave during the day, but at the end of the day, you all still have a choice about what to do, don't you?"

"Yes."

"Sometimes, you choose to be good and other times—"

"Kormah chooses to be bad," I interrupt.

"Sometimes you do things that get you into trouble, too. But if anyone, including Kormah, misbehaves and gets a whipping, that is their choice and what does that have to do with you? That is up to them, correct?"

"Yes."

"If Kormah makes a choice, whatever his choice—aren't you still free to live your life? Go to school? Eat milk candy? Get good grades?"

"Yes."

"Does being upset at Kormah change what he did or have anything to do with what you can do every day?"

"No."

"But maybe you should be mad at Kormah. Or maybe he should be mad at you when you misbehave."

"Why?" I ask her. "If Kormah makes a bad decision, that is him! I didn't do nothing wrong! What sense does it make for me to walk around upset?"

"Exactly" Mama says, patting my hand. "You can disagree with someone's actions, without allowing anger and bitterness to rise up in you. When you are angry, does it feel good?"

"No."

"So why allow what someone else does to make you feel upset any longer than you need to?" Mama hugs me again. "You can be disappointed and hurt. But after that, if you choose to have anger or bitterness, that is completely up to you. Look at you. You cannot even sleep because you are so angry. Auntie Korto and her choice are long gone, but here you are. It is getting in the way of your sleep!" Mama tickles me a little. "Quanei, even though Auntie Korto make a bad choice, only you can decide if you add anger and bitterness to it."

"Austin leaving is already sad enough," I tell Mama. "I don't want to keep these other feelings with it."

"Then the way to do that is forgiveness," Mama says. "When you forgive someone, you say, I do not agree with what you did, but I am not going to return hate with hate. Since there is nothing I can do about the past anyway, I am going to see your action, bless you and pray for you, and continue to live the happy life that I have."

I look at Mama. "That is how you are not angry at Auntie Korto? Even for this?"

"Just like Kormah's choice is his choice, Korto's is hers to live with. Even though you do not understand or agree with it, it does not mean that you have to ruin your life being angry about something that no longer has anything to do with you. We have far too much to do than to carry around the burden of negativity from someone else's choices, because you have the choice to forgive. I have what matters most to me in the world."

Mama yawns and I yawn too. She gets up and nudges me toward the door. Before I go, she kneels and looks into my eyes. "I have my family, my children, and my freedom. What good will it do for me to walk around angry at her when I have the choice to enjoy what all has been given to me? No matter what someone does to you, you still have that power and nothing anyone does can ever take that away from you."

"Mama," I say. "You are the smartest woman in the world."

Mama laughs a big hearty laugh, but she looks tired. "Now, off with you to bed. No talking late at night with Kormah. You need your rest. We have a big day tomorrow."

I feel like I have only been asleep five minutes when I someone is pushing me awake.

"Quanei." I recognize Mama's voice. "Up, little boy. It is time for us to get ready to go."

I am sleepy, but I sit up. I see Kormah is up, more awake than me, already on the edge of his bed. Mama tells us we need to hurry, get up and pack. We listen and go off to the bathroom where I splash some water on my face. I have seen Papa do this many times. He always told me it helps him wake up. I rub the water on my face, but I do not feel awake. When we go back to our room Mama is there, pulling out small travel bags.

"Pack a few clothes—shirts, and shorts for a few days." She looks at Kormah. "You know what to do. Help your brother."

I do as I am told, putting things in the bag. I hear Nyempu, Aunt Cecilia, and Uncle Thomas bustle around the house, taking directions from Mama. Mama swoops in and out of our rooms, checking, counting, and examining our bags before she is satisfied.

I am starting to feel better about this trip. It will be simple. When Papa comes home, everything will be as it was again. I decide to take my yellow sweater. It is my favorite because yellow is my favorite color.

"Quanei, you don't need to pack that."

Mama is standing in our doorway. "You should leave that one here. Only get the things you need. That sweater can stay. You have worn that one out. Plus, we will only be gone for few days."

"Oh," I say, pulling it out of the bag. My sadness returns.

"Quanei." Mama's voice is warmer now. "We will be back, Quanei, and you can wear the sweater as much as you like. But it is much too nice for this trip and I don't want it to get lost or for you to mistakenly leave it behind."

She's right, I figure. It will be good to come back to it. I quickly tuck the shirt away and grab another. If we go to Monrovia with all these things, my sweater may be lost. I decide I don't need my lunch box either. When I finish packing and Mama has approved my bag, I make my way to the front of the house to see that there are already many things by the door. I wonder when Mama had time to pack all this. There are bags, kerosene lamps, some food, and what looks like towels. It is still dark outside, but the sky is starting to lighten a bit.

Auntie Cecilia whizzes past me, holding something in her arms. "Quickly, Quanei! You and Kormah—come help me get these things in the bus."

The bus that Mama has told us about is indeed here. It is white, bigger and taller than our yellow car but not as big as the big trucks I saw on our way to Telecomm. The doors are open, and I hop in to see four long rows of seats. The bus is enormous, enough for all of us and many things. The smell reminds me of our car.

Scan this code with a QR reader or use the link below to follow selected chapters for a more purposeful Witness Experience

www.resources.witnessliberia.com

12

On the Run to Gaye Town Church

Eventually, we are ready to leave the house. Mama, Nyempu, Fungbeh, Kormah, Kulubah, Uncle Thomas, Aunt Cecilia, Uncle George, and I all climb in. Nine of us plus the driver. Mama tells the driver we are ready. The driver roars the van to life and we begin rolling through the dimly lit morning away from Sugar Hill. As we drive through our now abandoned community, I see a dark figure step into the road and wave us down.

"Slow down, please," Mama tells the driver.

I see the figure is Mr. Paye, Boye's father. Then I see Boye. I lean forward in my seat. Boye waves at me and I wave back, but neither of us moves. I am very happy to see him.

"Mrs. Karmue," Boye's father says. He comes to Mama's window.

"Good morning, Mr. Paye," Mama says. "Have you and Boye come to see us off?"

"If you are in fact leaving, then yes." Boye's father takes a deep breath as his eyes roam the van. "So, it is official. The Karmues are leaving Sugar Hill."

"We don't have a choice," Mama responds. "I have just come from Monrovia and the war is tearing Liberia apart. It is much worse than we ever imagined. Much worse than the stories we have heard. The rebels are taking over. I don't think it is safe for anyone now. We must go."

"I know." He sticks his hand in his pockets and drops his head. "You and Alfred are the most loyal to Sugar Hill. You have been the heart of this community. So, I know that if your family is leaving then, there is no hope."

"Oh," Mama says. "Keep hope. This will not be always. Just like it one day started, it will one day be over. Plus, we don't plan to be gone long. We will be meeting Alfred in Monrovia next week and we will all come back this way." Mama asks quietly, "Will you leave? Where will you and your family go?"

I don't hear his answer because they suddenly drop their voices. My eyes are locked on Boye, and he returns my gaze. I wonder when we will see each other again, if he will be here when we return with Papa. I hope that he and his family stay safe. I hope they find their own higher ground. Soon the van begins to move again and Boye waves at me one last time. I nod at him. As the van continues forward I look back through the windows, watching him slowly disappear in the morning dust.

Our journey to Monrovia is beginning and I am suddenly no longer concerned with Sugar Hill and what is behind us. Now, I am only thinking of what Monrovia will be like in the new era that has suddenly overtaken us. Mama tells us we are going to drop off Aunt Cecilia, then pick up others along the way. Before we go to Gaye Town church, we are going to get Grandma Yeayea and Mama's brothers and sisters. They too are running to some place safe until the rebels are gone and the war is over.

As the van bumps down the road, I look outside just as I always do when we're riding. The sun is up and the green, fertile undulating hills of the plateau are blanketed with its golden glaze. These used to be the best sights for me: the traditional huts that meant we were approaching our own village and would soon be loudly welcomed by family. But today, nothing feels right. As we drive, we pass lines of people walking along the road. They are going to a safer place too. They are being ripped from their environment just like us. No one is in the right place anymore. Sometimes as many as fifty people are walking together, carrying children on their backs and belongings atop their heads. I hope they do not run into rebels or Doe's evil government along the way. I pray none of them are killed in ways I have heard on the news and from Aunt Korto and Uncle Lawrence. It sounds like anything at any time can get someone shot dead or torn away from their family. I know why we have left early in the morning, before all of the commotion and activity begins, before rebel warriors and government giants get out of bed.

The vinyl seats in the van stick to my skin, squeaking whenever I move my leg. I keep moving my leg just to hear that little noise. No matter what is happening, how the van moves, or what the grownups are saying, when I move my leg I know I will hear that noise. I know it will happen, and that makes me feel okay somehow.

Just as we arrive at grandmother's village in Mahyah, Fungbeh starts to fuss. Nyempu gives him a toy to play with. Usually as we arrived in our yellow car, we would see curious kids chasing the car, peering at us, joking, eager to see who is arriving. I would feel rising excitement as my cousins eagerly swarmed us before we even got out of the car, then they would drag us to play hide-and-seek once we stopped. But there are no children running today. Mama doesn't have to tell us to stay put when the van stops. We already know this visit is not like usual.

Grandma is giving instructions, swiftly packing more into the van. It seems my entire family is running away now. Even in this strange visit, I am happy to see Auntie Garmen. She is around 17, the same age as Uncle Thomas, and they always joke together. Auntie Garmen is muscly and tough, playful with us kids. She is strong and can do any work a man can do; she often has an axe in one hand and she can climb trees faster than anyone I know. Mama says she has always been that way—like Kormah, not afraid of anything. Auntie Garmen is willing to do what most traditional village women would not even think of. Auntie Garmen is so cool and I am glad that she is coming with us.

Grandma climbs into the bus and solemnly greets us with a quick smile before turning to talk to Mama. Then comes Aunt Gormah who gives Mama a long, tight hug. I know that Auntie Gormah's husband, Nathan, died last week in a swimming accident. Mama and Aunt Gormah are as close as I am to Austin. Nyempu goes and gently takes Aunt Gormah's baby, Gerpili, from her. Her other little boy, Tinawoo, toddles behind her. I give Tinwoo a squeeze and scoop him in beside me. He is the same age as Fungbeh. I am glad that Mama and Aunt Gormah are together now. I can tell that Mama is happy too.

Mama gets Aunt Gormah's things in the truck as Aunt Ginger and her baby, Patricia, get in. As usual, Aunt Ginger is wearing bright lipstick and looks like a movie star. Usually she is laughing loudly and smiling, always with some new boyfriend hanging around, but today she gets in, just her and Patricia, squeezing in with Tinawoo and me. Uncle Michael, Uncle George, Uncle Chris, and Uncle Thomas, and a few others add their stuff and settle into seats. Once everyone is in, we start our journey. The van struggles up a hill and with every bump in the road, Aunt Ginger squishes us children into the side of the van. I pray the van has a strong engine.

Along the way, we drop off Michael, then Uncle George, wherever they have decided to go. I figure everyone has their own higher ground to get to, the place they are going to hide while the war blows over. Finally, we reach the giant Firestone plantation where they harvest rubber from trees to make tires. It is quite famous because our Liberian tires are put on cars that drive the streets of America. I have only heard about this great place, but this is my first time seeing it. Grandma is going to stay with her brother who works here.

Pulling up to the entrance, the company looks to be operating as normal, not like there is a war coming their way. I see people, white people too, going in and out of buildings and cars. Uncle Thomas helps Grandma out of the van. I see her hug Mama tight and whisper something in her ear—the same way Mama holds and whispers to us when we are afraid.

"Okay," Mama says when she is back in the van. She turns around to look at us. "Now we go to Gaye Town where we can rest and wait for Alfred."

Uncle Thomas, Aunt Ginger, Aunt Garmen, Aunt Gormah, and all our cousins will there with us. Hearing Mama say that we are close to the place where we will see Papa is the best news I have heard for days.

13

A Community of Whispering Strangers

"Quanei! Quanei! Wake up, kpaah!" Kormah gives me a shake. "Wake up, kpaah, we are almost there. We are almost to Gaye Town Church."

I sit up and rub my eyes. I must have fallen asleep. "We are here?"

"Almost." Kormah's eyes are locked on the scenery. I turn to look out the window too.

The van is pulling up to a place that looks like a nice country-side community. This place seems tucked away, far from the scary world that is overtaking Liberia. We pass a sign that reads Welcome to Gaye Town Church. The bus rolls into a giant garden compound, with the church at the center.

"We are here," Mama says.

As the bus pulls around the front of the church, we see more buildings, soft dirt roads, and children playing outside. There is a brick building with people going in and out and I realize it is a school. This community has a school of its own just like Sugar Hill, only this school is on the premises of the church courtyard. As our van approaches, a few people come out and stand in front of the main building. I see they have wide smiles on their faces. The man with the biggest smile and the woman next to him are waving.

"That is Brother Wesley and his wife, Sister Sarah," Mama tells us. "They run Gaye Town. Alfred and I have known them for some time."

"They seem nice," Aunt Gormah says. "Thank God they are helping you, Neyor."

The van stops and Mama opens her door.

"Hello, Sister Karmue! Welcome!" Brother Wesley calls out.

"Brother Wesley," Mama says, as she embraces him and then his wife.

"So glad you have made it safely," he says. His voice is full of warmth.

"Thank you for having us," Mama replies. "We know what a risk it is to have traffic in and out of your property. I know you don't want to attract too much attention."

"Think nothing of it. You and Alfred are like our family. Of course you are welcome here," Brother Wesley says.

Mama seems happy to see these people and it is the first time I have seen her smile in a long time. I am happy now too. Once our aunties and uncles are off the bus, Nyempu grabs Fungbeh. Kormah guides them both out and I help Kulubah down.

"These are the children," Mama says to Brother Wesley. "These are my sisters Garmen and Gormah and her children. This is my brother, Thomas. And this Alfred's sister Ginger and her daughter. Ginger is going to stay with another family close by in the area."

"Hello!" Brother Wesley reaches out to shake my hand. His hand feels warm and completely absorbs mine. I give him my best shake, the way Papa taught me. Even if we are strangers and in a strange place, I need to make a good impression. Brother Wesley has kind eyes. I like him. He introduces himself to each of us.

"And who do we have here?" Brother Wesley asks, nodding toward Fungbeh. "Look at this one, looking so much like Karmue.

He reaches out and tickles Fungbeh's tummy the way Papa does. Fungbeh reaches for him and they are instant friends.

"Oh, I am already in love with this one," Sister Sarah says.

I am used to grownups making a fuss over Fungbeh. He knows just what to do to get people to spoil him with hugs and kisses.

While the Wesleys are making us feel welcome, I see a few people poke their head out their houses around the church. They whisper to each other, then duck back inside. I am reminded that people don't feel comfortable with strangers entering their communities during such a terrible time. Even though Gaye Town Church seems like a nice place, the people here are scared, hiding from war just like us. Thankfully, these Gaye Town people have a great relationship with Mama and Papa and I am grateful that we have a place to stay.

"Okay, children," Mama says. "Gather your things."

"Yes," Brother Wesley says. "Let us show you inside."

Brother Wesley leads us through the double doors of the church and inside the main building. We clutch our bags and glance at every place Brother Wesley points out.

"This is the cafeteria," he says. "We all eat breakfast, lunch, and dinner together. And this is the main auditorium. We gather in there to listen to the evening news and to have worship services and prayer. Sometimes we get news from the front lines of the war."

"Front lines?" Aunt Garmen asks.

"Yes. The war is ongoing day and night, mostly in rural parts of Nimba and some part of Bong, where you're from. Most everyone outside the city has abandoned their home to come here or to other places of refuge. And when they come, they bring even more news. Also, there is a member of our church who is a soldier and part of the Liberian Army. He is a faithful member of our church and sometimes he comes to bring us news so that we can be prepare ourselves or even hide if we need to."

"What are they saying?" Mama asks. "What does he know?"

Brother Wesley stops and turns to face us all. "It is the most gruesome, hopeless thing that has ever touched Liberia.

The rebels are killing people and the President is terrified that rebels might hiding within our borders and spying among us. He is killing anyone suspected of supporting the rebel forces. He is killing families." Brother Wesley pauses for a moment and lowers his voice, speaking carefully. "But of course, that is not what is being reported on the news, since the government controls the radio."

Brother Wesley opens the door to what appears to be a Sunday school room. "Nevertheless, this is where you are staying."

I peek around Mama to see inside. The room is simple. There are a few chairs and the floor is lined with cots and blankets. All of us are to share this room.

"Thank you, Brother Wesley," Mama says.

"It is our pleasure," he says smiling. "Bathrooms are down the hall and some are outside in stalls in case the inside ones are occupied. Make yourselves comfortable."

"Come on, put your things down," Mama says to us. "Thomas, look after them. I need to go and speak with Brother and Sister Wesley." With that, Mama is off down the hallway toward the main rooms.

I step inside the room that is going to be our home for the next few weeks and find a place near the wall to make my bed. The faint smell of sweat and musk lingers in the air and I wonder if there was a family in here before us. The entire room is smaller than our living room at home, yet somehow we are all supposed to make do. Mama and the five of us, Aunt Gormah and her two kids, Uncle Thomas, Aunt Garmen—all of us will have to find a way to fit. I am glad to see the room has a window like my room back home. I miss home. I am ready for this war to be over.

'Come on, kids," calls Aunt Gormah, inviting her children to pick a spot and settle in.

"When is Papa coming?" Kormah asks plopping down on a cot. "I am ready to go home."

"Kormah!" says Nyempu. "Please be good." She takes a second to stare at him. "We all want to be home, but we just got here. Plus, we can't go home until Papa comes."

"Mama says Papa will come soon and then we will go home," I tell Kormah. "And when Papa gets back to Sugar Hill, he will do what he does best and make everything alright."

"Well, he better hurry up," Kormah says, crossing his arms.

Soon, the people Aunt Ginger knows come and take her and baby Patricia to their safe place. I am sad to see my sweet cousin go, but I am not surprised that Aunt Ginger is not staying with us. My father's sister sometimes has sharp opinions about anything that she does not agree with.

We make ourselves comfortable and lie on our thin cots until Mama comes to bring us to the cafeteria for dinner. I get excited when the members of the church start serving everyone plates of food. All the families are gathered to eat together and the cafeteria is filled with a light hum of voices and chairs and plates clinking. When we all have our plate, Brother Wesley calls the room to order.

"We are all grateful to be here today," he says, his arms outstretched. "And we thank God for being a light to others. Today, help us to welcome the new families who have come to Gaye Town and let us all bind together in love during these perilous times." He looks around at the crowd of families that are in the cafeteria. "Now, let us pray."

He bows his head, as does everyone else except for Kormah. Even in Gaye Town, Kormah needs to be rebellious. When grace is complete, we dig in. Some people are shoving food in their mouths and swallowing fast, as if they have not eaten in days.

"Don't stare, Quanei," Aunt Garmen whispers.

I do as I am told. I don't blame the people for eating so fast. The food tastes good and we are glad for a meal. When I look up from my own plate again, I notice families just like ours, with children our age. A young girl waves at me from across the room, smiling hard. She seems friendly. I slowly raise my hand too. She nudges her brother and he turns to look at us too. His smile goes all the way up to his eyes. He waves quickly before turning back to his food.

"Aye, Quanei," Aunt Garmen says. "You will have time to play with your new friends tomorrow." She gives me small nudge and a smile. I am slowly starting to like this place.

After dinner, we get washed up in the bathroom. Mama rubs each of us down with a warm towel, our face, our hands, and our bodies. "You have had a busy day, little boy," she says.

"Can I play outside tomorrow, Mama?" I ask. "Aunt Garmen says we can play outside."

Mama tugs my shirt and says, "You can play outside, when your little body has gone to sleep and you have gotten some rest. You too, Kormah," she says, giving him a hug.

When we get back to our room, Mama gathers us together near her cot. "Children," she says, "we are grateful to be here for a little while, while we wait for Papa. The Wesleys are very good people and the people here are just like us. We are all together." Mama rubs lotion on Fungbeh's little body. The smell of shea cream fills my nose, making me think of home. She continues, "There will probably be even more families coming, but we are guests and I want each of you to be on your best behavior. Do you understand?"

"Yes, Mama," we all say.

"And mind Thomas and Garmen." She pulls Fungbeh's shirt over his head. "You are to mind your manners and do not be speaking of rebels and war at this place, do you understand me?"

"But what if we hear guns at night?" Kormah asks, bouncing on his cot. "I heard a boy say he hears guns at night!"

"Kormah, settle down. That is nothing to celebrate. Stop jumping!" Mama snaps. "I don't care what you hear at night. You do as I have just said. All of you. Understand?"

We all nod back.

I'm not excited about the war and don't like talking about the rebels and the war anymore. Not since I saw the trucks on Ghanta Highway. Thinking about it gives me a bad feeling. This feeling, it is like a great wall of sadness and fear has come alive inside me. I don't know how to make it go away. If there are rebels out there killing people, and if, like Brother Wesley says, President Doe is killing families, then Mama is right: no one wants to hear about it. We all just want this to be over.

I crawl onto my cot beside Kormah and wrap the thin blanket around me. As Mama finishes unpacking, Fungbeh and Kulubah are already snoring. I hear Mama softly whisper to Uncle Thomas that she is going down to Brother Wesley's office to speak with him about Papa coming. I expect to stay up with Kormah, Nyempu, whispering about this place, whispering about guns, and even Papa, but I am asleep before Mama even leaves the room. I sleep through the night and wake up after the sun is up.

I roll over to see Fungbeh is cuddled up next to me. I hadn't even noticed him get in. Mama must have put him here. I rub his back while my eyes roam the room. Nyempu is still asleep beside me, but Kormah is gone. I look around and Aunt Gormah's cot is empty. So is Mama's. I hear people walking and talking outside and my stomach growls a little. It is time for me to get up and go find Mama. I pick up Fungbeh and place him in Nyempu's bed. She is sleeping so deeply she doesn't budge when I put Fungbeh down. I don't want to wake her. She works almost as hard as Mama, like a little grownup. I tuck a thin blanket around them both then slip out of our room.

I know that first thing in the morning I am to wash my face, so I go to the bathroom to find a sink to splash water on my face. When I am done, I wander down the hall where I hear noise. Maybe I will find Mama there.

"Quanei!"

I turn to see Kormah waving at me from the end of the hallway. He is standing with a group of kids. It looks like Kormah has made friends and I am suddenly excited.

"Go wake up Nyempu," he says with a big grin. "Come on and eat!"

14

Home on the Front Lines

When we are finally all together again at the breakfast table, the mood is different from dinner last night. The whole place seems lighter and happier in the daylight. More people are speaking to Mama and Aunt Gormah and they don't seem as wary or afraid. Mama even lets us go eat breakfast at the table with the other children. The girl and boy who waved at us during last night's dinner are sitting there. Robert and Oretha are their names. They happily welcome us to their table and tell us all about themselves. They are staying in one of the houses next door, coming over here for meals and Bible study.

"Where is your Pa?" I ask, stuffing some rice in my mouth.

Oretha, who has been talking the entire time, suddenly grows quiet and does not say anything and Nyempu nudges me under the table.

"I don't know," Robert says. "He went to go and pick up his mother from her village and he has not come back. But our Uncle lives with us and he says he will help Mama while Papa is gone."

"Our Pa is gone too," I say wiping my mouth. "He went to Ah—"

"Away," Nyempu breaks in. "He went away too. He is not back yet."

Kormah gives me a cold look from across the table.

"What games do you play here?" Kormah asks. "Where do you go to catch frogs?"

Robert brightens back up. "Oh, we go to a little pond nearby! We have to stay close to the campus, but we can still go if one of the big people come with us."

"I want to go!" I am bouncing in my seat. It has been forever since I went catching frogs. I forgot all about catching frogs.

"Yes, me too!" says Nyempu.

"I can show you where," Oretha says, smiling. This is going to be fun. The most fun any of us have had in a long time.

We find Mama and tell her we want to play outside. She gives us the rules for staying close and then finally we are free to go run and play. Robert is especially good at catching frogs, even better than me and Kormah. He knows exactly how to creep up quietly and he moves faster than any boy I have ever met. We also see who can throw rocks the farthest. Kormah can throw better than anyone and he makes sure to rub it in our faces. But I don't even mind that. It has been so long since Kormah has boasted about anything. Now that Aunt Gormah's kids are here, it feels like a family reunion. I run, laugh and play, feeling our souls happy again. We play all day and when we get hungry, we run back to the main building for lunch. We are excited now that we have friends. I guess it is true what Mama says—that it is not a house or material things that make you happy. She always says that real happiness comes from the joy you choose to make, no matter where you are.

Once we are done eating, we go back outside and play until we are called in. In Gaye Town, we can't play until the sun goes down. Coming in from catching frogs, we pass the main auditorium where the grownups are listening to the radio. They are gathered at the radio like flies on a piece of food. The grownups' faces are intense, ears locked to the sound of the voice on the radio. There is no interruption—not even from us. The news announcer says the same thing he has been saying for months. But this time, even I am forced to slow down and listen a little closer when I hear rebels are invading villages, towns and are now in Gbarnga City. They are burning homes and turning children into small soldiers and pushing their way to the capital of Monrovia.

My mind rushes to Boye and his family, to Sugar Hill, and our house on the hill. I can't stop wondering, did Boye and Uncle Paye, and Jemama ever leave in time? What if they did not leave? Did Boye turn into small soldier too? With no one living there, did rebels burn our house down?

As the news about the takeover in Gbarnga City continues, I hear Mama tell Aunt Gormah that we got out of the city just in time. That if we had stayed even one more day, we could have been dead. The entire room is heavy. I notice the worried faces of people sitting around, helpless as stones, wondering what will happen to all of us. The sun is going down, and it makes the mood even worse.

When the sun goes down here, just like in Sugar Hill, the people and the atmosphere change. Sundown brings about an evening fever that goes on throughout the night. The fever makes people walk quickly to their destination, keep their children close and their voices low. All you hear from grownups is a command to hush, and their murmurings of fear. With night comes more danger. The fever makes us all talk less and look around more. At night, we listen to the world with our entire body, waiting for any sound that may mean we must run for safety.

15

War is Real

One night, about ten days or so after we arrived, I am making up my cot when I hear a rapid pop pop pop. Then I hear tiny explosions. I jump up and look around with my eyes wide. I hear it again—a steady rat-a-tat-tat in the distance. I look at Kormah.

"Do you hear that?" I ask. My heart is racing. "Mama?" I call.

She comes in quickly from the bathroom. "Shhh! Lie down, all of you." She flips off the kerosene lamp.

"It's guns, Mama!" I say. My whole body is trembling. "Are the soldiers coming for us?"

Mama is in front of me. She is grabbing my shoulder. "No. Do you hear that? Those sounds are far away. They are in the distance. They are not close. We are in a church, Quanei. Churches are where God's people go to be safe. . ."

I am still shaking. The sounds continue. "Mama, I'm scared."

"I know. Lie down and be quiet," she says. "We are okay. Those noises are far away."

The sounds stop after a minute, and it gets quiet again. Maybe Mama is right. It could have been anything. Rebels fighting soldiers or just someone shooting in the darkness. Are we still safe here? Or is the war coming our way now?

"Quanei, don't be a baby." Kormah says, sliding his arms behind his head and looking at the ceiling. "Mama already said sometimes we may hear a gunshot. We are at war. We are not at home."

I give Kormah a look and shake my head angrily at him. I cross my arms and just try to think about home. But just as I begin to wish I were at home, I realize that home is not safe either. I lie awake for most of the night, listening for the soldiers who came to Sugar Hill, wondering if they will come for us. The fever that takes over the grownups has taken me now. And I want is for everyone to be quiet and keep low. I can't wait for the sun to come up.

At breakfast the next day, no one brings up the gunfire. Instead, we eat with Robert and Oretha, talking about what our plans for the day. This morning we are all scattered, having fula bread with mayonnaise and hot water for our meal. We are talking excitedly when a church member bursts into the cafeteria.

"There is a special report!" the man says. Everyone gets quiet. "On the news! A special report, Sis Neyor."

"Bring the radio in here," Brother Wesley says. People begin to murmur and look around. "Everyone, stay calm, please. We must listen and see what's going on."

The man returns with the radio and instantly I feel a rock in my stomach. Just looking at the radio gives me a bad feeling, because all the man on the radio ever does is give bad news. Everyone watches the man bring the radio to the front of the room. Brother Wesley turns up the volume. People shush their children. A male voice speaks.

This is a special BBC news update. The rebel advancement has continued into the Gbarnga area, where they have slaughtered hundreds of people in their attempt to push back government troops. On the coast of Liberia, rebel forces have set up camps, shutting down trade in and out of Liberia. Today, the Liberian government has issued a decree that all foreigners currently in Liberia need to leave the country within the next 24 hours. Again, anyone traveling in Liberia is being advised to leave immediately. It is no longer safe here. The United States Embassy is evacuating all Americans as of this afternoon. As rebel leaders call for the resignation of President Doe, he is responding with more deadly force for rebels.

The room is quiet as President Doe's voice fills the room. *I will not listen to the low voices of rebel convicts who are trying to destroy this county. We will not back down for criminals and looters and pests that desire to overthrow the power of Liberia and create their own anarchy. I will strike back! I will continue to cut down any person, any tree, any flower that goes against this government and its power.*

Everyone is stunned to hear the leader of our country. I am quiet. I know I am listening to the same voice that gave the order to kill the children I saw that day. The news broadcaster takes over again. *Additionally, to stop the activity of the rebels, the government is shutting down all major roads. The government will be closing off roads that lead in and out of the cities. If you are traveling on a major road, you risk attack by the rebels or being questioned by the Liberian government. Once more, President Doe has officially advised all those traveling in Liberia to leave the country now. Roads are being shut down and he is implementing a curfew on all Liberian citizens. No one is to be outside of their homes or offices after sundown. Anyone outside after sundown traveling or otherwise risks imprisonment by the Liberian government.*

I hear people gasp and see Uncle Thomas puts his hand over his mouth.

"It is getting worse," Aunt Garmen says. "To stop all travel? To cut off the roads? How will people find safety?"

Mama doesn't say anything. She is still listening with her hands clasped tightly over her mouth. Fungbeh is on her lap, beginning to fuss. He has figured out how to get whatever he wants when grownups are quiet or listening. Even though he is not old enough to get milk candy, he always wants money for it. He started doing this back when we would have Bible study at Sugar Hill. He would cry for money and someone would give him a nickel to be quiet. He decides to start fussing now.

"Want mo-ney!" Fungbeh whines, in a voice we know too well.

"Be quiet, child," Mama says.

"No, mo-ney for milk candy," he insists.

Uncle Thomas digs in his pocket and finds a single coin. "Here, now hush," he says. Everyone turns their attention back to the radio broadcast.

The Liberian government is shutting down all major roads and putting a curfew in place to cut off rebel activity." The news man continues. "Anyone traveling major roads or who is seen out after curfew will be suspected of treasonous activity. This has been a BBC News Special Report.

The music plays again, and the broadcast goes silent, leaving everyone stunned. The sun is shining brightly outside, but inside a cloud has formed over the Gaye Town Church cafeteria.

"This is terrible news," Brother Wesley says to his wife. "We have families who are coming here. How can they come if the roads have been shut down?"

I hear another couple whispering at a table behind us. The wife is upset at the news we have just heard. "How long can we stay here?" I hear the woman ask her husband. "If the government is shutting down roads, they are isolating us here!"

"No," the man says. "They are shutting down the roads to keep out the rebels. We are safe here."

"Haven't you noticed that food is getting less and less?" she asks. "More and more people have come here and if they are shutting down the roads, Gaye Town cannot get food in or out. The portions are smaller every day. If they run out soon, then what will we do?"

"Nancy, calm down," the man says. "We will stay here and eat what we can. We have no choice."

Until now, I have not noticed the food portions getting smaller, but then again, we have only been here a couple of weeks. I consider today's breakfast—we only had *fula* bread with a little mayonnaise. Everyone is upset that the Special Report has brought the night fever on our sunny morning.

16

Papa

Early April 1990

As soon as the news reports goes silent, everyone finds their children and goes their separate ways.

"Bye, Kormah! Bye, Nyempu! Bye, Quanei!" Oretha and Robert wave at us as they head back to their home next door. We wave goodbye and Mama ushers us back toward our room where we stay all day.

"Sister Neyor!" Brother Wesley calls from his office at the end of the hall. He walks briskly down the hall to Mama. "Come with me, please. There is more news. A PSA is circulating that you need to hear."

Mama follows him. We all follow behind her, but wait outside the office. Inside, I can see Brother Wesley, Mama, Aunt Gormah, and Sister Sarah gathered around a tiny radio. I cannot hear what is being said, but I can tell from the looks on their faces that it is not good. Suddenly, the radio signal picks up and the news voice is loud enough for me hear. *I repeat all travel, planes and otherwise, in and out of Liberia have been stopped. The American government is no longer allowing planes into the country and the Liberian government has completely shut down their airport. No one is traveling in or out of the country.*

I see Mama sit down and cover her mouth and Sister Wesley grips her hand. "That is why Alfred has not come. He cannot. They have shut down the travel."

I turn to Nyempu and Kormah who are all standing in shock like me. "Oh no! Is she saying that Papa is not coming Gaye Town? What will we do, Nyempu? How long can we wait for him?" I want to run in and ask Mama, but I do not. We all stand in the hallway stunned.

Mama sits for a long time and none of us move. "He isn't coming," Mama says to no one. Her voice is shaking. "He cannot come now. And there's no way to even talk to him."

Mama is still as a stone. Aunt Gormah slips an arm around her shoulder. "He cannot. At least he is safe, sister. He is safe and alive until the war is over."

"But me and my children are isolated here," Mama says. "We came here to wait for him. He was coming back early for us. And now he's not coming."

"You are not alone," Aunt Gormah reminds Mama, with tears in her own eyes. "I am not leaving you, Neyor. We have each other."

"I cannot believe this," Brother Wesley says. "I am so sorry, Sister, that this has happened. But you are not alone. We will look after you and the children until this war is over."

Nyempu tears away and takes off, running back down the halfway. I can hear her cries as she runs to our room. I want to run with her, but I am glued in my spot waiting for Mama, who looks distraught. I feel tears sting the side of my face and my chest begins to heave with sobs. We have waited here for Papa for almost two weeks and now they are saying he can't come to us. After all this—leaving home and waiting in this church, Papa is not coming to meet us. Mama is right. We are trapped here in Gaye Town, Monrovia and the soldiers are everywhere. The rebels are coming, and we are all going to die. Kormah walks away silently with his elbow cuffed around his face. He doesn't want us to see he is crying.

"Come, child," Aunt Garmen says to me. Her voice is as heavy as I feel. "Let's get you all ready for bed. Papa will come when the time is right, baby."

Kulubah immediately starts to cry at the news from Aunt Garmen. Fungbeh also becomes upset and starts to tear up, though I'm not sure he really knows what is going on. In a matter of seconds, we are all heartbroken. It is as if we received news that Papa is dead. Even Uncle Thomas has tears in his eyes.

Later, after the fever has pushed everyone into their rooms for the night, the hallway seems dark and hollow, matching how I feel. Mama comes into our room gathers us close. No one really says a word—we just sit in the silence. Indeed, the whole compound is quiet. Our sad silence is broken with the sound of Mama's warm voice as she starts to hum a soft melody. I know the sweet song Mama is singing and I am glad to hear it. I close my eyes and lean on Mama as I listen to the sound of her humming and singing the way she had done for us at home.

Kokoleoko, children, Kokoleoko, Kokoleoko, chicken crowing for day... Kokoleoko, Nyempu, Kokoleoko, Kokoleoko, Rooster crowing for day. . . Soon, Aunt Garmen, Aunt Gormah, and Uncle Thomas join in softy, then we all join in. We have transported ourselves back to Gharmue, to when our entire family's village was filled with comfort and joy. I feel a smile tugging on my lips and the dark room is filled with love and hope. The more Mama sings, the better I feel and soon sleep pulls on my eyelids. We all just lie there quietly as Mama softly hums *Kokoleoko. Hum hum hu huua hmm, Hum hum hu huua hmm, Hum hum hu huua hmm. . .* Kormah is snoring now. Nyempu's eyes are closed tightly. Soon everyone is asleep.

That night, when the gunfire wakes me, I do not look out the window. I lie there in the darkness facing the wall. I feel like I have been lowered into a deep dark hole. I miss Papa so bad it hurts. I feel empty and dry. I want to cry but I cannot. I am all cried out inside. I cannot think anymore. I am not even afraid when I hear the distant guns. I don't care anymore. I can only see the wall. All I want to see is the dark wall. Maybe the wall will suck me up and I will become a part of it and not have to worry about any of this anymore.

17

Fungbeh Wants Milk Candy

Two more weeks go by and there is no change. If anything, conditions get worse. All of Gaye Town is practically out of food and each night the sound of gunfire gets closer and closer. Sometimes gunfire seems right at the gates of the church. By now we've gotten used to hearing the shots. Many families have left the compound on foot, in search of a safer place and food to eat. At night, Brother Wesley boards up the windows and doors and says that it is best that all who remain in the compound sleep in the big room in the back. If soldiers or rebels come, they will think the place is abandoned. He tells us that if they break in the front door, we are all to huddle in the back. Likely, after searching a few rooms, they—whoever they are—will give up and move on.

Mama has gotten so skinny that her shirts are slipping off her shoulders. Whatever little food we get, we share during the day. Mama carefully distributes her own portion to us. We are so hungry during the day that my stomach hurts. The normal eating times are no more. We just eat one time a day and it is a small fistful of rice. I have to tie my pants up around my stomach, almost into my chest to keep them on.

Then, the entire compound is out of food. We go an entire day without rice. Thankfully, Auntie Garmen is tough and very brave. She knows how to do everything a man can do, like hunt and fish. During the day, she goes out into the dangerous war zone to look for food to bring back to us. She has found a lake nearby where she catches crabs and picks little shellfish off the leaves that grow in the water. Most days she comes back with just a handful of things for us to eat. But we are too hungry to care. We happily take down every crumb we can manage.

As we stay locked inside Gaye Town with a war roaring outside, I wonder how long we can stay here without food. I pray that we don't have to find out, but every day seems darker and darker. Mama's neck is becoming so skinny and everyone looks worn and tired.

We do not see Oretha or Robert anymore either. We have not been allowed outside for many days. It is not safe, the grownups say, even in the day. The firestorm of bullets continues every night and sometimes even in the daytime now. When that happens, everyone runs and hides in the darker parts of the church. Every night, Mama sings little lullabies to calm us. "Jesus Loves the Little Children" is so comforting when Mama hums. Sometimes, even on an empty stomach, these simple songs put us to sleep for a little while.

One night, about a month into our stay at Gaye Town, we are all lying down in the back room, quiet as mice, listening to rapid gunfire and loud booms down the road. As I lie next to Kormah and Aunt Garmen, I wonder how much longer we can do this. Every day is the same—locked inside, starving. Every night is worse—hiding from rebels and soldiers.

I try to pretend I am back home, but the sound of tires on pavement interrupts my thoughts. I lift my head. It seems everyone else has heard it too. Soon the sound of a single truck grows into the steady thunder of many trucks circling the campus. Fear fills the room as everyone looks around. Headlights shine against the building, spilling beams of light through the boarded-up windows and onto our walls.

"Aye! Over here! Check here!"

There is yelling all around us, then loud banging on walls and doors. We all duck our heads in the darkness, praying not to be discovered. There is much commotion outside with what sounds like an entire army filling the Gaye Town compound. *The soldiers are here. They have found us, Mama. They are coming for us.* My mind is wild. I want to speak but my throat is frozen.

"It's that soldier from the church, I know it is. He told them we're hiding here," Aunt Garmen whispers harshly.

"I knew it—he's a traitor," Uncle Thomas adds.

"Shhh! Keep it quiet. Come close to me, all of you." Mama is pulling me by the back of my shirt. She hauls Kormah and Nyempu into the corner directly behind the door. We are terrified. Everyone is trying to control their breathing so as not to make a sound. I can feel Mama's heart beating as she holds all of us close. "Jesus, we need you!" Mama whispers. "Don't let them come in here, Lord."

I see Mama close her eyes tight as she prays. As the footsteps and yelling encircle us, I pray too. I wish Papa was here to make all the bad soldiers go away. I hear the soldiers inside the compound. It sounds like they are going from house to house. I hear doors being kicked down, glass shattering. The main building where we reside is huge, so it can't be missed. Our only hope is that the soldiers will think it is empty because of the way it is boarded up and locked tight.

I hear another loud crash outside and yelling. Then I hear terrified screams that seem to come through the walls and right up to my face. The soldiers have broken into someone's house.

"Oh, my people! Please! I beg you, people! Nobody here but us!" someone pleads.

"Please! What you hiding for? You fucking people! People like you making the damn rebels come this way!" I hear soldiers yelling and cursing as they interrogate whoever they have captured.

"Sumo! Go check the house!" one soldier yells. "We will find out if you got rebels hiding here!"

"No! Just me and my children!"

"You lie to me and I'll cut your neck, you hear me? All your children and you will die today! Where you from?" Whoever they are interrogating is crying too hard to speak. "I say where your ass from, woman? What tribe are you?" the soldier insists.

As screams fill the compound, I hear soldiers kicking in yet another door. I am trembling so hard. I almost can't breathe. "Who is here? Who are you?" the soldiers yell. I hear them asking questions and I hear someone begging and pleading. The screams fill our ears and we are all too scared to move. I have never heard anyone scream so horribly in my life. I hold my head down and close my eyes tight against Kulubah and Fungbeh and Mama, trying to make it all go away.

Suddenly there is a loud bang on the main door of the church. Everyone hears it, but no one moves and no one breathes. Thank God Brother Wesley has bolted the door shut. The banging stops and whoever was knocking tries kicking the door, hard. The door does not give. The soldier walks around the building, shining a flashlight into the boarded-up windows. No one moves. The air is silent, as if we are all waiting for a bomb to drop. The screaming around us continues. I can no longer breathe. My heart beats inside my chest and in my ears so loudly, I fear the soldiers outside may hear it and discover us. Footsteps draw closer, heading toward the window of the room we are all crowded in. They are coming from around the left side of the building.

"Um, Mama." A small voice breaks the silence and everyone gasps. We all whip around to see Fungbeh tugging on Mama.

"Mo-ney!" he says.

Ma clamps her hand over his mouth and looks to see if the soldier's light has found us. Fungbeh wiggles his face free and says even louder, "Want mo-ney!"

"No, be quiet!" Mama snaps.

"Oh, my God, Neyor!" Uncle Thomas cries. His voice is trembling. "He will get us killed!"

Everyone glares at us with fear in their eyes. I cannot believe that Fungbeh is using this "quiet time" to get his way.

"Um, Mama, want money for milk candy," Fungbeh begs, holding out his hand.

Mama covers his mouth with her hand. "Shhh, baby." But that only makes him cry louder.

"Shut him up!" someone hisses from the corner.

"I don't have any money!" Mama says.

"Give him something!" someone else pleads. "Anything!"

It sounds like a soldier is closing in now, like a lion on its prey. The footsteps get louder, and we know Fungbeh could give us away. I feel like I am burning up.

"Mo-ney!" Fungbeh cries, as he kicks and throws up his arms.

"Does anyone have any money to give to this boy, so he will shut up?" a man in the corners asks.

"Funbgeh, be quiet!" Mama whispers. He knows better, but he is spoiled and wants to get his way. "Hush!"

"Here!" Someone shoves something at Mama. It is a nickel. Mama hurriedly gives it to Fungbeh, looking embarrassed and scared. Fungbeh takes the money, smiles, and tucks his nickel away in his shorts, satisfied. Everyone listens to see if he has given us away.

The soldier is now directly under our window. He flashes his lights inside, tapping and pulling the boards to try to see through a crack. I feel as if I am about to drop dead. I am sure the soldier is coming for us now. I am sure we will die. Another terrified and gut-wrenching scream erupts from a house next to us. Nyempu is gripping my arm so tight that it hurts.

"What you got over there?" the solider calls, walking away from the window. "What you got?"

More screams fill the air, the soldier's beam of light disappears. Just when I think the blood-curdling screams are more than I can take, they all stop. The next thing we hear is the sound of giant trucks rolling away. No one moves a muscle, not for the rest of the night. Not until sunlight is breaks through the cracks of the boarded windows.

18

My First Massacre

The next morning, I am jolted awake by the sound of screaming. I shoot out of my sleep like a rocket and look around to see that most of the adults have the left the room. Nyempu is also awake, her eyes wide. We both run out of the room looking for Mama and everyone else. The double doors in the front are open and we can see people outside. Where is Mama? *Where is Aunt Gormah?* Nyempu and I step into the sun's warm light. Mama is there to my great relief, and everyone else is next door at the Johnson's home, where Oretha and Robert live.

"Oooh, God! Oh no! Oh, my God!" Someone is screaming and crying. "Oh, God no!"

Nyempu grabs my hand, but I pull away. I push against the group of people standing in front of the Johnson's home. Finally, I break through. Immediately, I stumble backward, knocked over by a sickeningly sweet, metallic smell, which I would too soon learn is blood. I stand in shock before a river flowing down the steps of the Johnson's home. A man is lying down, covered in blood, next to a woman. I realize it had been the Johnson's screams we heard the night before. All the feeling leaves my face. I feel bile rising up in my chest, but I am stuck, unable to move.

"Oh, my God!" Sister Sarah drops to her knees, sobbing hard. "They are all gone!"

Everyone stares blankly at the Johnsons' lifeless bodies and blood-stained porch. The sick feeling fills my stomach as I look past the dead bodies and into the hallway of the Johnson's home. I see Oretha and Robert flat on their backs, Oretha's arm across Robert's stomach. My knees are weak. It is hard for me to breathe. I feel dizzy and the next thing I feel is the cool ground on my back.

Quanei! I hear an echoing voice in my eardrums, calling my name. Someone is shaking me. *Quanei!* I see only black, but I feel myself lifted into the air. I am floating away from my pain. I am lifted above the war. I am flying away. *Quanei!* I stop flying. I hear Mama's voice. "Quanei!"

Someone is tapping my cheek. I open my eyes and slowly Mama's face comes into view. She looks worried, but happy to see my eyes open. "You fainted, boy!" She hugs me.

"Mama, are Robert and Oretha dead? Did the soldiers get them? Are they going to get me?" I fall limp against Mama's chest, feeling dizzy again. "Are they getting us?"

Mama does not answer me. She just holds me tight as people begin rushing to their rooms in a panic. I am starting to feel better. I can hear scared voices.

"Come on, baby," Mama says, helping me get on my feet. "Let's go to our spot."

'It is not safe here," I hear several voices say.

"We have to go!" someone cries. "What will we do? What if they come back? What if they bring something to pry open the door Brother Wesley boarded shut?"

"Is he alright?" Brother Wesley says as Mama leads me into the church hallway.

"He is fine," Mama says. "I am going to get him some water." Mama pushes us all back toward our room.

I can see and hear everything around me, but I feel like a zombie. I keep seeing the blood running from Robert and Oretha's house and I tremble at the thought of what must have happened to them. I cannot believe Robert and Oretha are dead. How can they be dead when they were just sitting next door? *How could anyone look at Robert, as nice as he is, and Oretha, as sweet as she is, and just kill them? Adults are supposed to protect children, teach them the right way to grow up. Not kill them.*

As soon as we are all secure in the room, a troubled Aunt Garmen repeats what so many were saying in the hall. "It is not safe here. The government is coming down on us. That family is dead! They were sitting here in the auditorium with us yesterday and now they are all dead!" Aunt Garmen goes quiet, deep in thought. Uncle Thomas is pacing the floor.

Suddenly there is a knock on the door and we all jump.

"Neyor, it is me." I recognize the voice of Sister Smith. Mama opens the door. "Neyor, I have come to say goodbye."

"You are leaving?"

"Yes, we have no choice," Sister Smith says. "That family. They were massacred, and we were right here. I do not know why we are still alive, but I am not going to stay to find out. We are leaving right now, before the day is started."

The woman hugs Mama quickly and then she is gone.

"Neyor, we need to leave too," Aunt Garmen says. "We cannot stay here. Not one more day. I know of some people in villages off the main roads where neither rebels nor Doe cares to look. I am going back to our home village. I must go."

"But it is too far," Mama pleads with her.

"We cannot stay here, Neyor." She grabs Mama's shoulders. "Last night was a blessing from God. But it was also a warning. We cannot stay here and starve or be slaughtered. I am going home to Mahyah."

"Take me with you," Kormah says leaping over his cot and in front of her. "Mama, I want to go with Auntie. Let me go to Mahyah. I'm not scared—I want to go."

"No," Mama says. "We are staying together."

Aunt Garmen has already begun packing her things, making it clear that she is leaving no matter what.

"Mama, I can go!" Kormah cries. "I'm not scared!" he insists.

"Kormah, that is enough! Garmen, you cannot go," Mama says. "It is not safe."

"It is not safe here either, Neyor," Aunt Garmen replies.

"I agree with Garmen," Thomas says. He looks upset. "I am going to go too."

"It is not safe!" Mama insists.

"It is safer than here, Ma Neyor," Uncle Thomas says. "I am like Garmen. If I can go to the village, I want to go. I want to go home. And I have to take that chance."

"And you have to take me with you!" Kormah says, "Mama, you have to let me go!"

I can't believe Kormah is keeping up such a fuss about wanting to go with Aunt Garmen. Mama has raised her voice at him three times, and he still insists. Finally, when Mama refuses again, he turns over his cot and storms out of the room.

"You should let him go with me, Neyor." Aunt Garmen says.

"Absolutely not," Mama says. "My children are staying with me. We are all staying together. Even Kormah. I don't care how much he protests."

"Okay, then I protest." Aunt Garmen says. She lowers her voice and pulls Mama to the side. "Neyor, you have five children. Gormah has her own children to look after. Without Thomas and me to help look after the children, what will you do? You have so many mouths to feed and there is barely any food as it is. At least let me look after and feed one of your children."

Mama gives Aunt Garmen an angry look. "He is my son. My child. I look after my own children and we stay together. If you and Thomas need to leave for Mahyah, then I understand. But all of my children are staying in Gaye Town until I figure out what to do next. End of discussion."

Later that night, after several others have left Gaye Town and those remaining have settled down, I pass by the main auditorium and hear Mama and Aunt Garmen discussing the Kormah situation again.

"Neyor," I hear Aunt Garmen say. "I know this is not easy, but you know I can look after the boy. With me and Thomas together you know it will be no problem. I can take him home to our village where he will be with other family too. He will be safe from this war then. The boy wants to go. Do you really want to be dragging an angry Kormah through the streets of Liberia, with those rebels and everything that is out there? You have seen how well we get along. You know that he listens to me. You know that if he is your son, he is my son. I will look after him with my life."

"And what if you don't make it?"

"What if you don't?" Aunt Garmen asks. "Is it better for all of us to risk dying together or for at least some of us to make it home? Let the boy come, Neyor. You have been so smart getting us all here. You cannot continue to manage all of these children and the baby by yourself. Let me take Kormah and let me help."

"Fine," Mama says. She is crying. "Fine, I will trust him with you. Maybe, it is best, given everything, that he goes with you. If the soldiers come back here, I will know that at least one of my children is somewhere else."

"God willing, we will all be safe soon enough," Aunt Garmen says. "We know the plan is to meet up at the village no matter what. If you make it home, send word and we will come to meet you in Sugar Hill. Or you can come straight to the village and, God willing, we will be there. And then we will all be together, you hear? I promise."

"Okay," Mama says, letting out a deep breath. "But at least, please, stay a few more days so I can spend more time with him and you, before you go."

"Neyor, I have to get myself out of here. I have to leave at first light. With or without the boy. Don't worry, we will be together again."

The next morning, we all get up early and send Kormah, Aunt Garmen, and Uncle Thomas away with a long and tearful goodbye. Mama holds onto Kormah so tight and so long I think she might actually squeeze him to death. When she finally lets him go, Mama looks as if she is about to collapse, but Aunt Gormah slips her arm around Mama's middle and gives her a loving squeeze. "You are doing your best given the circumstances, Neyor."

Finally, once we have all said goodbye, they turn to go, starting their own journey to safety.

It turns out, Aunt Garmen was right. That night, the soldiers came back, with their footsteps and their voices and their guns, looking for any sign of life, anyone to question. We have become accustomed to hiding in the back, and there are fewer of us now. As the soldiers walk around, we all hold our breath and pray silently. We know if we are caught we will be killed like the family next door. As we sit in the dark together, just a step away from death, I wish that Mama had run with Aunt Garmen. So that we wouldn't be here now, with soldiers on top of us, waiting to be killed.

As we lie huddled on the floor, Aunt Gormah puts her arm across Nyempu and me. On the other side, she wraps her arm around her her kids, Tinawoo and Gerpili. Her eyes are fixed on the door in front of us and she is very still, like everyone else in the room. In the stillness, Fungbeh senses that all grownups want to be quiet, and decides now is the time to get more money for candy.

"Mama," he says in his crying voice. "Want mo-ney!"

Aunt Gormah's head snaps up and everyone else gasps and looks up at Mama, their eyes wide, but their voice quiet. They cannot talk for fear of being heard. Mama places her hand over Fungbeh's mouth again.

"He is going to get us killed!" Brother Wuo whispers.

"I want mo-ney," Fungbeh says in a crying voice.

"Dear God, please." Brother Maxwell, who is lying next to me, prays.

"Mama!" Fungbeh says, reaching out his hand with a sly look on his face. Even at two-years-old, he knows what he is doing. He just does not know that this quiet time is much more serious than any Bible study or television show.

"Fungbeh, hush!" Mama says, covering his mouth. He is crying for money still. I hear footsteps getting closer and my eyes are filling with tears from the fear alone. He will surely get us killed tonight.

"Here!" someone says.

"I am sorry," Mama whispers.

"Shhh." Mama slips the money into his hand and he is quiet again. Although his crying is over, the threat is not.

We don't hear any screaming or crying outside that night. There is no one else being tortured. The soldiers do not stay for long and, once again, we are saved by the grace of God.

The next night, before we go to sleep, Mama takes Fungbeh into one of the rooms. I can hear her say, "You have been a bad boy. Do not ask me for milk candy tonight."

"Mo-ney," Fungbeh laughs. "I want mo-ney!"

The next thing I know, Mama is whipping Fungbeh. "You will be quiet tonight!" she says. He is crying so hard that Brother Wesley comes to the door.

"Please don't whip him, Sister," Brother Wesley says. "He is just a baby. Don't whip him, please."

Mama does not listen, and whips Fungbeh, telling him again that he will not ask for money tonight, that if he does, she will whip just like this. Whatever she does, it works because that night Fungbeh is quiet as a lamb. And when the soldiers come, he does not make a peep.

19

Not the Chosen Ones

Late July 1990

There is no food left at Gaye Town Church and Mama has begun going out into the streets, risking her life to knock on doors for food. There is nothing left in the entire Gaye Town community. Every day, people are fainting from hunger. Most days Mama comes back empty handed because people have nothing to spare. They are starving themselves or they are too afraid to open their doors at all. Again I wish we had gone with Aunt Garmen because at least she knows how to catch food.

Just when I think that I cannot last another second of starvation, a miracle happens: Mama comes back with a cup of rice. Mama cooks and divides it among the eight of us. I am so glad to see the rice that I stuff it down, even though it burns my throat. I am so hungry that I am shaking. Everyone is quiet, quickly eating the rice. Mama takes her time and puts Fungbeh on her lap, feeding him with a spoon. All too soon, my small portion of rice is gone, and I want to cry. I am still hungry. Kormah and Nyempu are finished too. As we look up at Mama, we realize we don't know when we will ever get more.

"I have news," Mama tells and all of us.

"Oh, please say something good, Neyor," Aunt Gormah says. "Please, God."

"It is about how I got this cup of rice. I went to look for food and ask for rice today. I saw Edith, an old friend from high school. It is a miracle that I even found her." Mama wipes Fungbeh's mouth. "Edith is the one who gave us the cup of rice. She and her family are starving there too, but she was generous and split what they had left with me."

"God bless her and her family," Aunt Gormah says.

"Yes," Mama says. "She gave me the last of what they had. But, she told me of a Lutheran church two miles down the road. Edith says that the church is helping those who are running from the war, especially those who are running from Doe. She told me that the Lutheran church is taking in people. That they have food and more supplies."

"But we cannot go there," Aunt Gormah says. "It is not safe! What if they do not help us?"

"We cannot stay here either," Mama points out. "There is no food here or around here and every night rebels or soldiers are walking through this place, looking for someone to kill. I am going to walk to the church, to see if they will give us food. I have to do something or else my children will die of hunger."

"It is not safe to go, Neyor." Aunt Gormah warns again. "I have heard about this church too, and they are only helping those who are from tribes that are being persecuted by Doe in Nimba. He has made it very difficult for those who are not from his native tribe. He does not trust anyone."

"We should try anyways, as there is no more food anywhere," Mama says. "Edith is sure they will help us. She says that because the church is so big, they have enough to spare. She is taking her family there tomorrow too. They are going to check in there and stay until all this is over. We will not stay, but we will get enough food and bring back for the others here. That way, we can have enough food to survive." Aunt Gormah and Mama discuss this a little more before finally agreeing on a decision.

The next morning, Mama tells us we are walking to the Lutheran church to get food. I am so happy to hear this, but I don't have the energy to run or jump up and down. Also, if I jump, my clothes might fall right off my shrunken body.

We walk the two miles to the Lutheran church, along with Aunt Gormah and her children. On the way, we pass other people walking as well. They have all of their things with them, and they look scared. I think they are walking fast to get to wherever they are going before the fever sets in.

Two miles feels like twenty in the hot sun, especially considering that we have not had a real meal in so long. That last ladle of rice Mama fed to us in bits, and even that we were glad for. But it was not enough, which is why Mama is taking this chance. At this point we will follow Mama anywhere.

When we get to the Lutheran Church, I see many people already there. Many more than in Gaye Town. The church courtyard is surrounded by a stone wall with an iron gate, and there is a man with a clipboard checking people in. Verifying them. There are whole families being let in, seeking refuge in the church. A lot of the children look skinny like me and my brothers and sisters. They look sad and tired and hungry, just like us. I cannot wait to just eat something. I do not care what it is.

"Good Lord," Aunt Gormah says, looking around. "It seems as if they are indeed helping a lot of people."

"I am so glad," Mama says, as we approach.

"Neyor! Neyor!" We turn around to see a woman waving at us.

"Edith!" Mama says.

The woman comes over with her children. "You made it!" She hugs Mama tight. Edith and her children are carrying bags filled with things.

"Thank you, Edith, for helping us," Mama says. "And for telling us about this place."

While we are waiting, Fungbeh fusses and Mama shushes and sings to him. I feel as if I cannot stand up anymore. I think I may faint. I hold on to Mama as we move closer to the big gate.

There are tables with supplies. I can see what looks like food and water and plus a few blankets. Some people are going inside and some others are being given a bag of rice or a canister of something. My eyes lock on the food as we get closer.

"Are you sure you don't want to check in, Neyor?" Edith asks. "That way you don't have to worry about coming back out and getting more food. Who knows how much they will give you. It may not be enough to last the week."

"It is better than nothing," Mama says. "We haven't eaten in two days, Edith. My children are starving."

"Yes," Edith says. "In that case, something is better than nothing."

We wait forever, then finally it is our turn.

"What tribe are you from?" a man asks Mama.

"I am from Gbarnga City. I have come because my family is starving, and I know that you have food," Mama says. "Can you please give us some food to take back to where we are staying?"

"No!" the man says sternly, taking us all by surprise. "We are looking for people from Gbarnga City, but the Nimbadians and Gio people only. They are the ones being killed by Doe."

Aunt Gormah grabs our hands and pull us toward her when she hears the man raising his voice. Her eyes are set sternly on the man as Mama continues to plead.

"We are facing hardship too!" Mama says. "Please consider my children, please. We are so hungry. We have not eaten for days!"

"The answer is no." The man is firm.

Mama suddenly becomes desperate. "You cannot turn us away, please! We have come all this way for just a cup of rice. Anything that you can spare for my children, please! Please, I beg you, please. Please!"

Edith steps forward. "She is my friend. Please help her! I told her to come here with her children and that you would help. They have walked all this way."

"I am sorry," the man says. "You are not the chosen ones."

"Please," Mama says.

"You are not the chosen ones," he says again. "Get out of here."

"But my children and my sister's children—they will die!" Mama cries. "You have to help us."

The man looks at Mama and then glances over us. "Wait here," he instructs. He leaves, then returns with a man wearing a collar.

"This woman will not leave," the first man says. "She is begging for food. She is not from Ghanta. I told her we cannot help her."

"Lady," the priest says to Mama, "I am in charge here. We can only help the people who live here and are of the Nimba and Gio tribe. We cannot give our food away to different people. We can only take care of our own people."

"But we have come all this way," Mama protests. "Surely you can give us something. A bowl of rice, water. Anything that you have, we will take."

"We can only take care of our own," the priest says. "You are not of the Nimba or Gio tribe." He pauses, running his eyes over each of us. "But, if you want to check in here and bring your family to join us, we will feed you and your family only."

"But, I am already staying with another family and helping them. I cannot abandon them now."

"Either check in and eat, or go."

"I will check in," Edith says stepping forward.

"Where you from?"

"I'm from Nimba County," Edith responds.

"Very well. You and your children are welcome here."

"Thank you. We will stay here with you."

"Very well." The priest nods to the first man to open the iron gate.

"Neyor, just check in here," Edith says. "The Wesleys will understand that you and your sister had to do what you had to do."

"I can't," Mama says. She turns back to the man in charge. "Sir, if you just give us a small amount of food, we will go and never come back. But we can't abandon our family. They are waiting on us." Suddenly Mama begins to cry. "Please sir. You cannot turn us away."

"Then, I am sorry," the man says. "You are not the chosen ones. We cannot help you."

Mama's tears drop on the ground. "Please!"

"You are not the chosen ones," the man repeats. Then he looks past us. "Who is next?"

"Please!" Mama cries again.

Aunt Gormah pulls Mama's hand. "Come on, Neyor. He is not going to help us. You have done enough. Come now."

Mama is defeated. Her shoulders slump as she wipes fresh tears from her face. I feel like crying too. I am hungry. We are so tried. We have gotten right to the door of help and nourishment, and now we are being turned away. The man is so mean that I almost understand why Mama does not want us to check in there. They are nothing like Brother Wesley and the people of Gaye Town. We cannot be part of people who will turn away starving children. More people push past us to make their way to the entrance.

"Come," Aunt Gormah says. "We need not stay out here any longer."

"Yes," Mama says, her voice shaking. "We need to get back to the church."

We turn around empty-handed and start the two-mile walk back to Gaye Town Church. Clouds have begun to fill the sky and soon are dropping sheets of rain on us. Our baggy clothes cling to our skin as we walk in silence back to the compound. For once, I am glad for the rain because it masks the tears coming down my face. I am so angry that I am crying. I don't know if I have ever been so angry.

When we get back, Brother Wesley and his wife run out to meet us. Mama and Aunt Gormah tell them what happened. Inside, Brother Wesley tells us that another family has left the compound. There are just a few of us left now. Those who are still here huddle in the back room once again. As I lie down between Mama and Kulubah, my stomach is growling. But at night, that is the least of our worries. We are all scared. Listening and praying, just to make it through to morning.

I am awakened by a commotion outside. It seems as if all of Gaye Town has come back to life this morning. There are voices everywhere and people moving. I jump up looking for Mama, but she is not there.

Aunt Gormah comes in. "There is news! We are all in the auditorium. Hurry now."

Nyempu and I run. The double doors of the main entrance are open, and people are walking in and out. Some are carrying all of their belongings. There is a lot of talking and commotion and fear. There are people that I have never seen before, walking and running through the street. Heading this way and that way.

"Quanei," I hear Nyempu call. "Come inside!" I do as I am told and run to her.

"What is it?" I ask. "What is the news?"

"It is bad news, Quanei," she says, scooting me into the auditorium. When I get inside, I see a soldier who brings us news from the war. He is in plain clothes, looking distraught, talking to Brother Wesley.

"I cannot believe it!" a woman says. "The whole church— massacred!"

"What church?" Mama asks, running up to the woman.

"The Lutheran church up the road!"

"What!"

Mama and Aunt Gormah look as if they have seen a ghost. Mama is stunned. "No." Her eyes dart back between Brother Wesley and the solider. "Brother Wesley, what has happened?" Mama asks. "Tell me!"

"The Lutheran church," Brother Wesley says. "This brother has brought news. And the news is spreading through the entire city, causing a panic. Last night, Doe sent his troops to kill everyone at the Lutheran church. They are all dead."

"What?" Mama says shaking her head. "No! We were just there."

"It is true," the soldier says. "I was there." He hung his head. "I could not go inside. I could not do it. I have ripped my uniform off, and I am no longer a part of this terrible man's army. But it is true. He sent troops in the middle of the night with machetes and they killed all of those people—even the priest."

Mama sits down and the panic in the room drowns out their voices. People begin to scatter. "No, no, no," Mama says, again and again. "Edith and her children. I saw them there, yesterday. And they checked in there!"

"Then they are dead. You, your children, and your sister and her children were barely saved."

Mama looks completely distraught. She is struggling to catch her breath. After a moment, Mama stands back up. "We must leave," Mama mutters. "The Lutheran church is only two miles up the road! This place has to be next!"

I am terrified of what those soldiers can do. How close we were to being killed last night. I think of the blood I saw on the porch of the Johnson home. I can only imagine the rivers of blood that must be flowing from the Lutheran church. I know that Edith and her children are in that river, like Robert and Oretha were. Our worst nightmare has come true for them. And like the solider said, we were spared.

As the commotion continues around me, all I can hear in my head is the hard voice of the man at the gates. *You are not the chosen ones.* And now, he is dead too. If we had stayed, we would be dead. *You are not the chosen ones.* I think of Mama's tears and pleadings. *You are not the chosen ones.* I think of the rivers of blood. *You are not the chosen ones.* At that moment, I feel God talking to us through the dead man. The knowledge makes me feel old, not like the boy who shouted, "go around, go around" in our new yellow car that day. That dead man blocking us from safety had said, "You are not the chosen ones." We were not the ones chosen to die.

Aunt Gormah and Mama are consoling each other, looking lost and confused.

"The massacre at the Lutheran church has set all of Monrovia on fire," the solider continues. "For President Doe to massacre an entire congregation of his own people shows he has no fear. No respect for life. He is a monster, and nothing is off limits. He has killed even children. No one is safe. The rebels have taken this as their opportunity. The chaos, the fear. They are turning people against Doe, creating more soldiers, stealing and killing more. Monrovia and all of Liberia is in full blown war. There is nothing anyone can do."

"Then, we cannot stay here," Mama says again.

"What?" Brother Wesley says. "Where will you go? There is war and chaos everywhere!"

"We cannot stay here," Aunt Gormah repeats, almost to herself. She looks up. "That church, where those people are lying, dead, is only two miles away. Two miles! If they had come two miles down the road, we would all be dead!"

"Yes," Mama says. "We will be next if we stay. It will only be a matter of days and we cannot stay here and die."

"Sister," Brother Wesley says. He is holding his hands together, shaking them. "Do you not hear the guns at night? Shooting right outside our door? The rebels and Doe's government are at war. It's not safe outside these walls. And where will you go? You don't even know if your son and sister are alive."

"We cannot stay in this war zone," Mama says. "We have to go back . . . home."

"Home?" says Aunt Gormah. "The whole country is in war, Neyor."

"Gbarnga City is more than 100 miles from here," adds Brother Wesley. "How can you make that journey on foot?"

"Lady!" the soldier says sternly, used to speaking to even with those he does not know with great authority. "You cannot just go off marching yourself and your family into war! What is your plan?"

"My plan? My plan is to get my children through this horrible thing, this war. To stay alive. And by some miracle, I hope to see my husband again."

"The rebels are coming from that direction into Monrovia, and the government is fighting in Monrovia. There is nowhere to go," Brother Wesley protests.

"Exactly," Mama says, standing up and smoothing out her dress. "The rebels do not care about where they have come from, Brother. The rebels want Monrovia. Doe's presence is in Monrovia.

Monrovia is where he is killing his own people to protect himself. So, we must get out of here, far from Monrovia, before he comes back for more. If we stay, the rebels will come and assume we're part of Doe's people. We will head toward Gbarnga, even if we have to risk the rebel zone."

"Neyor," Brother Wesley pleads. "You cannot take those children into the war. You hear the guns at night. People are dying out there.'

"I agree with my sister," Aunt Gormah says. "This is crazy. It is not safe for us here. We cannot just wait here for them to find us."

"People are dying here," Mama says. "And I cannot stay here and watch my children die."

"Then leave Fungbeh with us," Brother Wesley says.

"No!" Aunt Gormah and Mama shout at the same time.

"But he is just a baby and his cries might give you away at night when you are hiding."

Brother Wesley is right—Fungbeh cries, even in the middle of the day now. But not for milk candy, not because he is spoiled; he cries because he is hungry. I look anxiously from Brother Wesley's face to Mama's and Aunt Gormah's. Even though Fungbeh cries, I do not want us to leave him.

"No," Mama says. She looks at all of us. Kulubah is leaning against me, wide-eyed and silent, Nyempu is trying to hush Fungbeh who is fussing against her shoulder. Aunt Gormah's sons are looking at the floor. "We stay together." Mama turns to Aunt Gormah, who is standing now. "We leave in the morning.

Not the Chosen Ones
Navigate to Ch. 19, read the reporting of the Lutheran Church Massacre in the
N.Y. Times (29 July 1990). Post a comment on Witness social.

20

Mama Is Taking Us to War

After we have all washed our faces and are ready for bed, Mama gathers us close. "Your Aunt Gormah and I have decided that we are all going back home tomorrow," Mama confirms. "We are going to leave before the sun gets up, just like we did when we came here. We are going to walk down Duport Road, all the way home."

All the way home? I'm not sure if we can make that journey all the way without being caught. I remember how long our first car journey to this area with Papa took. I heard Brother Wesley say home is a hundred miles away. But I'm not worried only about the distance. I look at sleeping Fungbeh and at Nyempu, whose dress sags off her shoulders as if her bones were a wire clothes hanger. Our legs are weak and our stomachs hurt all the time. I am tired.

"Mama," I say. "When we finally get back to Sugar Hill, we can stay, right?"

"I hope so," Mama says. Then she hugs us tight and puts us in bed.

Nightmares of angry rebels chasing me with machetes jolt me awake. My eyes pop open in the darkness. To my surprise, I see Mama is up too. I can hear gunfire in the distance. Mama is holding Fungbeh to her chest, staring outside the same way she did in the days before we left Sugar Hill. As the moonlight shines over Mama, I can see a cloudy storm across her face. It is as if she is thinking about a million scary things at once. I sit up quietly and look at her, but she doesn't notice me. Her eyes are fixed on something out the window. She listens to the sounds of war—the war she will be marching us into tomorrow.

I can see that Mama is worried, but to me she still looks strong as she looks directly in the face of danger. I imagine that Mama must be thinking about what happened at the Lutheran church and about her decision. She is probably wondering the same things as I am, as everyone else at Gaye Town is wondering. *Is it foolish for us to go? Is it a death sentence if we stay? Will we make it? Will we be gunned down? Will we starve to death?* As the loud pops of automatic rifles create their own song of violence and terror just beyond our gates, these are the questions I see all over my mother's face.

I start to feel sleepy and lie back down on my cot. My mind is too worn to think any longer. Besides, I trust Mama. She will protect us. Mama has brought us all this way, following nothing but God and her heart. It was her heart that had us leave Sugar Hill just days before the rebels took over Gbarnga City. It was Mama's heart that led us to Gaye Town church, where we were safe. It was Mama's heart that had her going out looking for food, where she found Edith who gave us the cup of rice. It was also her heart that told her not to stay at the Lutheran church, a decision that saved our lives. So, if Mama says that we needed to leave, then it is time for us to leave.

My stomach begins to hurt. I don't know if I am hungry or scared. I clutch the ache and pray for it to go away. I feel sleep pulling me back into its strong grip, I continue my prayer to God that He protect us tomorrow.

Before the sun is up, we prepare to leave. In the darkness of the early morning, we pack what we can carry. When we are done, Brother Wesley and his wife walk us outside. Brother Wesley tries again to convince Mama to leave Fungbeh, but it is no use. We are all heading back home to Sugar Hill together. Mama has given all of us strict instructions and together, Aunt Gormah and her children, Nyempu, Mama, Kulubah, Fungbeh, and I begin our journey toward home.

The compound is extremely quiet this early in the morning. It's so quiet you can hear yourself breathe. Mama and Aunt Gormah explain that we are to walk behind the houses, in the bushes, anywhere we can off the main road.

Mama is carrying Fungbeh on her back in one of her wraps, as tight to her body as possible. She is walking quickly. I watch her thin legs leading the way. I wonder what it will be like when we get home. I wonder if Sugar Hill will be the same. I don't have much time to think about it though, because we are alert for signs of danger, listening for any noise that might mean trouble.

There is this strange unpleasant smell that mixes incongruently with the typical dewy smells of early morning. It is cool, and the rains have not yet started. We move as quickly and quietly as we can, slipping between hollow streets and abandoned burned buildings. The only sounds I hear are our footsteps and our breaths.

We walk about four miles before the sun begins to come up. When it does, it brings the tropical rains of the season with it. The rain pours down, making my clothes feel ten pounds heavier than they are. Each step is harder as we sink into the sodden earth. My feet begin to hurt.

"Come," Mama says, sensing our group becoming weary. "We will rest and hide over here."

We approach what used to be a fruit stand to hide inside. It is empty. The rain drips all around us. Mama sets out a bottle to catch some water, and gives us each a drink. When the rain stops, we cautiously step back out and continue walking.

There are other people on the road now. Everyone seems to be going one place or another, but only on foot. The rebels will take any car they see, and kill the passengers on the spot. And if the government sees a car, they will assume you are a rebel and kill you. Either way, driving brings death. More and more people fill the streets, carrying backpacks and children. Now we are a part of the steady line of people leaving Monrovia, a silent exodus toward survival. We don't speak to anyone; we just walk. We don't have any food. I guess we will find some along the way. Whenever a car passes, people look around with panic in their eyes. As we walk, I wonder if Auntie Garmen and Kormah came this way.

We are approaching a big intersection, I see many more people up ahead. It has become busier as the morning goes on. Mama gathers us closer and pushes our skinny legs to walk faster. We don't see the attack coming. We just hear gunfire. Then it is suddenly upon us.

"Get down!" a man yells out. Instantly, we all drop low. Nyempu holds Kulubah, I grab for Mama's hand. My heart races as rapid gunfire fills my ears. The line of travelers scatters quicker than papers in the wind. Everybody is running, but Mama pulls us down to the ground and close to her as the shooting continues to erupt. I can't see where the shooters are, but I see Mama looking around frantically. People begin to scream and run for cover and that now familiar sweet and metallic smell of blood mixes with the dusty, sulfurous smell of gunfire. I breathe in sharply and shudder.

"Run!" Aunt Gormah screams, as she scoops up her children and runs for her life. Suddenly we are all running at once, and I am swallowed up in the frantic sea of people. I let out a terrified cry as rapid rounds pop in the air. I run toward Mama as fast as I can, but I feel like my feet are moving in slow motion. I don't know where everyone else is, but what fills my head is that I don't want to die like this. I see Oretha lying on that porch.

There is screaming, crying, and the loud rat-a-tat-tat of guns on the road. The shooting is so loud and so close that I can feel the vibrations in my chest. My ears are ringing. People continue to scream and run in all directions. I am completely lost in the crowd, but I see a woman wearing a bright green dress running in front of me and I just follow her. I run as fast as I can toward the woman when suddenly she is struck by a bullet. I see in slow motion a red spot spread across the green dress. Then she falls to the ground. I let out a terrified scream as the woman's warm blood spits out onto my face.

"Mama!" I stop running, too afraid to move. Bullets are flying past me, zinging past my ears. All around me there are sparks of blinding light as bullets zing around and ricochet off things. Another person falls, right in front of me. Her blood splatters on my feet, forcing me to leap over her. I jump then keep moving. I am running again.

"Mama! Mama!" I scream as I run. I don't see any of my family. People around me are dropping like flies. Finally, I catch a glimpse of Mama. She is running too, and I run like crazy after her. I see others from our group with her.

"Run toward the trees!" I can hear Mama's voice over all the commotion.

Zpht! Zpht! Bullets whizzing past my ears make me run even faster. A man in front of me is hit. I trip over his body, slamming the ground hard. I know that it is no use. I am going to die today. I see Nyempu, Kulubah, and the rest of our group running, slipping farther out of sight. A bullet flies over my head, forcing me to duck in the grass next to the body of another bleeding man. I crouch there for a moment, seeing Oretha on the porch. *This is my time to die. I am finished.* I start to panic. I feel like a rabbit hunted by wild dogs. I lie frozen, watching people run past me, panicked for their own lives. I cover my ears with both of my hands as bullets continue to fly all around. I close my eyes tight, flinching with the anticipation of a bullet killing me at any moment.

Suddenly, I feel a strong hand grip the back of my shirt, lifting me to my knees, then dragging me several yards. My knees scrape sharply, painfully against the hard ground, and I try to get my feet up under me to run. I hear a familiar voice screaming, "Quanei! Come on! Come on! Let's run! Boy, don't give up! We must go, I got you! I will never leave you behind!" Mama has suddenly grown wings like an eagle and strength like a lion and she is dragging me along. My terrified little brother is still strapped tightly on her back. Breath enters my lungs again and hope enters my soul. I get to my feet and I am running, running, running. I am gasping for breath. Sobs are escaping my throat as the woods come into view. Mama holds my shirt all the way until we make it into the woods, inside the safety of the tress, out of the way of the gunfire.

My heart is beating wildly in my chest. I can hear the gun fight continuing the road behind us. Aunt Gormah and her children are there too, and everyone is breathing hard and crying. Mama turns around, her eyes surveying us, counting with a touch on each of our heads.

"Quanei, Nyempu, Kulubah. Where is Fungbeh? My people, where is Fungbeh!" Mama cries. She turns this way and then that, looking all around.

"Neyor!" Aunt Gormah says her arms wide. Mama stops and lets out a breath, realizing that the baby is still on her back. She swings her arms around to untie the cloth and bring him to her bosom. "Oh, my baby! Shhh, Mama's right here with you."

My legs are still trembling as Nyempu rushes over and hugs me. "Quanei! I thought we had lost you!" She holds me so tight.

The gunfire is still erupting behind us. I look back to see a field of bodies and grass.

"Come, let me look at all of you," Mama says, still running her eyes over everyone. She and Aunt Gormah are like mother hens gathering their chicks.

"We are all here and safe, Neyor," Aunt Gormah says. "We are all here."

Mama drops to her knees and pulls us close. "Oh, thank you, God," she says with tears streaming down her cheeks. "Oh, thank God!"

As I hold onto Mama, I am still shaking. I am shaking so hard I cannot even stand up on my own. I wish in that moment that I can hold on to Mama forever. I never want to let her go. Mama rocks back and forth as she holds us all and prays.

"Oh, my God," Aunt Gormah says hugging her children tight. Her eyes run wildly over the dead bodies lying in the field behind us. She pulls herself from three-year-old Tinawoo and starts to wrap baby Gerpili in her *lapa*. "Neyor, we have to move."

"Yes," Mama says. "We have to move now. And we must stay off the road."

She pulls herself out of our arms and starts to tie Fungbeh onto her back. "Listen to me. We are going back to the church. We are only four miles up the road, we can walk back. We have to leave here quickly."

We don't have time to catch our breath, to think, or to cry. We just move. I don't ask any questions because I am afraid that even one second of wasting time will get me killed. Gunfire is all around us. I look back at the people lying on the ground, in the same places where we just took steps. Then, I cannot move. Again, I am breathless, sick and terrified as my eyes take it all in. I feel Mama pulling on me.

"Come on! Move, boy!"

I run alongside her. We follow Mama back in the direction that we came, deeper into the brush. My knees are still bleeding where they scraped the ground. My skin is being newly torn by the sharp brush. We are still shaking and scared, walking so quickly that we practically run the entire way back. I hear our feet swishing the dirt and snapping twigs. There's a stream of people all around us, headed in the same direction. Screams and gunfire are still audible. Fear alone keeps me moving. For four miles, we keep a steady pace and we don't stop until we recognize the clearing that leads to Gaye Town Church.

As we approach the church, we see someone up ahead. They dart into the main building and return with what looks like Brother Wesley and his wife.

"Come on," Mama says. "Hurry." She grabs my hand and scoops up Kulubah with her other arm. We begin to jog toward the church.

"Oh, Sister Karmue!" Sister Wesley runs out and wraps her arm around Mama, taking Kulubah from her. "What happened?"

"There was an ambush. Rebels are here," Mama says, catching her breath. "We were almost killed."

"Oh, my God!" Brother Wesley says. "Come in, let's get you inside!" He quickly rushes us back toward the main building.

By the time we make it to the main building, almost everyone in the Gaye Town community has gathered outside and all are saying "Oh, my God!" and "You poor children!" and "Oh, thank God." We get what seems like a hundred hugs and everyone seems shaken, as if they too had almost been killed.

"Sister Neyor," a woman says, once we have made it inside. "God has been with you. It is a miracle."

"Yes," Mama says, wrapping her arms around us again. "Come here, my babies."

"Please say that you will stay here until all of this is over!" Brother Wesley says.

Mama stands up and looks at Brother Wesley. "We will stay the night."

When she is met with silence, she goes on. "When we were caught in the attack, it was just four miles up the road. The rebels have taken over the area and the government was coming through. The rebels headed them off. But it is definitely not safe here. The rebels are coming, Brother Wesley. They own the country now. In a few days, this whole place will be turned upside down. I appreciate what you have done, but we can't stay here much longer than tonight."

"But—"

"No," Aunt Gormah cuts him off. "My sister is right. We are not staying here. We just need to leave earlier in the morning next time. But we cannot stay, Brother Wesley. We just can't."

We are quiet as Mama pulls us to her again. It's the first time since the ambush that we have stopped long enough to breathe.

This feels like the first moment in a long time that we are not running for our lives. All at once, the fear and everything I have been holding in comes rushing out. I am sobbing and shaking. I cannot stop. I can hardly breathe between the deep heaves. Nyempu is crying. So is Kulubah. Mama squeezes us tight and we all just lean on her and cry. Even though we are in the middle of the main building of Gaye Town, it is like there is no one there but Mama and us. I think about Mama darting through my bullets to save me. I sob even harder. I am practically screaming. Mama did not leave me behind. She loves me. Even today, as I live in the safety of California, I have never forgotten how I was so overcome by the knowledge of Mama saving me, by the fear of being trapped between two sets of soldiers shooting among everyone I loved. In that moment, I just want to hug and kiss her forever. I want to hug everyone.

As we huddle together crying, it sinks in how differently this day could have turned out. I understand what Mama meant when she told us: as long as you have your life, you have everything. I have never before been so grateful for my life, or for my Mama. My hero. Whatever Mama says, I decide, I will always do. If she says we stay, we stay. If she says we go, we go. Even if that means going into the shadowy early morning, right back into the middle of war tomorrow.

21

Escape from Monrovia

The next morning, I wake to Mama's gentle voice pulling me out of my dreams. I feel her warm hand on my back. "Quanei, baby."

I roll over and squint at Mama. It is still dark and our room is quiet, but there she is smiling at me as if she is seeing me for the first time. Or maybe she is trying to remember my face forever. I look at Mama and wonder what makes her know that it is okay for us to leave here. I wonder what makes her think we even have a chance to make it.

I remember the Bible story Mama reads to us about Moses and the children of Israel, how they left on a dangerous journey with nothing but faith in God. I imagine this is why Mama is willing to give leaving here a try. I know that Mama has so much faith in God. I have heard so many grownups say that with faith in God, anything is possible. I think that if God and faith are strong enough to make Mama believe that we will be safe, then He must be a really big God and faith must be something amazing. Faith has to be something powerful because it is what is making Mama take us back out into the middle of this war.

"Time to get up," Mama says, interrupting my thoughts. I see Nyempu stirring in the corner as I sit up. I can see Aunt Gormah is waking her children too.

"Come and get up," Mama says, picking up Kulubah, who snuggles into her, still sleeping. "It's time for us to go."

And just like that, our second attempt to escape from Monrovia begins. This time, we all move swiftly, like tiny soldiers gathering our things, folding up blankets and getting ready to follow Mama. Even though it is dark outside, what we are getting ready to do is clear as day. We all know we heading into the war zone soon. After almost being shot in the ambush, we know exactly the kind of danger we are headed to.

The terror of yesterday is still ringing in my ears as I get ready. I want to tell Mama I am scared, but I know her mind is busy. I wonder if her heart is beating fast like mine as she quickly and quietly ushers us into the hallway. We already know the plan. We are leaving much earlier this time. It's two o'clock in the morning, so we will travel mostly in darkness.

I step into the hallway and turn to look at our room one last time. I feel this room is suddenly the safest place in the world. Now that I have seen the explosions of bullets and warm blood spraying through the air, I wish we could stay in this room that feels as safe as the one Papa has in his office. Couldn't we can just lock ourselves in the room and stay forever?

"Come, Quanei," I look up to see Aunt Gormah looking at me. "It is time for our journey to begin, little one."

To my surprise, I see the hallway is not empty. Others who have been staying at Gaye Town are there too. I see Brother Wuo, Bro Maxwell, Brother Pyne, Sister Hemelay and her children, all standing in the darkened hallway with what appear to be their belongings.

I place my hand on my sister's shoulder. "Nyempu," I say. "Are they coming with us?"

Nyempu nods at me. "Yes, I think so."

I am even more surprised when I see Aunt Ginger and her daughter, Patricia, walk through the double doors just up the hall. They are carrying their belongings and Aunt Ginger quickly explains to Mama that if we are going back home, then she might as well too.

At first, I am happy that we will have people with us on this journey, but then I am suddenly worried. Do they not know how bad it is out there? Did they not hear what happened to us? They must be really desperate if they would dare make this journey too.

Fungbeh is nestled snuggly on Mama's back. We are each given something to carry. Nyempu is handed a small bundled of clothes and Mama ties them in the traditional African kentia on her head. I look at Nyempu with her dark skin, her long neck, and the kentia on her head. She looks like a woman now: older, so different and serious, not like the big sister who argued with Kormah for the front seat of the car.

Mama gives me a small water jug to carry on my head in case we get thirsty. I am glad to have such an important job like keeping the water, and I know I am going to do a good job. A small pang hits my stomach as we all gather in the hallway, but I know I cannot think of hunger now. Right now, we must focus on the journey ahead, and hope that we all make it home without trouble.

Brother Wesley is there again, with his usual worried look. I see the former soldier from Doe's army is with him too.

"Please come in here," Brother Wesley says, ushering us into the auditorium. "I know that you don't have much time."

"Yes," Mama says. I can hear a bit of impatience in her voice. "We need to get out of government territory as quickly as we can."

"Even if you do," the solider breaks in, "know that there is no place that is safe. I need to tell you how you can survive out there."

Once we are all in the auditorium I see that his eyes are sharp, full of concern.

"We are listening," Brother Wuo says.

"The rebels have infiltrated almost every area outside of Monrovia and some of the outskirts of the city," the solider tell us. "If you encounter rebels, or if you encounter soldiers, God only knows if you will be safe. The rebels have set up checkpoints throughout the territories they have taken. If you are going back toward Gbarnga City, you will have to go through these checkpoints at some point. Listen to me carefully." He looks at us all, one at a time. "If you so much as look the wrong way these rebels will slit you in half right where you stand."

As I hear these words, my eyes grow wide. I am shaking in my shoes. Visions of angry rebels with giant guns and machetes dripping with blood fill my mind and I do not want to leave now. I do not want to see more dead people or guns. I do not want to leave.

"How can we stay safe?" Mama asks, holding Fungbeh close. "Tell us what to do."

"No one is safe," the solider replies. "There is only hope that you will not be killed. The best thing to do is to not appear to have any affiliation with the government or Doe. You cannot look like you have money because they will think that you are associated with Doe." He looks at all of us. "You must not make eye contact with these rebels, unless they tell you to, or they will kill you. Keep your head down, answer questions simply and be as simple and forgettable as possible." He pauses and looks around. "If you don't get shot or starve to death first, it will be a miracle, but if you do anything that looks suspicious, the rebels will kill you mercilessly anyway."

"We understand," Aunt Gormah says, speaking for all of us.

"Okay," Brother Wesley says, massaging his palms. He lets out a deep, heavy breath. "Then, you must go."

He walks to Mama and takes her hand. Then presses what appears wrinkled old money into her palm and closes her hand over it. "Just in case you have to buy anything like food from anywhere for the children," he says.

Sister Sarah has been quiet the whole time, looking like she has already lost our entire family. She hugs Mama and pushes a piece of bread wrapped in an old newspaper into Mama's hand. "Bread for the kids to eat."

Mama looks just as emotional as Sister Sarah, but I know she is focusing on the trip ahead. "Thank you so much," she says. "You have done so much. I will never forget all that you have meant to us in the absence of Alfred."

"Take hold, Neyor. Let God clear your path," Brother Wesley says. "Let God clear your path."

As we leave through the double doors, I take a deep breath, like I am getting ready to jump in a big lake. Then I step out into the early morning air.

We follow almost the same route again. All of us huddled together, moving quickly and quietly behind buildings, through bushes, staying off the road. Every noise we hear stops us in our tracks. We look around quickly before even breathing again. We continue to move forward. I know that home is at least three hours away in a car, so I can only imagine the long road that is ahead of us. I wonder how long we can keep this up. Mama and Brother Wuo lead the way as we slip through the city of Monrovia, headed toward the main highway that leads from Monrovia straight through the heart of Gbarnga. We pass through narrow alleyways, into the woods, and through swamps to keep off the road. The mud in the swamp is sticky and hard to walk through, but we keep pushing forward.

There is a smell in the air, almost the same one that pricked my nose yesterday, but stronger. Sometimes the smell is so thick, my stomach lurches and I feel like I'm going to throw up. It smells like a latrine and old meat. It is the smell of death, I realize. Sometimes when the wind rustles the trees, the smell is even stronger, and I feel like doubling over. I gag. There is no place to escape it. I realize I had smelled this sometimes at Gaye Town. I shiver at the realization that while we may not have seen it much from the safety of the church, death has been all around us.

We do as the soldier tells us. We stay low and move through the darkness quickly. No one is speaking, but I know that we are all moving as one unit, thinking the same things. What if we are spotted? Will we be interrogated? Will we be shot? What if more shooting starts again?

We keep up a steady pace and soon I see morning breaking over the countryside. The city will be waking up soon.

"We have been walking for quite some time," Brother Wuo says. "We need to rest."

"I agree," Mama says.

"There," says Brother Wuo pointing ahead. "There are some bushes and trees there, enough into the woods and high enough to hide us all. Let me go and check it out to make sure."

"Please be careful," Mama says.

"Let him go, Neyor. Someone has to," Aunt Ginger says. "Better him than any of us."

"I will go with you," Brother Maxwell calls to Brother Wuo. Together they start off.

As I watch them go, I hope that the place in the bushes is safe. My feet hurt from all the walking, but I know we are all too scared to even think of stopping. Mama unwraps Fungbeh and kisses his head.

"There, baby," she says. "We will rest soon."

"Here, let me take him." Aunt Gormah says. "Give your back and arms a rest, huh?"

My stomach growls again and I wonder when we will eat. I picture the piece of bread Sister Wesley gave to Mama and my mouth waters. I want Mama to share it soon. I can feel my body withdrawing and the pain of hunger settling in. We had nothing to eat at all yesterday. We have been living on just water and fear. I feel weak and tired and I wonder how long we can continue like this.

"It's safe!" Brother Wuo and Brother Maxwell call, and we eagerly follow them to the area they have cleared.

We settle down in a huddle and drink some water. Mama and Aunt Gormah go and pick berries and come back with some wrapped in a cloth. We all eat them quickly. Uncle Thomas reaches for his jug of water on the ground, but suddenly gets up and walks toward a patch of overgrown weeds. At first glance, you cannot tell that there is sugarcane intertwined in the bushes, but Uncle Thomas plows through the long grass to uncover the sugarcane sticks. Brother Maxwell notices and hurries to help him root out some of the stumps for us to eat.

Mama unwraps the old bread from The Liberian Daily Observer and beaks it into small pieces for us. At the sight of the bread and sugarcane, my hands trembled and my heart leaps. It has been too long since we have eaten. The bread is only a small piece and does not even cover half of my tiny palm, but I was glad and satisfied just to see food. Mama says we can only have a little bit, and that she will keep the rest for when we really need it. I rush a piece of the bread crust into the corner of my jaw and almost bite my finger. The crust is hard as piece of old leather and I chew the it for a long while. I figure the longer I can feel the food in my mouth, the longer my hunger will be satisfied. I chew and swallow, picking up small crumbs that fall to the ground. When I'm done, I gulp down my portion of water from the jug. I forget about the sugarcane until Uncle Thomas starts to break it over his knees and distribute pieces. We sit for about thirty minutes, catching good air and looking at the sky brighten little by little. All too soon, the sound of scattered voices on the main road hits our ears.

"The streets will be busy soon," Brother Wuo says. "If we try to stay in the woods too much and get caught, the rebels may think we are with the government—spies or something. We cannot take any risks."

"Yes," Brother Maxwell agrees. "If we want to move forward safely, we will have to go through the checkpoints."

Mama nods as she slips a piece of sugarcane into Fungbeh's mouth. "So, we will."

"Let's rest our legs for a little longer. Then we must move forward," Brother Maxwell says.

Mama begins to rock Fungbeh and hums a small tune. I lean on her and she puts her arms around me and rocks us both. In the warm hum of her voice, even hiding in the bushes, I am safe.

Soon, it is time for us to get on with our journey. We gather our things and start to walk toward the main road. As we make our way through the high grass and out of the woods, I can see the road in the clearing ahead. It is fully morning now. I wonder if we will find food again later. Brother Wuo uses a stick to push back grasses almost as tall as we are. I imagine that he is a great warrior, clearing the way for his people.

"Quanei," Mama says, grabbing me by the shoulder. "Where is the water?"

I look at my hands even though I know the jug is not there. I left it.

"I forgot it!" I tell Mama. "I can go and get it!"

I take off running back to our rest spot before Mama has time to speak. I know exactly where the jug is. I can get it and catch up with them in no time. The grass is so tall that I wish I had Brother Wuo's stick. I run fast and use my arms to push the grass away. I know that Mama thinks I am too small for this. But I can show her. Nyempu isn't the only one who has grown up quickly because of these troubles. I will get the jug and be back so quickly that Mama will know that I am big like Nyempu and brave like Kormah.

I push back more and more grass until I am stopped dead in my tracks. A woman and her baby are lying right in front of me. They are fully clothed, the mother is clutching a suitcase, her child is wrapped in her other arm. Their eyes are closed. I know they are dead. They look like they are simply sleeping, the baby cuddled in the mother's arm. The suitcase has popped open, revealing clothes and a Bible. My mouth is open as I stare at them. Suddenly, that smell is sharp in my nostrils and buzzing flies and my own shallow breaths are deafening. I don't know how to move backwards or forward. I'm just stuck there, as motionless as they are. Goosebumps trickle down my back. I take a few steps backwards, my heart beating wildly. I realize too late that I have wet my pants.

I hear a faint voice in the distance, but my eyes are stuck on what is in front of me.

"Quanei, baby, come here."

I am still looking at the mother and baby. Taking in their brown skin, the white blanket around the baby. I am trembling.

"Quanei."

Mama stands next to me, but she does not touch me. I can feel her looking at me.

"Mama," I say, reaching out and placing my hand on her. Immediately she scoops me up in her arms. She holds me tight. I hold on to her. Neither of us moves for a while. She just holds me. I see the water jug next to Mama and I wonder how she got it, but I don't care. Back with the rest of the group, I am silent, but no one seems to notice. Mama hands me the water jug and we are on our way.

22

Death by the Thousands

With the sun up, the morning grows humid. The smell of death is faint now, but it never completely disappears. We step out onto the road and continue walking. There are more families walking, swiftly headed to a destiny many once called home. The road ahead is long, and the sun is climbing higher in the sky. We are too hungry and weak to make conversation, so we just keep walking. Sometimes we see groups of people walking ahead and we walk behind them. Oftentimes, we pass small villages that look empty. Maybe those people have escaped to some place too.

Mama starts to hum a song and Nyempu and I sing with her. When Mama sings to us, it is almost like we are not running for our lives but back home in Sugar Hill. After quite some time, the main road turns to dirt, then the dirt road disappears into flat land.

"We will cut through here," Brother Wuo says, pointing into the distance. "The other road is the way. It will lead us to Gbarnga City."

We all walk on through a field where the grasses are no longer as high. We are thirsty, but there is no more water. We must walk through the fields until we get someplace safe to hide and rest. There is nothing but grass as far as my eyes can see. I wonder where this road is, but I trust the grownups.

"The road is just ahead, over that big hill," Brother Wuo says, pointing to a large hill in the distance. "Once we get to the top, there is land up there and we will see the road and be able to walk right to it."

We do as he says and start to climb the hill that is more like a small mountain. All of us together make our way up. We are exhausted, but we keep climbing. I can see that we are almost to the top and I am so happy. My legs are hurting and climbing uphill is hard, especially under the hot Liberian sun. As we get closer to the top, a few flies slap me in the face. I swat them away and keep walking. Finally, we reach the top of the hill where we are granted a vast and wide view of the grassy field, strewn with of hundreds upon hundreds of dead bodies.

My breath leaves me and I leap back, right into Nyempu, who looks as if she is about to vomit. I turn back to the bodies and hear a noise escape my lips. I want to run, but I know I cannot. There is no way to escape what I see. Bodies lie in the field, like blankets laid out in the sun. As close as ten feet in front of me lie dead men, women, boys, and girls of all ages. I can see a white blanket that I imagine is covering another dead baby. The smell of death stings our nostrils, sickening our stomachs. I turn my head, spanning the entire field. There are dead and bloating bodies as far as our eyes can see.

"Oh. My God," Sister Hemelay cries, covering her mouth. "Oh my God," she repeats over and over.

The hum of flies is so loud that I can barely hear anything else. There are bodies on top of bodies, heaped together like piles of trash. I have never seen this many people in one place in my life— let alone dead. Arms, legs, and hands are strewn everywhere inside the heaps. People. Dead. As I look around, I notice there are families lying side by side. A woman with her arm across a man's chest, their suitcase spilled opened on the ground. New grass springs up between body parts. Another man's arm is reaching out, as if for help. My mind flashes back to the man who fell beside me on Duport Road. I could see the pain on his face and the terror in his eyes as he cried out. I know that his was the same fate of every single person in this endless sea of bodies.

"We have come to a killing field," Brother Wuo mutters. His voice is as heavy as I feel. "God, please bless these souls."

"They wanted us to see. The rebels. They want people to see," says Brother Wuo, his eyes still on the field of dead bodies. "They want us to be afraid."

"So, we must go through?" Mama asks, holding Kulubah's hand.

Brother Wuo looks down at Mama and squints his eyes against the blistering sun. "Yes, Sister," he says. "We must go through."

"Absolutely not!" Aunt Ginger says, looking around as if for another route, or any others who will agree that to go through is madness. "It will be terrible!"

"We don't have a choice," Sister Hemelay says. "Right, Sister Karmue?"

Mama does not respond, but instead takes a deep breath and runs her eyes over all of us. Her eyes are filled with something that I cannot as explain.

As I look out over the field of bodies, I finally feel like I fully understand what Old Man Jackson was saying on his porch that day. There must be something serious about that Charles Taylor rebel leader, if he has the power to make other people do something like this. As we stand at the top of the field, looking over the bodies, I wonder how we will ever make it through.

"Neyor," Aunt Gormah says, touching her arm. "We must do what we must do. We are all together, so we will be okay." She turns to look at Aunt Ginger. "You can stay here if you want, Ginger."

"We don't have much time," Brother Maxwell says. "We cannot linger here too long." He is not looking at us, but at the bodies. "Let's keep moving."

With that, Mama grabs my hand and we follow Brother Maxwell. I grab Nyempu's hand as we move into the field. As we walk by the hundreds of dead bodies, the smell of rotting flesh becomes so thick that I want to throw up. My feet don't want to move. I feel like I am going to faint and die. Then Mama begins to hum our favorite nighttime song softly under her breath. I hold onto the sound of her voice and take another step forward. Flies buzz all around me. I see that some of the bodies are swollen big, as if someone has pumped them full of water. I see a man looking right at me with his eyes wide open and I turn my head and bury my face in Mama's side.

"Come, baby," Mama says, as she continues to move us forward.

Aunt Gormah and Aunt Ginger are holding their children's hands and we are all delicately maneuvering around the bodies laid out all over the place. There are barely any places to step. Mama starts to hum a happy tune. All I see are bodies and all I hear is Mama's voice. The bodies lie in every direction, as far as my eyes can see. I blink a few times and look around to make sure this is real. Most of the bodies have no shoes, and some even have no clothes. I see a naked man and a naked woman lying together, blood covering their bloated bodies. As we get closer, I see the woman has no feet and her legs are bloody, mangled sticks. I feel the sugarcane coming up in my mouth and I can't hold it in. Ahead, I see something moving on top of the bodies. Black birds are tearing at the once human flesh. They seem unbothered by us. This is their field now.

Not all the bodies are lying down. Some are leaning against each other as if they are watching television, their shoulders slumped over, their hands tied and bullet holes in the back of their heads. I cannot believe that these bodies are here, right off the road, thrown in the field like trash for everyone to see.

Mama's song gets louder and soothes the war inside me. I close my eyes and, because I must, I breathe in the hot, rancid air. I try to think of something pleasant. I listen to Mama sing and my mind takes me back to Sugar Hill. I feel the uneasiness in my body going away, like I can take another step.

I know that if Mama were not here, singing and holding my hand, I would have fainted long ago, that'd I'd be with the dead families of Liberia, bleeding out and rotting under the African sun. Then I feel another wave of fresh vomit rise up. This time I will myself to force it down.

I try to concentrate on nice visions of home and Mama's singing, but I can't help thinking about the people here who used to be families like ours. I wonder if they had to watch their loved ones die. Even though I don't want to, my mind imagines my own family lying here—all of us, even Papa—and I can feel the pain and anguish in my chest as I see us all in the faces of the dead and bloated around me. I would do anything to keep something like this from happening to my family. Anything at all.

Brother Wuo warns us there is likely a checkpoint ahead. He reminds us of what the soldier said. That, at least, takes my mind off the bodies we are stepping over. This is where the rebels interrogate and hurt people, even kill them, as we can see. They kill them and then bring them here, to the very fields we are walking in now.

Mama hums a little more and squeezes Nyempu's shoulder. Nyempu looks as if someone has taken all the light out of her eyes. Her thin, beautiful face is expressionless. The lips that were quick to smile are dry and cracked. But she is walking, so that is good. For all the times I have walked beside my sister on the dirt roads to our school, I have never imagined that we would be walking side by side through anything like this. But this is what our life has become. We are no longer the full, happy children skipping to school. We are the tired, hungry, lost family running for our lives, trying to find footing as we walk through this field of death. I wonder if Kormah and Aunt Garmen are here, among these bodies.

"Look up, Quanei and Nyempu," Mama says. "Keep your eyes on the horizon. Keep your eyes up toward the light. We are almost there."

As I step over yet another body, I look up and see a road up ahead. I am still holding tight to Mama's hand. I can see people on the road in a line that looks a mile long. This must be the checkpoint.

Scan this code with a QR reader or use the link below to follow selected chapters for a more purposeful Witness Experience

www.resources.witnessliberia.com

23

Meet the Rebels

I am scared as we walk through the grass and onto the road. I am thinking of all the things the soldier has told us. There are hundreds of people in line—families, men, women, and children, each person carrying something. At first glance, this doesn't look so bad. There seem to be two poles and some sort of sign marking the beginning of the checkpoint and where we are to get in line. We walk toward it. The dirt road is dry and cracks under our feet as we join the large group of people. There are babies crying. In the hum of voices, I hear people are speaking in several languages, revealing their tribal tongues.

As we approach the entrance to the checkpoint, Sis Heme-lay lets out a cry. She is covering her mouth and looking up at checkpoint poles. It is then that I realize the poles have human heads stuck on top of them. They are two males. Blood stains the top part of the tall poles and trickles down. The heads stare down at us. This marks the beginning of our first checkpoint.

"Don't stare!" Brother Wuo says. "Don't be obvious. Just get behind these people here and remember what we have been told. We will be okay."

We all know that is not necessarily true, but we have no other choice. We are simply in a gamble for our life.

As soon as we go under the sign with the heads, I see a bloody rope covered with flies. I turn my head. It smells like rotten human flesh, maybe an intestine. My stomach knots up again as I realize the rebels have built their check point out of human body parts. What kind of people would do this to other people? It isn't too long before I have my answer.

A truck comes down the road on the right side of the line. As it approaches, time slows down. I can see the terrifying faces of the rebels, hear their rowdy, profane calls and threats. Bandanas cover their heads and blood stains their faces as they wildly jeer and jab at the people in line. They are like wild animals, wielding giant guns, their eyes fierce with rage and amusement. Their mouths dangle open like hyenas on the prowl. I have never seen anything or anyone like these men in my life. Most of them look like teenagers, which makes me even more afraid. One is holding a human skull in his hands, glaring down each person as they drive by. His eyes are cold except for the dash of amusement and his stern mouth wears the faint hint of a smile. He looks no older than some of the boys I go to school with, yet he is the scariest human being I have ever seen.

The truck stops a few feet ahead of us, and the rebels jump off. I know I am not supposed to look at them, but I am so terrified and surprised that I cannot pull my eyes away. These rebels are not what I expected. I look at them, with their cigarettes in their mouths, bandanas on their heads, crazy eyes, and sick grins on their faces. They have an air of pride about them as they sling curses at the crowds and push people for no reason at all. Some are wearing masks with wild hair attached. They are carrying guns and machetes, wielding the deadly weapons like tiny toys. One shirtless boy has fresh blood splashed all over his chest. He is pounding his chest and smiling as he passes by. They are not soldiers. Most of them are wild boys just a few years older than Kormah. Their shirts are bloody. One has an ear hanging on a neck- lace. They are much scarier than anything described to us. They all seem possessed by something evil. These are the monsters responsible for the field of bodies.

Mama pulls us close as we keep moving forward. I can feel her breathing quickly as we are pushed along with the moving crowd. As the soldier boys approach, I feel my legs going out from under me. Mama holds me tight. I know I must stand up and stare straight ahead. Mama looks over us quickly the second the rebels have moved away.

"Brother Maxwell," she whispers. "Your watch!" I had barely noticed it. It is brown leather and simple, almost matching his skin.

Brother Maxwell looks at his watch, then back at Mama, then to Brother Wuo. "It was my father's," he says.

"Take it off and throw it in the grass quickly," Brother Wuo says. "Before the rebels decide they want it and chop off your hand!"

Brother Maxwell lets out a deep breath. He takes off his watch and throws it into the high grass on the side of the road. We get closer to the front of the checkpoint where even more rebels are along the road, smelling like blood and death, and staring and jeering at the crowd. Some are questioning people in the crowd. Someone screams up ahead and my stomach goes to knots. I see a man and woman being dragged from the line. They are kicking and screaming, drawing the attention of everyone in line. They must have done something wrong. Something inside me wants to reach these people and save them. Their cries silence everyone in the line.

"Please! Please! No!" the woman is crying. "My children! Please!"

"Take me! Leave her with our children please!"

I cannot see anything. I can only hear their terrified pleas. I want to cover my ears but I do not dare move. Rebels are walking past us, looking at everyone in the line. I can smell them without even seeing them. I keep my eyes on the ground as I watch their shadows pass on the ground. When I look up again I can see that the commotion surrounding the man and the woman has moved off the road onto the field. The rebels are dragging the man and the woman to the killing field. The other young killers seem to enjoy this sight and an another one runs off to help, whooping loudly and pumping his gun in the air. We hear the pops of guns and my stomach sinks to my feet. I know that the woman and the man are dead.

As we go through the line, I am so afraid I feel that I might shake right out of my shoes. I think of the people in the killing fields and I say a prayer to God. I pray so hard that I wonder if everyone in line can hear my thoughts.

Dear God. Please, God, help me us to make it through this. I am so afraid of these rebels. I am so scared they are going to hurt us or kill us. God please don't let us get hurt. Don't let anything happen to us, God. If you will please, please just let us make it through this checkpoint alive and spare my family, I will do anything. I will give You everything I have. I will give up my bed and my clothes and my toys and even our yellow car. You can have it all. I would gladly give it all, if You can just leave our family in one piece. Please, God, help us make it through alive.

It seems as if we are standing in the line forever. Ahead of us, people are randomly being pulled out of the line for no obvious reason. Some are pushed back into the line, others are not. Some are tied up along the side of the road and guarded with guns. And suddenly we are facing the main soldier at the checkpoint. He is older than the rebels. It is clear he is in charge here. He looks at all of us and then at Mama.

"Where you from and what you doing on my road?" he asks loudly.

I am so scared that I might fall right over and get us all killed.

Mama looks at the man and speaks in Kpelle, *"Ku kwrah Gbarnga. Ku ka kpella Mu. Nunee ja nya, kwa lei ku poi tah."* We are from Gbarnga City. We are Kpelleh people. My children and I are going home.

The rebel solder says nothing. Suddenly he turns his attention to something behind us.

"What is it?" he asks.

We turn to see two young rebel soldiers holding a man who is tied up.

"Commander, da Krahn man, here! The same tribe as Doe." They say this with a grin, as if they had just won a prize. "This stupid fool lied to us. Tried to trick us that he and Doe not from the same Krahn virginal!"

"We will deal with him today, boss man," says the younger boy. He looks no older than 14 years old.

"No!" the man replies. "Chief, I was not trying to lie! My people. . . I just thought your people were going to kill me on the spot. Please! I beg you, chief! Please!"

"This filth lied to us. Tried to trick us."

"No!" the man says. "I am not a liar. I was afraid!"

The soldier in charge steps away from his post. He looks the man in the eye and then looks up at the two young soldiers.

"Give him government *farina*—make him pay for it. Him and all his tribal people need to go! The man is good to go!"

"No, boss man, please, I beg you!" the man cries. "Please! Please, Papa, I beg you, please!"

"Make him pay for it," he says and then walks back to his post.

"No!" the man says. "Please! Please!"

His begging is so desperate I can feel each cry in the pit of my stomach. I can't even swallow my spit because I am so consumed with fear. My feet are heavy and numb. I know the man is as good as dead. He is a piece of meat that has fallen to hungry lions. The teenage boys drag him away through the small wooden, green door as he collapses in their arms. His hands are tied so tightly behind his back that it looks like his ribs and shoulder bones will break through his skin. In just minutes, he will be dead.

Then his cry changes. He becomes like a little boy begging for mercy. He is crying for his mother and praying to God as he is dragged to the side of the road and forced down. The big soldier turns his attention back to us and begins snatching up each of our bags to search. The man on side of the road screams as he is pinned down and his mouth is pried open by blood-stained rebel hands. One pours sand down the man's throat. The man screams and gags.

"Gbarnga City?" a soldier asks Mama again, as he takes one more look through her bag. He looks over all of us, taking in our skinny frames. He looks at our clothes and I feel as if my whole life is on fire under his gaze.

"Yes," Mama nods.

"Fine." The man pushes Mama through. "Go!" This one believes Mama. The man seems satisfied for now and waves us ahead.

"You!" The rebel soldier points right at Aunt Gormah, who is still behind us, waiting to be waved through. My stomach does a flip as I turn to see if she and her children will make it through. "Come on! You wit them?"

"Yes," Aunt Gormah nods quickly.

"Move it then!" he says, waving them and the rest of our party through.

It seems as if God has answered my prayer, but even so, I do not breathe until we have passed the guard and he is talking to other people. Even then, I keep moving, as he could call us back. I know that we are not safe. The man drowning in sand is still screaming. I look over to see him being dragged off the road toward the field of bodies.

24

An Impossible Choice

We walk in silence for miles. No one utters a word for a very long time. We just walk with the crowds on the road. We do not see any other rebels, but we do see more dead bodies in the streets. Some lay beside suitcases broken open with the belongings scattered but I don't have much time to think about what happened to them. I must keep walking. Two older men pass us, going in the opposite direction. I turn around to see them stop and pick over the suitcases of the dead people. One of them selects a couple of shirts and then they both continue on their journey.

Later we find an abandoned village far off the main road and stay the night in a few of the empty homes. Brother Wuo and Brother Maxwell take turns keeping watch while we sleep. As I lay next to Kulubah on the dirt floor of the clay hut, I think of the mother and baby I saw our first day after leaving the church. I think of the white blanket. And in this moment, we are lying just like them, except we are breathing. We all cuddle close to Mama. She kisses us all and holds us tight until we finally drift off to sleep.

We get up before the sun again and are back on the road. We have found a rhythm now, and we know when to step off the road, when to walk in the woods, when to get back on the road, and which fields to walk through. Each checkpoint is still terrifying and gruesome. Some of the checkpoints are small and simple, while others are set up like small cities, with areas for parking trucks, sleeping, and even doing business. No matter the size of the checkpoint, each one leaves me feeling more and more shaken.

This day, after several hours of walking, Brother Wuo announces that we have finally left the heart of Monrovia and will soon be in another town. I can tell that we are also getting ready to approach another checkpoint. It's always easy to tell when you are coming up to one. The smell of death is so thick that you can taste it. You can hear gunfire and the faint screams of those sentenced to die.

As we get close enough to see the next checkpoint ahead, we all begin to prepare ourselves for what is to come. I already feel the fear. Flashbacks of bloody faces and dead bodies from previous checkpoints cloud my mind. We have been lucky so far. We have followed the rules the soldier taught us. We keep our heads low. We look plain. We speak Kpelle and we keep our answers the same no matter what. As we approach a line of people on the road, there is a man lying dead in the street. I step over him quickly to make sure that I keep up with the others. We wait our turn to get to the front of the line where the rebels are asking questions, rummaging through belongings, and getting in people's faces. When it is our turn, we listen as Mama goes through the routine.

"What are you doing here?" The rebel asks looking at Mama. "Why are you here?"

"Ku kwrah Gbarnga. Ku ka a Gpella. Mu. Nunee ja nya, kwa lei ku poi tah." We are from Gbarnga City. We are Kpelle people. My children and I are going home.

The rebel interrogating Mama looks over us and then back at Mama. His fierce eyes stare at her without blinking, his face unmoving. He says nothing for a moment. "You are a woman with four children? Traveling alone?"

"Yes," Mama answers in Kpelle.

The rebel snatches up Mama's bag and begins to look through it. Then he looks back at her. "What woman has four kids with no husband?" He is leering at her. "Where is your man?"

"Mo grown," Mama says. *I don't know.* My heart skips a beat as I watch Mama try to keep her composure. I know that Mama cannot tell anyone where Papa really is, and she never lies and says that her husband is dead. The rebel holds up his hand to stop other travelers from taking another step. The rebel lowers his gaze to Mama's face and leans in so that there is no space between them.

"You don't know where your own husband is?" he asks. "What woman doesn't know where her husband is? Where is your husband?"

"I don't know," Mama tells him again. "He left to go get supplies and never returned. I don't know where he is."

"Perhaps he is in Doe's army and you just don't want to tell me! I don't believe that you don't know where he is, woman!"

"No." Mama's voice is shaking. "I am telling you the truth!"

Aunt Gormah freezes in her tracks and grabs my hand, pulling me back. "Quanei, Nyempu, by me," she says quickly.

"You are lying to me," the solider shouts. "Who are you with? What tribe are you from? Who do you work for?"

Mama tries to tell the man but he cuts her off.

"You are a liar," he says, his voice dripping with anger and contempt. "Your husband probably works for the government. You are probably going to meet him now, aren't you? You and your children."

"No," Mama says. "I told you. I do not know where he is. He left."

To my complete terror, the rebel solider waves over some help. My eyes grow wide and I lean back against Aunt Gormah. We stand there trembling as he explains the situation to the other rebels. The new rebels look at Mama for a moment before they join in.

They ask her the same questions over and over. Mama's voice is shaking as he tries to explain everything she has just said over and over again. I am holding on to the water jug so tight that it is starting to hurt my hand. *Why won't they just listen to Mama? Why won't they just let us through?* The other rebels begin to snatch up our bags and go through them as two stay to interrogate Mama. I know this is not good and I wonder what is going to happen to us if we cannot convince these rebels of who we are.

"I have heard enough! Enough of these lies!" the first rebel says. He turns to his counterparts and nods. "She is good to go."

She is good to go. When I hear this, blood freezes in my veins and terror grips my heart. I have heard this at the other checkpoints and I know what it means. It means that they are going to kill this person.

"What? No!" Mama says. "I am telling you the truth!"

"No! You don't mean that!" Aunt Gormah steps forward. "She is telling the truth!"

But it's too late. Right in front of us, one of the rebels grabs Mama's arms and she quickly hands Funbgbeh over to Aunt Gormah.

"No!" Aunt Gormah calls out as she holds on to Fungbeh. "Neyor!"

I drop the water jug. A sharp cry escapes my lips. The rebels have my mother and they are pulling her away from us. Brother Wuo and Brother Maxwell look on in horror. The whole world has slowed down and all I can see is Mama's terrified face.

"No!" Mama says, struggling against them. "No! My children, please! I am telling you the truth! If you kill me, my children will be all alone! Please!"

I try to run to Mama but one of the smelly soldiers pushes me back so hard I fall on the ground. "Mama!" I scream after her. Little Kulubah is screaming and crying now. She runs toward Mama, but Aunt Gormah grabs her up just before a rebel solider goes to strike her.

"Keep moving!" he says, pointing his gun right in Aunt Gormah's face.

I hear the soldier's command, but I cannot move. I am looking at Mama. She is pleading for her life like I have seen so many others before.

"Please! My children! No!" she begs.

"Okay, you want your children?" one of them asks. "Fine!" He shoves her back toward the line. For a moment, it looks like they have changed their minds.

"Mama!" I call as they begin half shoving, half dragging her back toward the line.

"Please," Mama pleads as they march her back over to us. "Please, just have mercy!"

I am glad to see Mama coming back, but it hurts me to see her treated so roughly.

"You whine about your children. Here they are!" The rebel is still holding Mama by the collar of her shirt. "You so worried about what will happen to your children? Then I will fix it for you. We either kill them or kill you! Choose!"

Mama whips her head around to look at the man holding her. "What? No. Please sir. Just leave us. We are no trouble for you!"

"Either I will kill you or kill your children. You did this! Now choose!"

Mama looks at all of us and then up at Brother Wuo, Brother Maxwell, Brother Pyne, Sister Hemelay, Aunt Ginger, and Aunt Gormah—and finally at all of us children standing there. Fresh tears stream down her face. Her voice is shaking. "Take me. Let me die. Just let them go, please. Let them all go! Please!"

"Well, let's go!" the rebel says yanking Mama away again.

"Gormah!" Mama calls out. "Take care of my children, Gormah! Gormah!"

Aunt Gormah is standing in the sun, holding on to Fungbeh, staring at Mama in shock. Her chest heaves quickly as her sobs escape. Kulubah wails as Mama is dragged away from us again. She begins to squirm and fight against Aunt Ginger, who is trying to hold on to both Kulubah and her own small daughter, both are screaming at the top of their lungs.

I stand in shock, feeling helpless and weak as I watch them drag Mama away. I am trembling and crying. I can barely see Mama, as tears threaten my view.

"Mama!" I cry at the top of my lungs. I fall to the ground, my knees hitting the dirt. "Mama!"

"Get up!" a rebel soldier yells at me. I feel his rough hands scratch my neck as he pulls me up by my tattered collar. "You better keep walking before I kill all of you!"

The soldiers drag Mama, sobbing, forcing her to walk. She turns and calls back to us, "I love you!"

"Get up!" one of the soldiers yell again at me. He shoves me into Nyempu, who stumbles backward, tears streaming down her face. She too is sobbing, but somehow, she manages to steady us both.

"We have to keep walking," Brother Maxwell says. He is trembling. "Please, keep walking."

"No! No! Where is Mama? Where is Mama?" I ask frantically. "I cannot leave her behind."

"Go!" the rebel says. Kulubah is still screaming at the top of her lungs, as the rebel solider pushes us forward with his gun.

"Go now!" the rebel says louder. Kulubah is still screaming at the top of her lungs, as the rebel solider pushes us forward with his gun.

Sister Hemelay looks like she is trying not to break as she holds tightly to us and helps Aunt Gormah move us through the line and onto the road. Sister Hemelay and Aunt Gormah gather us all together. Tears are streaming down the grownups' faces, hitting the sand like rain in a desert. Aunt Ginger holds Kulubah's hand while trying to quickly pick up our things before the rebel soldiers decide that we are next. At the same time, she is pushing her own daughter forward. Suddenly, Kulubah wriggles free of Aunt Ginger's grasp and lands on the ground in a heap.

"Kulubah!" Nyempu cries, rushing to scoop her up. But she misses and Kulubah is pushed along by another rebel soldier.

"No!" Nyempu cries, her eyes wide with terror. "Noooooo!"

I watch as my baby sister runs away from us, in the direction they took Mama. I watch as Kulubah's tiny body moves swiftly through the crowd of people and into the grassland. Nyempu is screaming at her with every fiber in her body.

"Kulubah!" Nyempu cries, trying hard to see her. But it is no use. Nyempu is being pushed by the soldiers, blocked from running after Kulubah. The moment Kulubah is completely out of sight, a deep howl escapes her lips. I have never heard anyone make such a sound. It sounds as if Nyempu's heart is being ripped right from her chest.

We are forced to continue to move through the checkpoint. I feel my very breath being taken from me. Kulubah is gone and Mama is being marched to her death.

Impossible Choice

Scan the QR-Code and navigate to Ch. 24. Join the conversation and connect with other Witness readers. Post a short video about your experience of this chapter and you can win a Witness shirt.

www.resources.witnessliberia.com

Part Three

Terror. Survival. Death. Miracles.

*Art credited to Liberian children, survivors of war now living at
Christ's Children Orphanage Home on Sugar Hill, Liberia-Oct, 2018*
WITNESS: IN PARTNERSHIP WITH SAVE MORE KIDS, INC

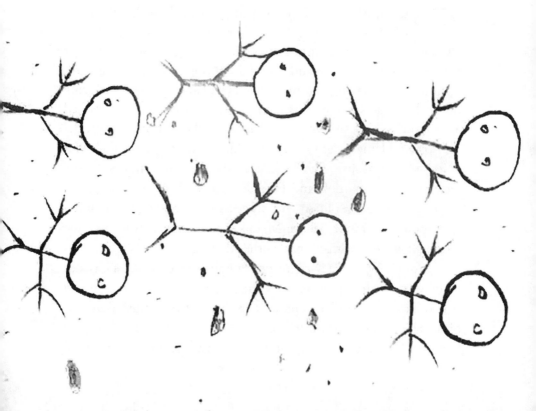

25

She Did Not Walk Alone

Early August 1990
60 Minutes After Duport Road Checkpoint

Dust swirls around me as it finds its back to the dirt road. My head is aching. My eyes are burning, my ears are ringing, and a million noises are banging in my skull. Hot tears run down my face and I'm still fighting to catch my breath. I am barefoot, having lost my shoes some time ago, and each step on the hot road sears my sore feet. The sight of Mama being pulled away from us is fresh in my mind as the soldiers push us forward.

Sister Hemelay grabs my shoulders. "Let's go, babies." Her voice sounds deeper. She looks scared. The harsh noises of the checkpoint commotion and Fungbeh's cries fill my ears as I look around at the rebel soldiers and other families moving through the checkpoint. I cannot believe Mama is gone. Taken from us. Just like we have seen with so many others before.

Brother Wuo is trying to get Fungbeh to be quiet so as not to draw any more attention. As the line moves forward, I am so scared I can barely place one foot in front of the other. Fear and Sister Hemelay's hand on my back are the only things moving me forward. Nyempu walks like a zombie, just a few feet in front of me. She stumbles a little as she takes small steps forward. Every now and then I see her shoulders heave and I know that she is still sobbing. Our group moves together tightly, each one holding on to someone else. We are all too scared to let go, for fear that any one of us may be stripped away. Tears hit the ground as I walk, and I wonder if I will ever stop crying.

As we keep moving through the checkpoint, I can hear Brother Wuo praying to God under his breath. I am praying too. I pray that we make it through this checkpoint without any more of us ripped away. I look over my shoulder, hoping to see Mama or Kulubah from the distance just once more. I desperately want to turn back and find them. Why did Kulubah have to run away? How come she did not just stay with us? Now the rebel soldiers will surely kill her too. Or, once Mama is dead, they will turn her into a monster child warrior, like all the ones Uncle Nenwon told us about. All of these terrifying thoughts are in my head as I wipe new tears from my face. We are all trembling as we walk. Eventually I see the end approaching.

"Let us just get through here together," Aunt Gormah says. "Hold on to me, babies. Hold on." Her face is wet. I can see that she is trying to be strong. She keeps us moving.

As we cross over the checkpoint, Brother Wuo and Brother Maxwell grab our hands. "This way," Brother Wuo says. Suddenly, we are all moving as fast as we can. I know that Brother Wuo is trying to put as much distance as he can between us and the checkpoint. I move as fast, but I also don't want us to leave too quickly. I realize that the faster we walk, the more distance we are putting between me and Mama. My heart breaks with every step because I feel like I am leaving Mama alone. I know she is dead by now, but I still don't want to leave her. Brother Wuo swiftly leads us to a little clearing off the main road. As soon as we stop, we are free to all start hugging one another and sobbing out the pain. Aunt Gormah is holding all of us in her arms and crying so hard that she is shaking.

"Why, God?" she sobs. "Why?"

I bury my face in her clothes and squeeze my eyes tight as I am wondering the same thing. I can still see Mama being dragged away. I can still see her face and hear her telling us that she loves us. It is starting to hit me like a rock. My Mama is gone now. She is dead. She has become another victim of this war that devours our life bit by bit. Another bloated body stacked in a field. Never did I think that Mama would be taken from us. How will we survive now? Where will we go? We came here because of her. We only survived this long because of her. What will our lives be now?

Nyempu and I are leaning against Aunt Gormah, silent now. I am exhausted from screaming and crying. Fungbeh has collapsed helplessly on Aunt Gormah's shoulders.

"What will we do now?" Brother Maxwell asks.

Sister Hemelay says, "It was Neyor's plan to go back home to Sugar Hill. She knew the way. Do we just do her plan without her?"

Aunt Gormah is too distracted to speak. She looks around to see who will take over as leader, who will decide where we will go next. Nyempu wipes her face and looks at the adults. I can tell she is thinking the same thing. Do we just keep walking? Do we go back and try to find Mama? Are we even safe here?

"Neyor was not the only one with ties to Gbarnga," Aunt Ginger says. "My brother's house is still there, and our father's village is near, so I am still going."

"I don't think I can make it," Sister Hemelay says. "I can't keep going after that. My heart is broken to pieces!"

Brother Wuo says, "We need God's strength. We need to pray for Neyor. We must pray that her soul may find God's peace."

"Yes," Sister Hemelay nods. "And for Kulubah, wherever the poor child is. Dear God." Her voice breaks. She begins to sob.

"I still cannot believe this." Aunt Gormah continues to cry bitterly.

My chest is still heaving and sometimes a random cry escapes my lips. I cannot believe that I am never going to see Mama again. My heart is aching more than I ever thought it could. My worst nightmare has come true. Once again, I want to lie down and die. I now wish I had insisted that I die with Mama. For some reason, I feel better to think this way. It just hurts to be alive.

Just when I am ready to slip right onto the ground, Brother Wuo forms an even tighter circle and the adults begin to pray and cry out to God. This now makes me feel better. I realize that I am not alone. Everyone is grief-stricken and shocked. We are standing in the middle of the wilderness with our hearts ripped to shreds. For a moment, I am glad that Brother Wuo has grouped us together, praying to God. Mama turned to God all the time. Even when she did not know what to do, Mama wanted us to pray. Whether for happiness, for sadness, for tough times, Mama wanted us to turn to God.

I have no idea how Nyempu, Kormah, Fungbeh and I will live without Mama and Papa. Will our aunts and uncles even be able to take care of us as Mama did? Or will they leave us like Auntie Korto and Uncle Nenwon did back at Sugar Hill? Who is going to feed us? Who is going to hold me at night and sing to me when I am scared? I cover my face with my hands and lean against Aunt Gormah. Brother Wuo leads us in prayer. He prays for strength and guidance for us all. I know I need it, but I don't even know if God is listening. Where is God? I'm so confused. Even though I don't know what is coming next, I listen to the group pray and decide that I feel a little better knowing we are doing something that my mother would have wanted us to do.

As our group stands on the side of the road, consoling one another and looking to God for answers, a strange rumbling from the bushes catches our attention. The rustle is consistent, like an animal trying to make its way onto the road. Nobody pays any mind to the movement at first, but I hear it and I pull at Brother Wuo's hand. The rustle grows louder, stronger, stopping our prayers. We are all fear-stricken. My first thought is that it must be a rebel looking for someone in the woods. Maybe we have wandered too close to another killing field. Brother Maxwell grips my shoulder. "Get behind me."

The bush is thick and heavy, and it is a dark afternoon. Clouds gathered up above, announcing the next tropical shower and blocking out the sun. It is hard to see clearly. All I can feel is terror in my stomach. Whatever is in the woods is getting closer and my blood freezes in my veins. Shouldn't we run and hide? I'm sure

that the rebels are hunting someone. The thing seems to be carefully moving forward, like a hunter creeping toward its prey. If it
is rebels, it makes no sense to run. Everyone's eyes are locked on
the dark and heavy bushes as we prepare from whatever is about
to meet us. I peek around Brother Maxwell, my heart racing.
I begin to see what looks like red and black clothing silhouett-
ed through the bushes. Then I see the outline of a body emerge,
causing us all to take a nervous step back. To my complete shock,
I recognize our new visitor.

"Mama?"

Mama and Kulubah suddenly appear from the bushes.

"Mama?" I hear myself say again. I frown and blink rapidly
trying to understand if my mind is tricking me.

"Neyor?" Aunt Gormah says in disbelief too. "Wha. . . what?"

"Sister Neyor!" Brother Wuo's eyes are stretched wide. We are
gaping at the vision in front of us, but no one moves. We are all
looking at a ghost.

"Mama? Kulubah? Is that you?" Nyempu says.

The vision we believe to be Mama stands smiling at us, with
tears streaming.

"Mama! Mama! Kulubah! Mama!" I run toward both of them.

"Oh, thank God!" Mama says and starts running toward us.
Suddenly, everyone is now rushing behind me to get to Mama and
Kulubah too.

"Neyor!" Aunt Ginger is stunned and motionless.

My mind cannot catch up with what is happening right now.
I know that Mama is dead, but it looks as if she and Kulubah are
standing right in front of me, not dead. I wonder if I am dreaming.
But even if I am, I don't care. As I reach Mama, I stop just a few feet
away and look up at her. My chest is heaving and sweat drips down
my face as I peer up at the sight in front of me.

"Quanei, it's okay," Mama says. When I hear her voice, I know
that it is her. Mama is not dead. Mama is back. Mama kneels down
and looks me in my face as a wave of tears rushes over it. "It's okay,
baby," Mama says again. "It's okay. Mama is here now."

I hold on to Mama and sob my heart out as the others circle around us. Nyempu jumps up on me and Mama keeps hugging me tightly. I can hear everyone around us creating a commotion, looking in disbelief, asking questions, and giving thanks to God. Still, I do not let go.

We have also attracted a little attention from people walking by. Few people nearby are simply standing and looking at us. There's a woman and her family who have even put their luggage down to just stand and look at us.

"We have to move," Brother Maxwell says, looking around. "People are looking. No one can know about this miracle. No one can know that you have escaped! They will send rebels after us! We need to get as far from this checkpoint as we can. We have to move."

We are all moving again as one unit, trying to put distance between us and the horror of the checkpoint. All the grownups are moving swiftly and I am holding on to Mama's hand, which I haven't let go of since being reunited with her. Finally, Brother Wuo decides that we have moved far enough to stop and hear Mama out.

"Neyor, what happened?" Aunt Gormah asks.

"Yes, how did you get away from those boys?" Brother Maxwell asks.

"It. . ." Mama begins, trying to catch her breath. "It was. . ."

"This is a miracle!" Brother Wuo says.

"It was a miracle," Mama says. She tries to answer everyone's questions. "I was taken to the fields, stripped down. I swear, they were about to kill me. But the God we serve is a miracle-working God! I did not walk out of that field alone." Mama pauses and looks around, cocking her head to one side. She is looking at her sister. "How did Kulubah even get away from you people?"

Aunt Ginger was on the other side of Aunt Gormah. She shakes her head, and says with a plea in her voice, "I was holding her back when the rebels were dragging you away. I was holding Patricia too, and also trying to keep Fungbeh calm. Everybody was in this confused state of mind, Neyor. All the children were crying for you and all of us were so busy crying that this little girl—" Aunt Ginger points to Kulubah. "She ripped out of my hands. Before I could even realize what happened, all I could see is her back disappearing among the rebels and running toward where they were taking you. Neyor, I'm so sorry. I don't even know how she found you."

"Oh, Ginger, no need to be sorry. Kulubah was part of God's miracle. She's why I'm alive right now. I can't even begin to tell you how brave this little girl was when she found me at gunpoint in the field, standing on top of all those dead people." Mama sighed and shook her head.

"Really?" Brother Maxwell is in shock and all of us are now looking at Mama to give us more details.

"How did all this happen, Sis Neyor? We had given up and did not even think you were still alive. When people get in the hands of those savages, it's like red meat thrown at hungry hyenas," Brother Wuo says.

"They stripped me down naked and were about to shoot me, I tell you! I couldn't breathe because of the stench of the dead bodies. So many, they were piled on top of each other, like clothes in a heap. I couldn't stand. They had to carry me the spot in the fields where a young boy, no older than my Kormah, said 'your turn' to a girl. He said, 'Do what you need to do. The woman is good to go!'" Mama is even imitating the way the soldiers speak, and the hand gestures and posture of the children who tried to kill her.

"But there was this man there. He was fighting for his life because he wanted to get back to his pregnant wife and baby. He even broke away at one point. He created such a commotion that the rebels were distracted. And while they were distracted, I was just standing there praying. Oh, I really thought I was finished.

"You should have seen the child that they ordered to kill me. She was barely two or three years older than my baby, Nyempu, and she was holding this heavy AK-47, trying to point it at me.

I looked at her and I was wondering what this girl was before she became a murderer. I was praying to God, asking Him to spare you all, and praying that they didn't catch Quanei and Kormah and turn them into killers.

"That man was screaming so much, and he was big, he was fighting the young rebel boys. They couldn't control him, and he got away. He was yelling 'My wife! Please God, our baby!' He was out of his mind fighting, so desperate that he shoved down another of the boys and almost got to the road. The girl who had her gun on me was watching them, like she wanted to go help them.

"I had made my peace with dying but when I looked into that girl's eyes, I thought of all of my children. All five of them. Would they become like her without me? I closed my eyes and I prayed. I promised God that if I made it through, I would find a way to become mother to children like the girl in front of me. I would serve Him and take care of the orphans who had been turned to monsters. I was praying and then I heard a rustle in the grass.

I thought I was dreaming when Kulubah came running out. I screamed at her 'Kulubah, go back!' But instead, the baby runs straight to me and puts her arms around my neck. She is looking at me, at the girl, crying, 'Mama, are they going to kill you? Mama, are they going to kill you? Why are you naked, Mama?' and I am crying because now they are going to kill me and kill my baby. I look at this girl and I say, 'Please,' and just then the commotion of the fighting man grows louder. They cannot hold this man to kill him.

"This girl, this child, she looks at me with no emotion in her face and she says 'Take your clothes and go. Quickly now, Old Ma, before they come back with me and kill you. Go, na! Move quick!' The poor girl had mercy on me and sent me and Kulubah away while the other rebels were distracted."

"What?" Aunt Gormah asks her eyes wide. "I cannot believe it!"

"It's true!" Mama says. "I grabbed my clothes and my legs were like water but I just jumped over so many bodies and I ran, holding my clothes in one arm and carrying Kulubah in the other. I just headed to the woods and didn't look back. I didn't even know where I was going or what would be on the other side. We ran and ran through the woods. Look at my face—all scratched because the twigs and branches were slapping me!"

"Oh, my God, that is so dangerous." Brother Wuo says. "If the rebels had found you sneaking through the woods, to avoid the checkpoint, I cannot image what they would have done."

"It is better than being killed in the fields. Plus, I only had one direction to run. Thank God all the rebels' attention was on that poor man. I ran so fast. I thought I was being chased. Kulubah was so brave. She just kept holding on tight. I thought they were surely going to chase me. Then I knew you all had to keep heading this way, so I used the woods to go around the checkpoint. I knew I would find you all on the road."

Even as Mama describes how she got away, it sounds unbelievable. Everyone keeps asking Mama questions, but I don't say much. I just stand looking up at her for fear that if I take my eyes off of her, she will disappear again. I am still trying to understand everything that has just happened. I feel like my whole life has become nothing but close calls with death and I am happy but I also wonder how much more I can take.

26

Rest at Ma Barclay

When everyone has rested, we begin our journey again. Brother Wuo tells us that the next town up is Ma Barclay and that we should be safe there, because we are now on the outside of Monrovia and fully into rebel territory. We no longer have to worry about answering to two different fronts. We all walk together. Sometimes Mama, Aunt Ginger, and Sister Hemelay sing along the way. Occasionally, I stop walking and look up at Mama.

"Mama?" I say to her.

"Yes, little boy, I am here," she says. Satisfied, I walk a while more.

"Mama?" I say again, still holding tight to her hands.

"Yes, little boy, I am here," she says. I don't know how many times I do this. But some part of me still wants to make sure that Mama is here and that she is never going anywhere ever again. Every time she replies, I know I am not dreaming, that Mama is here with me. God has indeed spared her life and given my mother back to us. Whenever her hand grows tired from my squeezing, she releases my grip, stretches her fingers, then brings her hand right back down for me to grip again. Nyempu walks on the other side of Mama, sometimes holding her and sometimes throwing her arm around her waist.

The hunger, exhaustion, and heat are no match for the joy we feel. When my aunts start singing again, I join in, swinging Mama's hand and skipping about as we make our way to our next stop. I am sure I have never felt so happy in my life.

After hours of walking, Brother Wuo spots something up ahead. "It looks like there is a village ahead or something," he says.

I am still holding on tight to Mama's hand. I squint my eyes to see what he sees. I am not as tall as the grownups, so I don't see anything yet. After a few more steps, I begin to see the outline of the village.

"Do you think it is safe?" Mama asks.

"We are in Ma Barclay now," Brother Wuo says. "The rebels are not concerned with this area. It is mostly old tribal villages. If it checks out, this may be a place where we can rest for the night."

I suddenly realize just how exhausted I am. I feel like I have hit a stone wall, or maybe like a stone wall has hit me.

"Let's just be careful," Aunt Ginger says as we approach.

"Brother Wuo and I can go check it out," Brother Maxwell says. "All of you stay here. We will go."

Mama takes a moment to unwrap Fungbeh from her back and rock him a little bit. She kisses his face a few times and then holds him tight. As I look up at her, part of me is still scared that at any moment she will snatched away. I am still staring up at Mama when Brother Wuo and Brother Maxwell return.

"It looks good!" Brother Wuo calls out, with a touch of excitement in his voice. "A lot of the villagers have left, but there are a few people remaining. They are nice enough. They have green, young papaya and palm cabbage for sale."

"What?" Sister Hemelay gasps. "Thank you, God!"

"Oh, thank God," Mama says as she holds Fungbeh close. "Let's go then."

After about a half mile, we come up on the village. We all quickenoursteps when we see a small fruit stand at the front of the village. A man and a woman sit comfortably and wave at us from the distance.

When I see the mounds of papaya on the table, my heart skips a beat. It is the most food we have seen in days. But I wonder how it will taste. I have never eaten it that green before. In Sugar Hill, the ones Papa would pick for us were so juicy and ripe. But my stomach is just for anything that will taste like food. Not to mention that the woman at the table is smiling at us. It's like a dream come true.

"I have some money," Mama tells Brother Wuo as we approach the table. "From before. I managed to keep a little. I think I can buy something for us."

"I have a little too," Brother Wuo says. "It's just that money is almost of no value now. All of the businesses are ransacked, and the government has basically shut down." He waves back at the woman. "Do you think they will even accept it?"

"We have to try," Mama says. "Why else would she be standing out here?"

It turns out Mama is right. The woman gladly welcomes us all to her table and Mama is able to use the money she has tucked away to buy the fruit for us. As we all fawn over the green papaya, the people at the stand tell us about the village. The older man at the stand shows us around. His name is Moses Kwelleh. "But call me Mr. Mo," he adds. Mr. Mo is tall and slender. He speaks proper English and his voice carries lots of bass for such a thin looking man. He tells us that we are welcome to rest in this village for as long as we need.

"Are you sure it is safe here?" Mama asks, looking around the abandoned village.

"The rebels have already done their damage here," he says. "They have not come around here for several weeks. There's nothing left after they looted and rampaged months ago. They killed many people and left the village almost bare. Since then, they have moved on to their real destination, Monrovia. So, they have no interest in anything here. The people who used to live here were either slaughtered, captured, or ran away when the war first started. You all can pick any place you like to set up camp and rest. No one is going to bother you."

In a way, I am happy to hear this since we have been sleeping on the side of the road for days. I can't even remember the last time any of us slept through the night. But there is also a part of me that feels a deep terror about what Mr. Mo just explained.

Once everyone has properly thanked Mr. Mo, Mama wastes no time finding a place for us. She picks a simple clay house that is very small and unlike the others, the door at least partially closes, and I think that's probably why Mama chooses it. It is much better than anything we have been inside in weeks. The house only has three rooms. One is big, one small, and there's a kitchen hut outside, behind the house. There's also a wood charcoal place for cooking. There are three wooden reef beds in the single room with just the sponge for the mattress and no sheets.

"This is good Mama," Nyempu says looking around. "I can set our stuff up in the room and I can help you clean it up."

"Me too," I say peeking into the kitchen. "Me and Nyempu can clean while you cut up the papaya."

"Okay," she says. "Let's do it."

"Brother Wuo and I will fetch for firewood to make hot water for later," says Brother Maxwell.

Even though I am afraid to let Mama out of my sight for even a second, I follow Nyempu into the room with our things.

That night, we all eat as much papaya as our tummies can handle. The papaya is not ripe, so it is bitter and hard to chew, but we do not care. We are so hungry that we just stuff it down. After we eat, we push all the beds together and sleep in one giant bed. We all huddle together in our makeshift bed, and for the first time in a long time my entire family sleeps through the night.

In the morning, I wake to the sound of Nyempu throwing up. I sit up to see Mama rubbing her back as she vomits into a pail. As I stand looking at them, I notice that my stomach does not feel that well either. Suddenly, I too am heaving. I jump up and run outside to the tiny front porch and hurl myself over the side just in time for the vomit to leave my lips. My stomach is spasming. I am shaking as I lean over and throw up again and again.

"It is the papaya." I turn around to see Brother Wuo standing behind me. "It is raw and not ripe. It hits the stomach and makes you sick. Are you alright?"

I nod at him and wipe my mouth. "But Nyempu is sick too."

"I imagine everyone will be," he answers. "But what can we do? We need to eat."

It turns out that Brother Wuo is right. When I go back inside I see that Kulubah and Fungbeh have begun to throw up as well. Later when I walk around the village, I see that the woman with the stand is gone. I wonder if maybe she sold all her fruit or if she moved to the next city to sell more. Either way, I hope that she comes back soon. Brother Wuo, Brother Maxwell, and Sister Hemelay come out of their newfound homes to tell us that they searched the other homes for anything of use. They tell us that there are few other people in the village, but that food is still scarce.

"It's okay," Mama says, gently rubbing my shoulder. "We have made it this far, we will be alright."

"One family told me they are going to Fender City, to the refugee camp," Sister Hemelay says.

"But Fender City is rumored to be terrible," Mama responds. "I heard the city is overrun with poverty, measles, and all kinds of disease. And it is run by the rebels."

"Yes," Aunt Ginger says. "We cannot go to Fender. The rebels may never let us leave. And we will not have a place to stay. Plus, the children may contract something horrible."

"Well we cannot stay here forever," Brother Wuo says. "It is not our final destination. Fender City is on the way to Gbarnga City and Nimba County."

"On the way?" Brother Maxwell asks. "Gbarnga City is still almost a hundred miles from here. We haven't even gone part of the way!"

For some reason this all makes us erupt into laughter. It is almost as if the journey has forced us to burst into laughter to peel away the stress of the past few days.

That night, we are all starving but terrified to eat the papaya again. No one wants to be sick. But no one wants to be hungry either. Thankfully, Mama is one step ahead. While we are out exploring and playing in the village, Mama finds some palm trees, digs out some palm cabbage, and makes palm oil to mix up with the papaya. Mama says it will take away the acid that made us sick. I look at the new mixture in front of me and decide that eating this mixture is better than being weak and hungry. So, I am the first to grab my food. I am glad that the food won't make us sick anymore, but that doesn't change the fact that raw papaya mixed with palm cabbage and palm oil tastes disgusting.

We spend almost an entire week in the abandoned village. While we rest at Ma Barclay, Mama lets us sleep in all morning. In the afternoon, we run outside, listening to stories from Mr. Mo and peeking into the abandoned houses. Pretty soon though, the papaya runs out and we are back to searching for food. After a couple of days, we are desperately hungry again, almost as hungry as we were back at Gaye Town Church. There is a fresh creek nearby so we have a little water, but we are getting weak again. During the day, I hear the grownups outside talking, and I know they are trying to decide our next move. I too wonder what we will do. Where we will get our next meal?

"We have to go to Fender," Brother Maxwell says. "We have to at least try."

"There could be anything there!" Mama says. "The rebels run

the entire town!" I can hear the fear in Mama's voice even as she says the very word rebel and I don't want Mama to be scared. I can imagine Mama's fear at the thought of seeing a rebel soldier again.

"Sister," Brother Maxwell says. "It is a refugee camp for people who are escaping the war or maybe even escaping the government. Even if it is a rebel camp, they are not looking to hurt people who are coming to them."

"Brother Wuo is right," Aunt Ginger says. "It may be a chance we have to take. There may be better chances for food there. We have been lucky to stay here all this time, but we cannot let the grass grow under our feet. A troop of rebels could come through at any moment."

"But what about Doe, and him bombing the area?" Mama asks. "I have heard that he tries to take out as many rebels as he can!"

"Okay listen," Brother Wuo says. "We have all heard terrible things about Fender. We know what kind of place it may be. But we cannot stay in this abandoned village and starve. And we can't eat any more palm cabbage or that might kill us too." He takes a deep breath and looks around. "How about, Brother Maxwell and I make the trip to Fender. It is only a day's journey. We can go see what is happening and come back."

"It is too dangerous!" Mama says. "You are going to a rebel refugee camp. Anything can happen."

"Neyor, the children are starving," Aunt Ginger says. "At least there is food at the refugee camp and there are plenty of things we can take from here to trade. We have to do something."

As I am listening to the grownups, I decide I agree with Brother Maxwell's idea. If he says Fender City is safe, then maybe we can go and get some food. All I can think about is the growling in my stomach and the fact that I don't want to eat any more of that nasty palm cabbage.

That same day, Brother Wuo and Brother Maxwell leave for Fender City. The day after they return with news. We all eagerly gather around. Mama is sitting on the floor with her legs crossed. Fungbeh is collapsed in her arms and she rocks him gently. I'm wide awake and agitated. It could be because we had only crumbs to eat this morning. I'm hungry and there's nothing anyone can do about it. All of the children in the group sit down to listen. I'm sitting along the wall, my skinny black legs crossed underneath me like butterfly antennae. Nyempu is next to me with Kulubah lying across her lap, huddled right next to Mama. Sister Hemelay and her kids are across from us and Aunt Gormah is sitting on the log next to her. Brother Wuo and Brother Maxell are sitting on the wood bench in front of everyone, as if on a stage. Brother Wuo tells us what they have seen and discovered about Fender.

"The place is quite disturbing and depressing to see," says Brother Wuo. "It is overrun with refuges, sickness, and rebels. Oh, my people. People are really suffering because of this war."

"Not to mention, every day people are getting killed by stray bullet from rebels," Brother Maxwell adds. "It's a death camp—especially for children. More people are starving to death in the camp than we could have even imagined. No one has access to any kind of food. If you're lucky, occasionally, you can get your hands on sugarcane sticks."

"Well if it is so bad, then we can't go there," Mama says.

"It may still be the best option yet," Brother Wuo says.

Brother Maxwell says, "While we were there, we discovered there may be a way to catch a truck to Gbarnga City or some of the other counties. Fender is like a transportation hub."

"What!" Aunt Ginger says. "That is such good news!"

"So, it is possible that we will be able to catch a truck home?" Sister Hemelay asks, her voice full of anticipation.

"Yes," says Brother Maxwell. "There are trucks leaving every day, and if you can make your way on one, then you are good. It looks like we all may be able to head home at some point. But we cannot take advantage of that if we do not go into Fender."

"But what if we get sick or die before we can get on one of these trucks?" Mama protests. "What you are describing sounds too terrible to risk."

"Do not be discouraged," Brother Wuo reassures. "It turns out God has been looking out for us. There is a chance that we do not have to stay inside of Fender but can take refuge in a house outside the city, away from the chaos."

Mama starts to say something then stops. She does not look convinced.

"We found a single room, the only one available for us to stay outside the camp," Brother Wuo says. "We will have to share, but at least we will have a place to stay outside the city. I have already talked to the people and they will hold it for us if we come soon."

I can tell Mama is relieved. "Well," she says, looking at everyone happily. "I say we leave in the morning."

It is settled now. Even Mama agrees that Fender is probably the best next move for us as long as we don't have to live in the camp. We get up before sunrise to pack and prepare for the journey to Fender. As I put my few clothes in my bag, I think about what is coming next. The lady with the fruit stand never came back to Ma Barclay, so Mama is right that we cannot just stay here and starve. Even if Fender isn't all that great, it will be worth the risk to get a ride to Gbarnga and closer to Sugar Hill. I look around our resting place. I know the next stop will not be as fun but I hope our stay there will be short. I'm pleased, though. We are now closer to getting home.

World Hunger Awareness
After finishing this chapter, scan the
QR-Code and navigate to Ch. 26. Read the article for a powerful connection
to the group's plight.

www.resources.witnessliberia.com

27

Risking it All for Fender

We make the few miles journey to Fender City in short time. Fungbeh is wrapped tightly on Mama's back and I am carrying the water jug again. Nyempu walks up ahead with Aunt Gormah and her children. It is still early and not yet that hot.

I can tell we are approaching the city because the road started to fill with people and trucks. At one point, a truck of rebel soldiers approaches and we all just stand aside, motionless. I hold my breath as they pass and try not to make eye contact, but they just ride on by, ignoring us, as if all of this is normal.

The closer we get, the more clearly I see that Fender City is jammed with people. There are crowds everywhere as we approach the mouth of the city. And Fender turns out to be even worse than I thought. The entire place is overrun by little tin shacks set up all over the place. From a distance, the tin shacks looked like thousands of pieces of clothing spread across a giant field. The grownups decide we will at least go into Fender and see if there is any marketplace to buy food and supplies. As we make our way through the town, I get a closer look at the tin huts crammed with families. They look piti-ful, sitting in the dark as if waiting for a miracle. There are people bustling all around amid the noise. Most here look worse off than us. Some look sick or near death. Their eyes are weary.

We walk through the tin city and come to a place with actual buildings. We make our way downtown to what appears to be a main building. A man at the door is checking people in and pointing them in the right direction. It doesn't take long to figure out that he is a rebel, but he is the first one I have seen not acting like a murderous monster. All the rebels in Fender seem busy, carrying things from one place to another, talking and busy conducting all kinds of business. They are still carrying guns, but they are not as mad as the ones who carried Mama away. Still, there is no doubt in anyone's mind that they will kill at a moment's notice.

Brother Wuo leads the way inside the rebel headquarters and we all file in after him. The place is dimly lit and smells of old must, sweat, and lots of people.

"Stay here with Sister Hemelay and your aunts," Mama tells us. "I'm going to find out how things run here." I watch Mama as she talks to several people. A couple of times, she gestures toward us as she explains something. After quite some time, Mama returns.

"It looks like we will be better off on the outskirts of the city. There is no real marketplace here. Everyone is just trying to survive," Mama says. Brother Maxwell and Brother Wuo have also been talking to officials within the building and hear the same things.

"Well, we don't need to be in Fender long," Aunt Ginger says. "Just enough to find a ride out of here."

"I agree," Sister Hemelay says. "No one can stay in Fender forever. I want to find my way to Nimba county as soon as possible. I heard there are trucks and sometimes buses that come and take people to other cities."

"Aye, but I heard it is impossible to get on one of those trucks," Aunt Gormah says. "Even on the way in here, I saw people trampling over each other, trying to get on some sort of truck. Some people were left behind, some people fell off. It is hard enough getting a single body onto those trucks let alone as many as we are. We would never make it."

"Well, we can't worry about that right now," Mama puts in. "We are all so exhausted that we can barely stand up straight. And the children are hungry. We must get going and find a place to lay our heads before night comes."

"Well then let's go," Aunt Ginger says, "before that room those people are holding for us gets filled."

We walk back through all the hustle and bustle and end up on the quiet outskirts of the city. Though I had been excited about the idea of camping out on the giant university campgrounds, I am relieved when we leave the overwhelming commotion of the center and go to a calmer place with fewer people. We easily find the place based on Brother Wuo's hand-drawn map and after a conversation with the landlord, we are directed to a tiny house with a porch. Mercifully, when we get there, the room is still available.

Even though we will all have to squeeze into one room, being in a house is better than being on the street or sleeping in bushes along the side of the road. Brother Wuo introduces us to the people there. The families occupying all the other rooms seem nice enough. We quickly go to the vacant room and place our things inside. It will be cramped but it will do for now. I am so tired and hungry that I want to fall on this floor and never get up. My stomach has been growling for two days straight, and I can't remember the last time I ate anything that wasn't palm cabbage. I never want to see or taste palm cabbage again, but I know in these conditions, we may not have a choice. The people in the house seem to be no better off than we are. Everyone is skinny, with long necks, drawn faces, and empty bellies.

I sit on the floor in the tiny room and lean against the wall for support. Nyempu does the same and we sit in silence as Mama organizes our things. After some shuffling about, Mama turns to us. "Look at you two," she says with love in her voice. "My babies are tired, Lord."

"I am not too tired to help, Mama," Nyempu says.

"Ah," Mama says, placing her hands on her hips. "But are you too tired to walk with me to buy some sugarcane?"

"Sugarcane?" I ask, sitting up.

"We get to eat sugar?" Nyempu sits up too.

"Something like that," Mama says, scooping Fungbeh up. "I heard a woman next door sells some. It will help hold us over for now. "

We follow Mama next-door where she buys some stalks of sugarcane for two dollars. We hungrily gnaw on the sweet stems right where we are—sucking out every bit of substance we can. We even eat the straw from the cane. I know we are not supposed to, but I don't care. I will do almost anything to make the gnawing feeling of hunger go away. It's only a taste of sweetness, but it helps, even if it is just telling our minds we are eating something.

That night, Mama, Nyempu, Fungbeh, Kulubah, Brother Maxwell, Brother Wuo, Sister Hemelay, Aunt Gormah and her two boys, Aunt Ginger and her Patricia, and I all pile into the single room to sleep. We are packed in like sardines, but at least we are all together and safe for now. Already I am hungry again. The sugarcane was sweet, but did not help for long. I know that if I can just get to sleep I can escape the hunger for a while. I roll over to take a peek at Mama. I just want to make sure that she is still there. To my surprise, Mama is looking right at me, and she smiles when our eyes meet. She is sitting with her back against the wall, like an angel of love looking out for us all.

The next few days at Fender are filled with resting, searching for food, and trips into the city to learn more about how to get on with our journey. Brother Wuo and Brother Maxwell have taken charge of going into the city because they think it is unsafe for the women. One afternoon, while we sit outside on the porch, Brother Wuo comes running up as if lions are chasing him.

When Sister Hemelay sees him, she stands up quickly. "What's the matter?"

Mama stands up too, looking concerned. "What is it Brother Wuo?" Mama asks. "Is something wrong?

"No." He runs up the steps and trying to catch him breath. "Not at all, sister. I have some news! I have found a man from Nimba County who says he can help us get back there. He is of the Gio tribe like me, so he is looking out for his people."

"So, what are you saying?" Sister Hemelay asks him. "This man is willing to help us?"

"Yes," Brother Wuo says. "The man used to work for my father at Limco, so he was very nice about helping us. But he is only willing to help people from his own tribe get back to Nimba."

"I've talked it over with Brother Maxwell. We think that since this is the closest we have ever been to getting back to Nimba, we should go and meet with him now. Before it is too late."

"I agree," Sister Hemelay says. "We are so close to home and this is a great chance for us."

"I agree then. You must go." Mama says nodding. "You have to take that chance and the opportunity. We will be fine here until we get our chance. I am glad you are going home."

"We don't want to leave you and the children like this," Brother Wuo says.

"You are not leaving us," Mama said. "We knew it was the plan all along to come here to find a way to our destinations. You have been with us all this way, and we are family. We have each other still, even in spirit. I am just grateful to God that He managed to bring us all this far together."

"Are you sure you will be okay?" Brother Maxwell asks. "Please don't stay in Fender too long."

"We won't," Mama tells him. "We will make our own plan for leaving. You must go and take the chance you have to return to your home."

Brother Wuo lets out a deep breath. "So be it." He looks at Sister Hemelay. "Do you want to go with us? We will need to go there now."

"We'll gather our things," Sister Hemelay says, rushing into the house. "We need to get home."

Although I am happy to hear that Brother Wuo, Brother Maxwell, and Sister Hemelay have a way home, my stomach constricts just thinking of this big change. I try to hide my panic. I understand what Mama has said about each person needing to do what is best for them. At this point, I would give almost anything to be back with my whole family again. I wonder if Kormah, Uncle Thomas, and Aunt Garmen made it back to Sugar Hill. If there was a way to Sugar Hill, I would take it right away.

When Brother Wuo and Sister Hemelay have gathered everything they need, they meet everyone back at the porch.

Mama reaches over and hugs Sister Hemelay. "God be with you, Sister."

"Oh, my God, Sister," Sister Hemelay says as she wraps her arms around Mama, "God be with you."

"Quanei, take good care of your Mama and be a good boy. You hear me?" Brother Wuo kneels down to look at me. "You are a good son and she is going to need your help to look after you all."

"Okay," I say smiling at him and sticking my chest out like a big man. "I will."

"Good," he says as he rubs a hand on my head. "You keep your eyes open, you hear?"

I nod as he stands back up and begins to point Mama in the right direction. As they walk away, I feel torn inside. It is a sad but happy goodbye. We must go our separate ways but Brother Wuo and the rest have a chance to make it back to their home. This moment reminds me of the unripe papaya—a little bitter but necessary to keep going.

28

Rebels or Friends

Although the extra space in the room is nice, over the next few days everyone realizes there is not much to do besides sit around and be tired and hungry. The sugarcane is gone and it did little to keep off real hunger. Mama has already gone out to see who has food or knows where we can find any, but she quickly learns that the only real food in Fender is with the rebels. The majority of the town is either waiting for a miracle or trying to get home. As the days pass, there isn't much running around and playing because we are just so hungry. It seems like there is nothing to do but wait for something to change.

Sometimes, just to get out the house, we go and sit on the porch with Mama to watch the cars and the people go by. One of these times, we see a troop of rebel soldiers pass the house. They all walk together in a big group. Unlike the wild rebels we have seen who sometimes paint their faces, wear wigs or masks, laugh, taunt, and scream, these rebels are stern and serious. Still, they are nothing to be messed with. I take a big gulp and my stomach turns as they walk by. I try to not stare but I can't help but notice the AK-47s around their bodies.

These men aren't as young as the boys on the street either. They look like they are in their 20s and 30s, some are uniformed, and they all seem very sure of themselves. This makes their presence feel even more dangerous. Everyone outside notices them and freezes as they walk by. It's obvious to me that everyone is trying not to move while also trying to appear to keep up business as usual so that their mere stillness does not bring about the wrath of the rebels. It doesn't matter that the rebels don't bother anyone in Fender. They are still rebels and we are still in war. Anyone can be plucked from their home and killed instantly for doing anything rebels don't like.

The commander of the group is fashioned with a thick chain of bullets across his chest. He looks strong; he is tall and slender, wearing long camouflage pants and a black tank top. His army boots are strapped up tightly. The others are dressed in what seem to be mismatched outfits—some have red cloths tied around their head like Rambo, others have button-down shirts with one long sleeve and the other torn off. As the group approaches our house, everyone drops their eyes to the ground. I hear the steady crunch of gravel beneath their powerful boots, creating a terrifying rebel marching. I wait as patiently as I can for the scary soldiers and their gravel song to disappear so we can all breathe again.

Suddenly the steady crunching stops. I look up to see why. To my horror, the tall, strapped rebel commander is staring straight at us. My heart skips straight into my stomach and I hold my breath. The soldier catches my eye as soon as I look up, causing me to draw closer to Mama, sitting next to me on a wooden log. All the rebels have stopped now. Through the bright sun, I can see the commander's eyes scanning my face. Then he shifts his gaze to Mama and I feel like I might die. My entire body is shaking. I can hear Mama's breath quicken.

The commander takes a step toward us and I want to run and hide. I don't know what the rebels want with us or why this one focuses on Mama. I stand trembling as the solider continues to take steps toward us. I don't have to hear it to know that Mama is praying. Everyone on our porch and in the houses next door are staring in fear. None of us knows what the commander is thinking or what has caused him to stop. In the silence under the sun, the he takes a few steps closer, his eyes still locked on Mama. He looks back at his troops for a moment and I wait his order to kill us all.

Then he squints at Mama. "Neyor?"

My eyes grow wide upon hearing this rebel soldier utter my mother's name. Mama is in shock too, because she doesn't say a word. Everyone is staring at Mama with their eyes as big as eggs.

"Neyor, daughter of John Lorpu Kollie? Is that you?" I feel Mama stiffen at the sound of her father's name coming from a rebel. His stern face bursts into a grin. "Neyor! It's me, Abraham. A.B., from school!"

"Ah. . . uh, A.B.?" Mama says, her voice small and unsure.

"So, you do remember me!" the commander says, spreading his arms wide. "Ha ha!"

I am still staring at the man and barely breathing. How can anyone that knows Mama ever be a part of the rebel army? The commander walks right up to the house and puts his hands on his hips. "What are you doing here?" Everyone within earshot turns to hear Mama's answer.

Mama places her hand on me. "Me and my family, we had to come here," Mama answers, her eyes darting past him to the group of soldiers who are still in position.

"Neyor," A.B. says. "Don't be afraid. I mean you and your family no harm. It is okay." He looks at me, Nyempu, and Kulubah all huddled in fear next to Mama. "Your mother and I were great friends in school. She was so smart and used to help me with my homework." He looks past Mama at the tiny house we are crammed in.

"You are staying here?" he asks.

"Yes, we are for now," Mama says.

He nods, still looking around. "It looks like the war has been hard on you. And your family."

"God has been faithful," Mama responds. "We are all still here."

"Neyor, you don't have to stay here. Me and some others, we

have plenty of nice houses where you can stay. In the best part of town. Why don't you come with me? Let me take you and your family to some place better than this."

"A.B., that is so nice of you to offer," Mama says, "but it has been years since school. You don't owe us anything."

"No," he responds. "But you are one of the few people from home that I even know. I won't let you stay here hungry. You don't have to be afraid. You can trust me. You can come with us."

"A.B.," Mama says, her voice still trembling. "My sisters are here. I can't leave them."

I stand next to Mama, waiting to see what the rebel leader will say next. Will he try to force us to go to his house?

A.B. seems to be thinking deeply. "Okay," he says finally. "At least let me help feed you and your family, Neyor. You can't stay here like this. You are all as skinny as weeds. Send someone with me to get some food for you."

"I don't know," Mama says.

"I'll go," Aunt Gormah offers.

"Gormah!" Mama looks at her sharply.

"I'll go," Aunt Gormah says louder, ignoring Mama.

"Well good," A.B. says. "Come then. I will wait for you."

Aunt Gormah goes into the house. Mama, Nyempu, and I follow, glad to be out of the sight of the rebel soldiers.

"Gormah, you cannot go with rebel soldiers," Mama says inside.

Aunt Gormah whips around to look at Mama. "Neyor, I have to go. My children need food and your children need food. As do yours, Sister Ginger. Of course, I am afraid, but this is a chance I have to take—that we have to take. Let me go with him, Neyor. He is your friend!"

"He was a classmate," Mama says. "But this war has changed people. They are not the same people as they were. You don't know what he had done. What he may do."

"Well, what I do know is that we are starving, and he says he wants to do this for you. So, let him. We need this!" Aunt Gormah whispers sharply.

I stand listening to them debate in the dark room. Part of me is still terrified, but I am so hungry that I am almost willing to go with the rebel solider myself. After a little more discussion, Mama finally helps Aunt Gormah gather a few things and everyone goes back onto the porch.

"I'm glad that you agreed!" A.B. calls, still standing in the same spot. All the soldiers are staring at the neighbors.

"Thank you," Mama calls back. "Thank you for doing this. We are so appreciative."

"Neyor, I am here for whatever you need. As long as you are in Fender, you don't have to worry about a thing, okay?"

"Okay," Mama says quickly. "Thank you, A.B."

"Your sister will be back tonight," he says, still smiling. "With food."

He looks at me, standing by my Mama's side and does a small salute before turning around to go back with the group of soldiers. Aunt Gormah is beside him and I think that she is for sure one of the bravest people I know. As we watch her walk away, I can feel Mama praying for her sister's protection, praying to God that it not be the last time she sees her.

Much to our delight, Aunt Gormah returns that night with ten pounds of rice. As soon as she walks in the door, we all swarm her like bees. We are happy to see her, and we are even more excited to see the food. I have never been so happy to see a bag of rice in my entire life. I squeeze through and hug it. My mouth is already watering at the sight. It's the most rice we've had since Gaye Town.

Mama's eyes are wide with disbelief. "Oh, thank God!"

All the of the kids watch with joy as Mama, Aunt Ginger, and Aunt Gormah go into the kitchen and began to prepare the rice. The second the warm rice hits my lips, I feel as if my soul is soaring. There's no salt or anything else to eat with it, but the white rice is just what we needed. I literally want to burst out laughing at the sheer joy of the experience. We are excited and happy that night as we sit in our room, eating until our hearts and our stomachs are content.

29

A Bloody Proposal

The next day, we actually play in the small front yard. We finally have the energy to run and skip about. Mama, Aunt Gormah, and Aunt Ginger are sitting on the porch watching us. I am drawing in the dirt when I catch the sound of their voices in a serious discussion. I pretend not to listen as I draw.

"I know that the rice will not last us forever," Aunt Ginger says. "Maybe three more days. And then we are back where we started."

"That's true," Mama says. "I think tomorrow, I am going into town. When I was in town before, I saw a truck that had Phebe Hospital on it. I want to go and talk to the driver. If the truck is from Phebe, maybe it can take us home."

"That is good news!" Aunt Gormah says. "Why didn't you say anything before?"

"Because I may have to offer these people money to give us a ride. And I didn't know if we would need money for the house. Or to buy food. But now that we have food and a place to stay, it may be worth a try."

"Neyor, I have seen people trying to get on those trucks," says Aunt Ginger says. "It is near impossible. I have seen people get trampled, get separated from their families, even get run over as the trucks are pulling off. That is if whoever is in charge even allows you a chance to get on the truck. There is no way we can all make it."

Mama is silent for a moment. "I know. But Fender is overrun. And I cannot rely on A.B. again for help. That was a miracle from God."

"Then what will we do?" Aunt Gormah asks.

"I don't know. I just don't know."

The next day something even stranger happens. A rebel soldier walking by stops in front of our house. We all freeze and pray he doesn't stop for long. To our complete shock, he opens his mouth and asks Mama to marry him, right in front of everyone. I have heard stories of rebel soldiers taking random woman as their wives, so I am terrified. Mama quickly tells this rebel soldier that she is married. After much convincing, she is finally able to send him on his way. But the next day he comes back and asks her again. This time, Mama rushes us all inside. I can hear him telling Mama that he is a powerful person in the rebel army and that he can take care of her. That he has already taken wives before and that he wants her to come with him and be one of his wives. Mama tells him that she is a woman with sickness and that she would not make a good wife for him. I am terrified as I listen, hoping that Mama does not say anything to make the man upset. If she does, it will not end well.

After quite some time, Mama finally convinces the man to go away. But when she comes back in, she looks shaken. Aunt Gormah is terrified, but Aunt Ginger seems to want to make some sense out of the situation. "Neyor, maybe you can just agree for some of these men to help us. The man looks like he can be okay."

"What? Ginger, are you serious?" Aunt Gormah jumps in before Mama can even respond.

"I mean, first the school friend tried to help us, but Sister Neyor said no. And now another man is here and can maybe even arrange for more help, but—"

"Enough, Ginger!" Aunt Gormah says sharply. "You want so much help, why don't you marry all of them yourself?"

I don't take my eyes off of Mama. I know she must be itching to say something sharp to Aunt Ginger, but then I see her look at Nyempu, who is also glaring at Aunt Ginger.

In a measured and stern tone, Mama finally says, "Ginger, in case you forgot, I'm still married to your brother. I am not going with any man except my husband. And that is that."

But the next day, the same man comes back again. He walks right up to Mama, holding a machete covered in blood. He makes sure he gets everyone's attention and then holds his blood-stained weapon high in the air. He tells Mama that he has just finished killing an entire family and to celebrate, tomorrow he plans to make her his wife. Everyone stands in shock as he turns to address everyone within in earshot. To finish his big announcement, the rebel lets everyone know that if Mama turns down his marriage proposal tomorrow, he will kill her and every last one of us with the very blade he is holding. And then, just as simply as he came, he turns and walks away.

Mama stands in terror as she watches the rebel depart. As soon as he is out of earshot, Mama reaches down and scoops up Fungbeh. "Everyone, go and pack your things. We are leaving."

"What? Where are you going to go? We can't leave!" Aunt Ginger says. "You are crazy to go in to Fender so close to evening. You and your kids won't make it through the night."

"You can stay if you want, Ginger. But me and my children will not be here tomorrow when that man returns."

Within an hour, we leave without Aunt Ginger or little Patricia. We abandon our room and walk into town, headed to the campus to sleep outside with all the other families. We are so terrified by this soldier stalking Mama that we don't even ask any questions or complain. Besides that, we are practically out of the rice A.B. gave us, so we are just a few hours away from being hungry all over again.

As we walk into Fender, the stench of war, sickness, and desperation greets us. The streets are filled with people going this way and that, all trying to survive somehow. Families are huddled together like spoiled sardines in a rusty can. If they are not mourning someone who has just died, they are squeezed around a child who is sick with something.

Mama seems to know exactly where the campus is. As I imagined, it is crowded. Families have claimed different sections and settled on the bare ground with whatever they have. We find a place that is wide enough for all of us and Mama lays down some of the blankets from the Ma Barclay village. We are settled and resting when Mama spots a truck in the distance.

"That's the one," Mama says, jumping up. She lifts Fungbeh to her hip. "That's the truck that says Phebe Hospital."

Aunt Gormah stands up too. "Aye, it does."

"I need to go talk to the driver."

"I don't think it's that simple, Neyor!"

"I'm going," Mama says, grasping Fungbeh tighter. "Watch the other children for me."

"Not me!" I say jumping up. "I'm going with you."

Mama seems too distracted to argue and quickly grabs my hand and pulls me along. She walks swiftly toward the truck, which is similar to the ones that I have seen carrying soldiers and supplies. It sits parked off the side of some building, partially open with a tarp covering the back. We are not the only people who have spotted the truck. An eager crowd has gathered in front of us. As Mama and I get closer, I can see that some people are already being turned away by whoever oversees the vehicle. When we finally get close, the driver speaks out to us.

"Look, lady, I have told all the others the truck is not going anywhere tonight. I am parking for the night and there are only a few that I am taking tomorrow. This truck is not for everyone."

"I work at Phebe Hospital," Mama says. Suddenly, Mama stops and peers at a woman leaning on the side of the truck. "Mary?" Mama calls.

The woman looks up to see who has said her name. For a moment, it looks like she recognizes Mama, but she does not reply.

30

Mary, Mary, Quite Contrary

Late August 1990

"Mary? Mary Suah!" Mama says, with rising excitement. She turns to the man I can now see is a rebel soldier. "I know her!" Mama smiles at the woman. "Mary! Are you still at the hospital?

"You know her?" the rebel soldier asks Mary, looking intrigued.

"We are coworkers. Nurses together at Phebe!" Mama answers, half laughing. "I cannot believe this!" Mama is happy to see a coworker and I am happy for her, but this Mary woman is acting very strange.

Mary acknowledges that she knows Mama for the benefit of the rebel's curiosity, then back goes to her side of the truck.

Mama follows her. "Can you help me and my family, Mary?" Mama asks. "We need to get home to Sugar Hill."

"No," Mary says dryly. "I know you, Neyor, and I know that you and your family are not Gio or Mano. This truck is for people from Nimba, Gio, and Mano tribes. It is not for everyone. I am sorry. I won't be able to help you."

I am not surprised to hear this because I know that the rebels treat those who are Gio and Mano from Nimba the best. Everyone believes Nimbadians to be the true heart of Charles Taylor and his rebellion, and loyalty among African tribes is tight. If you are from the same tribe as a person, even if you have never met them, they are like your family. Unfortunately for us, although Charles Taylor is Kpelle, the Nimbadians are the ones who helped him start his revolution and they are only loyal to their own.

"Mary," Mama says. "Surely you will not turn us away simply because our families are from different tribes. You know me!"

"I am looking for my own people," Mary responds, not looking at Mama. "And so is he. This man is a rebel soldier. He is from Nimba. I can't do any favors for you or your family, so you better not even ask."

"But Mary, you know me! Surely you can help me. Speak to him."

"No, I told you! He is rebel."

"But is he a human being? Do you think that he would turn me and my family away and leave us here in Fender to die? Let me speak with him."

"I already told you," Mary snarls. "The truck is not for you! It is for our people who are supporting the war in Nimba County! I don't care if you are from Phebe. We are here for our people. Not you."

"Fine. Then I will speak to him myself and beg for him to have mercy on me and my family." Without another word, Mama marches away from Mary and toward the other side of the truck.

"Sir," Mama says, addressing the man who is leaning up against the truck. "I am a nurse at Phebe Hospital. I have worked there for years. With Mary. I need to get home. My home is only a couple hours walk from Phebe. I need to get back there. I know you want to keep this truck for people from Nimba, but I need you to make an exception to take us with you tomorrow. Please, Papa, I beg you."

The rebel soldier steps forward and glares at Mama. "A nurse, eh? If you are a nurse at Phebe, how did you get all the way here? And why are you going back?"

"We had to leave our home, because of the Doe's army. They were interrogating and killing everyone," Mama tells the man. "We hid at Gaye Town Church, but after Doe killed everyone at the Lutheran church, we escaped and came here." I can see that the man believes Mama. Where ever we go, everyone knows about the massacre at the Lutheran church. But the man only looks away without saying a word. Mama continues, "We were there when Doe's soldiers drove the children from Nimba through Gbarnga City. Me and my son, we saw them. Me and my family left for Gaye Town Church not long after that. Mary will tell you that I worked at Phebe and I know Dr. Gwenigale, one of the administrators there, very well."

"You know Dr. Gwenigale? He is the head doctor and administrator there now. Some of your people who used to be there are dead."

I wonder if rebels killed them or Doe's army killed them. Mama seems to ignore this news. "So, you know who he is. And if I know him, then you must know I am telling you the truth."

The man says nothing, but turns his attention to Fungbeh, who has climbed down from Mama's arms and is now standing directly in front of her. "What a cute little baby boy," he says, as if Fungbeh reminds him of someone he knows. To my surprise, the solider reaches into his pocket and pulls out a five-dollar bill. He smiles at Fungbeh and kneels down to give it to him.

Fungbeh lets out a shrill scream and runs behind Mama's legs. "No, no, no!" he screams as Mama scoops him up. "I no want your money! Get away! Get away! No! You men hurt Mama! You hurt Mama!" He is sobbing now, and he buries his face in Mama's neck.

Mama says nothing, but the rebel soldier looks shaken by Fungbeh's outburst. I am surprised as well, and I wonder if once again Fungbeh is about to get us into major trouble. I lift my eyes to the rebel soldier, to see what he is thinking. He seems hurt that a little baby would think of him as evil. With his eyes on Fungbeh, he says to Mama, "Okay. I will do you and your children a favor. I will let you on the truck tomorrow. How many children do you have?"

"Four. But I am not just traveling with just them. My sisters and their children are traveling with me as well. We all need to get back home."

"Woman, you are crazy! Now I have tried to help you, but there is barely enough room for the people we were sent here to get. Do you know how many people try to get on the backs of these trucks? The truck is not big enough. I can't take you and your entire family."

"I can't leave them behind. I've seen these trucks carry lots of people at once. If you can make an exception for me, you surely have spare room for them as well."

"No. Take the offer and leave them behind or take nothing at all."

"I won't. We depend on each other. They are my family. So, you can take your truck and your nurse and go!"

Mama turns around and begins to walk away. I can tell she is frustrated at how things have turned out because Mama rarely raises her voice at anyone, let alone a rebel solider.

"Wait," the soldier calls.

Mama turns around, still holding Fungbeh close to her chest.

"In all this war, I have never seen someone willing to sacrifice themselves for their family. I admire that. I will help you and your family. I will send a second truck tomorrow for you and your family." Turning to the truck, he calls, "Mary!"

"Yes, Othello?" Mary replies, emerging from her side of the truck with her arms crossed defiantly.

"Tomorrow, make sure you bring a second truck and find Neyor and her family. We are going to help them get back to Gbarnga."

Mary says nothing but stares at Mama as if she has just committed some cardinal sin. Mama says nothing to her scowling former coworker; she only thanks the rebel for his kindness. She turns and walks away as Fungbeh and I follow.

Back at the campus grounds, Mama can hardly wait to tell everyone the good news. No one can really believe it, but they are all so excited that we have a chance to go home. Once again, Mama has come through for us. We are leaving in the morning.

That evening, as the sun begins to set, we all settle in our little area and begin to relax when we hear men shouting in the distance. The voices get louder and closer to us. It seems like they are rebels having a terrible disagreement. Then suddenly, pop, pop, pop. Gunfire erupts just a few hundred feet from where we are lying. As soon as we hear bullets, we plant our faces and bodies firmly in the mud. Mama yells, "Stay down! Stay down!" I do as I am told.

I feel the clay against my skin. My heart is pounding into the earth. I can do nothing but wait until it is over and hope things do not get worse. Aunt Gormah flings her arms over all of us kids and everyone remains still. The shooting goes on for several minutes but no one in our group moves a muscle. I can tell from the screams that people have been hurt. Still I don't dare to move. I know from the ambush that first time we tried to leave Gaye Town Church what one stray bullet can do.

After several minutes, the shooting stops. Still, we don't move. When everyone is certain the threat has passed, people slowly get up and begin to look around. Aunt Gormah slides her arm off of us and tells us to wait. She stands up first, her eyes darting quickly around the grounds to make sure everything is okay. Mama is doing the same. Finally, Mama and Aunt Gormah look at each other and then each grab their own children, holding them close as the chaos continues around us.

We hear people searching for their loved ones. Some are screaming for those who have been shot. For a moment, our entire group remains in our spot, shaken. I knew Fender was unsafe but had no idea I wouldn't go a single night without firefight. I can tell that Mama and my aunt are frightened. They quickly decide that there is no way we can safely stay here tonight. I wonder if they are thinking the same things I am. What if the shootings start up again? What if the ones who had the dispute come back for revenge? What if the shooting brings more rebels or even government soldiers?

Mama and Aunt Gormah decide that we need to go back to the house for the night. They figure the rebel who has been stalking Mama would be long gone by now, because it is so late. They decide we will leave the house before dawn to be safe. But for tonight, we cannot stay here. We gather our things and in no time we are headed back to the house.

Aunt Ginger is standing in the doorway, staring us down from the distance as we approach. She is grinning as if she knew we would not survive one night there. As soon as we get close, she calls out to Mama, "The rebel came back here looking for you. I told him you and the children left town. He was not happy, Neyor. I think he's looking for you now."

I honestly can't tell if Aunt Ginger is scared or enjoying telling Mama all of this. Either way, Mama seems too tired to care. "Ginger, get some rest. Tomorrow morning we're going to be out of here. I found a truck that will take us to Gbarnga tomorrow."

"Oh Neyor! Really?" Aunt Ginger's face lights up. "Then we are getting out of this place? Oh, thank God! I don't know how much more of this I can take."

As we file into the house, Aunt Gormah stops and looks at Aunt Ginger. "Yes, Ginger, we are all fine. Thank you for asking."

The next morning feels like a repeat of the day we left Gaye Town Church. We leave at four o'clock in the morning, before there is even a hint of sun in the sky. We walk swiftly, and before long, I can see the outskirts of the city. Even though it is early morning, I am a little scared to go back into camp after last night's shooting.

We all walk in silence again, out of sheer exhaustion. There really isn't much for us to talk about anyway. We already know the plan. Mama went over everything before the shooting at the campus and then again at the house before we went to sleep. We are to wait around at the campus grounds until Mary Suah from Phebe Hospital comes to let us know that the second truck has arrived. Then we are to hurry and to get our place on the truck. We will finally be headed home.

31

The Fight to Get Home

When we reach the campus ground, it feels like the previous shootings never happened. It is quiet, and people are just beginning to stir. Anyone who had been hurt or killed in the shootout now lies on the side of the road. Once again, the campus is just a field filled with families. When the sun finally comes up, the grownups make small talk with the families around us and we find a few children to play different stick games with. I don't know why, but I like being around all these people. Even though we are in the midst of Fender Camp, all these families together remind me of home, reminds me that even though we are all running away, we are all still people.

I am in the middle of one of my stick games, when I hear my mother's name being called across the campus yard. I look up to see Aunt Gormah calling from across the field. "Neyor, get your things! I see the truck!" She is running across the campus, waving her arms to get Mama's attention.

"Mama!" I say, running over to my mother and tugging on her dress. "Aunt Gormah says the truck is here!"

"The truck!" Aunt Gormah says breathlessly, panting due to the exertion of sprinting to get Mama's attention. "Neyor, it's here! I saw it! I saw that truck. It's the afternoon so this has to be the second truck!"

Mama looks stunned. "But Mary is supposed to come and get us!" she says, scooping up her sack. "The truck isn't even at its usual place!"

"Forget that woman," Aunt Gormah says gathering her children. "She never wanted to help you anyway. I saw that truck with my own eyes."

"Then we need to go!"

I get my things and grab Fungbeh's hand to lead him to stand next to Nyempu and Kulubah. Quickly, Mama gathers everything else and then we are all running wildly in the direction of the truck. I can see a large and very noisy crowd has already gathered there and they are surrounding the back gate.

"Oh, my goodness!" Aunt Ginger exclaims as we approach. "Will we get on, Sister Neyor?"

"Yes!" Mama says, shoving her way through the crowd of people. Mary is standing at the truck, next to a rebel soldier that we have never seen before. When Mary sees Mama, she turns her back, but Mama calls her name so loud that even the people around us stop talking for a moment.

"You moved the truck!" Mama says. "Why didn't you tell us you were here? My family is here, all of us."

"I already told you," Mary replies. "This truck is for the people of Nimba County. Not your people."

"But the man, Othello, he told me that he sent this truck for me and my family and people from Bong County."

As Mama is talking, more people try to push and negotiate their way onto the truck. It suddenly feels like there are a million people all around us. With every second that goes by, the crowd and the frenzy increases. I am struggling to even stand on my own feet, as I am being pushed and moved by the crowd. I hear Mary telling Mama that she is not going to let her on the truck. My heart begins to sink. We have come all this way and now the little chance we had of getting home is being scraped away.

"Mary!" Mama says sternly. "We are supposed to be on this truck!"

"I can't take you, let alone all of you people. Now leave me alone!" She opens the front door of the truck and climbs in. Mama doesn't waste a second in going to the other side of the truck to speak to the rebel driver. People are trying to pull open the back hatch and weasel their way on. I see Mama trying to reason with the rebel to explain our story, but he quickly moves her aside so that he can clear people away from the truck. Suddenly, in the midst of all the commotion, he points his gun at the crowd.

"Back up!" he yells. "Back up now—all of you!"

Aunt Gormah grabs my hand and pulls me backward as everyone quickly steps away from the truck. Even though he pushes everyone back, the crowd continues to push against each other and try to get to him. Mama stays next to the driver's side door and waits patiently for the man to return. I can see from where I am standing that Mama looks worried. I am worried too. This does not look good for us. People are running from all over the campground to try to get on this truck.

I see Mary get back out of the truck to help with the commotion. She starts talking to people in the crowd and allowing some of them to come forward. Apparently, these people are from Nimba County and she is letting them on. I even see one man hand her a wad of money. Then he and his wife are allowed past the others. The crowd is deafening. I can't see Mama anymore, but I know that she is somewhere pleading for us. I just hope she does not get hurt. At this point, the only thing keeping the truck from being completely overturned is the rebel's AK-47. People are continuing to push past us and get on the truck under Mary and the rebel's watchful eye.

"Mary!" I hear Mama's voice again. I squeeze through people's legs to see her trying to reason with the woman who was sent to help us.

"Mary, why would you turn your back on your own coworker and leave me and my family here helpless? When we get back to Sugar Hill, I will give you whatever I have if you will please just help my family get home."

Mary pretends not to hear Mama.

"Besides, what will you say tomorrow when Othello asks you why you have not done as he told you? What will stop him from killing you for going against his word?"

Mary stops in her tracks and looks at Mama. "Fine," she says. "We are leaving now but the truck is full. So, if you and your family can get on, we won't stop you." With that, Mary turns around and nods her approval to the rebel soldier to let us get on.

Mama quickly runs into the crowd, calling all of our names, trying to get us onto a rapidly filling truck. People are packing themselves into it and others are still running from the campground to try to get on.

"Come on!" Mama says to all of us. "We must fight. We are going to get on!"

We all push through the crowd and try to follow Mama as best we can. I have heard stories of families having to split up or children being left behind when their families get on trucks. I am not going to be left without Mama again.

"Come on!" Mama calls. She pushes Fungbeh into the truck. Next, she grabs my hand and pulls me up. The truck is humming underneath us as the driver fires up the engine.

"Nyempu!" I see my sister fall to the ground as a man and woman shove past her and make their way on. The truck begins to move a little. Aunt Gormah grabs Nyempu and puts her in the truck as Mama hoists Kulubah in. Mama rushes to grab Aunt Gormah's children. She pushes them in next to me. I take my cousin's hand and Nyempu grabs the baby by his shirt, pulling him the rest of the way in. My heart is pounding, and I am straining to see Mama get on the truck. There are so many people in front of me that I can't move forward to reach Mama.

"Mama!" I cry. My heart is in my throat as I the truck begins to move. I realize that Mama is getting left behind.

"Mama!" Nyempu screams, as the truck picks up speed.

Mama is with a very pregnant woman who can barely run because of her belly and another baby in her arms. She is almost close enough. She is trying to put her baby on the truck. The truck lurches forward. Mama takes a big leap and grabs onto the railing, pulling herself on at last. I let out a huge sigh. Even though I can't get to her, I am glad she is on.

The woman and other people are still running and pushing, trying to get their way onto the truck. The pregnant woman is holding her baby up to the truck when she trips and the baby starts to fall. Mama reaches down and grabs the baby just before her little body hits the ground, but she loses her balance and is hanging out over the back. Aunt Gormah reaches through several bodies and grabs Mama who is still holding the baby.

"Neyor!' she screams. "You almost fell out!"

Another man leaps on to the side of the truck and squeezes his way in, pushing Mama and the stranger's baby back toward us. There are about fifty people smashed together in this truck. I can't see Mama now because a few more people have made their way on and we are packed together, unable to move. I can't see her, but I hear Mama frantically calling.

"Quanei, are you here?"

"I am here Mama!" I say as loud as I can.

"Kulubah!" she cries. Kulubah answers and so does Aunt Ginger and the rest of the people in our group.

I listen to everyone tell Mama they are on the truck, and I know I have just seen another miracle. I keep turning around and looking at everyone around me, in complete disbelief that my entire family was able to get in. As the truck moves forward, I feel a mixture of shock and intense joy. I wish I could be near Mama, but I am squeezed up against some strangers and it looks like we will be stuck together like this for the entire ride.

Dust kicks up all around us as the truck powers down the road back toward our home. I still can't believe Mama managed to get us all the way from Gaye Town Church to where we are now. I cannot believe that after all of this, we are actually headed back to Sugar Hill. I wonder if the pregnant woman made it on the truck. I do not see her. I peek over to glimpse at the child Mama is holding. I guess that she is around two years old, about the same age as Fungbeh is now. She looks terrified and must surely be wondering where her own mama is.

The truck bounces up and down and everyone holds on and stands or sits in their spot. The baby that Mama saved fusses. I can hear Mama rocking her and singing her little songs as we ride. Pressed against one of the rails of the truck, I can see the outside as we ride. As we pass trees, villages, and farmlands, I think about how long it would have taken us to walk all this way. Before long, I begin to feel the truck slow down and I see more and more people on the side of the road. My stomach lurches as I realize we are approaching a checkpoint.

I look at the people gathering at the checkpoint, recognizing the fear and terror in their eyes. Wild rebels, like the ones we first encountered, are terrorizing people with their guns and machetes. I see one rebel with a green wig, yelling with his gun pointed in the air. I ball my fist up as tight as I can and try to make my heart be still. I know the truck must go through the checkpoint like every other vehicle or person on this road. With a rebel driving our truck, hopefully no one aboard will get killed. As we approach, I say a silent prayer.

Our truck passes everyone on the side of the road, slowing at the head of the checkpoint. With one look at the driver, the checkpoint rebel gives a quick nod and wave, and we roll right through. The same thing happens at every checkpoint, as if the truck is our magic dragon, carrying us over the long roads of Liberia and through the dangerous rebel strongholds. Everyone knows simply crossing the street could mean a death sentence. But not for us. Not for those who are traveling in trucks driven by the rebels themselves. Now I see why the desperate, hungry, and sick people of Fender fought so hard to get on trucks leaving town. As we bump along the road toward Gbarnga City, I am grateful for this truck.

I glance over at Mama and the babies hanging on her. Mama has squeezed into a spot that is closer to us and, somehow, Fungbeh has made his way to her. She is now leaning firmly against the truck's railing with Fungbeh and the stranger's baby resting on her chest. As the truck bumps us all along, I just stare and admire Mama so much for being strong for us.

After three hours of riding, the roads and landmarks begin to look familiar and I know we are close to home. When the truck pulls into Phebe Hospital, I notice that it looks less like a hospital and more like a military camp. Trucks and rebel soldiers guard the outside and a few doctors and nurses mill about. As people begin to move around in anticipation, I lose sight of Mama. I feel a hand grab mine and I look up to see that it is Nyempu. She has wiggled her way through the grownups while they shifted around, preparing to get off.

The second the door to the back hatch opens, everyone begins to make their way off. I can no longer see Mama or my aunts. I am pleased to be holding Nyempu's hand. Finally, I see Mama, still holding tight to Fungbeh and the baby she grabbed.

"Gormah, stay put to the side for just a minute, let these people off," Mama instructs. "Nyempu, move behind me to this side here with Quanei, next to Kulubah and Auntie. Let the people go through first. I want to make sure everyone is okay."

After everyone else is off the truck, Mama motions Aunt Gormah to get off with her kids. Then, I notice someone waving at us.

"Neyor!" a man's voice calls. "There she is! Neyor!" A woman's voice follows: "Oh, my, she has been reduced to the size of a toothpick!"

"Oh, my God!" Mama says breaking into a smile. "Dr. Gwenigale! Ma Etta! Is that you?"

I am surprised to see my father's sister, Ma Etta, standing in the parking lot next to a man in a white coat.

"Yes, it's me! Oh, my goodness!" Ma Etta responds.

"How did you know we would be here?" Mama asks, giving her a big hug.

"I am just glad you all made it here in one piece!" Dr. Gwenigale exclaims. "When Othello came back with the story of your family, I sent word to Etta. We have been anxiously waiting for you to arrive!" Dr. Gwenigale grins at Mama and they embrace. They both look so excited and happy to see someone they know.

"Neyor," Ma Etta says. "It was such a relief to hear that you and the children made it through so far. Oh, my—Ginger!" Ma Etta runs to embrace Aunt Ginger and her daughter.

I remember Dr. Gwenigale when he was Mama's supervisor, before the whole world went to hell. He was always such a nice man, a great friend to both Mama and Papa. Though only a few months have passed, Dr. Gwenigale looks years older to me now. His skin is dry and greyish, and his eyes are sunken and weary. I know he lived through a terrible massacre at Phebe Hospital. That story is almost as well-known as the story of the Lutheran church massacre. Only at Phebe, everyone was killed by rebels, not government soldiers. The rebels have now set up command at the hospital to treat their wounded.

"Please, all of you, come inside," Dr. Gwenigale says. "I can give you and your family some rest here."

Mama's eyes dart around the hospital grounds and I know exactly what she is thinking. There is no way in the world she is going to go into that place and surround herself with those rebel soldiers.

"Doctor, you know that I appreciate it greatly. But my husband's sister is here. Thank you for getting her here. We will go to her house and rest."

Dr. Gwengale nods. "Are you sure you are not too tired?"

Mama looks at the building and then back at him. "I am sure."

Dr. Gwenigale runs his eyes over all of us for a moment. "Well then at least allow me to have some water brought to you and your family so you can refresh yourselves before you go." He places both hands on Mama's scrawny soldiers. "And maybe something to eat?"

"Thank you," Mama says smiling. "Your generosity will not be forgotten."

He is smiling too. "Speak nothing of it. I am thrilled to see you and your family together and well. You and Alfred are like family to me, Neyor." His eyes roam over the hospital grounds. "It is sad to say that you are one of the few people that we have left."

"God has been faithful in bringing us all here now," Mama says.

"You are right. Now, you and your family stay grouped together and I will get someone to help me bring the water and a little food to you."

As Dr. Gwenigale walks away, Auntie Gormah calls to Mama. "Neyor! Look! It's the pregnant woman from Fender. She made it on. I see her." Aunt Gormah is pointing and already walking. "Look—there!"

"Oh, my goodness," Mama says, her eyes wide. "It is her!" I stretch my neck to see a woman standing next to the truck looking around.

"Hey!" Mama calls, waving at the woman. The woman turns around and I can see her big belly and great surprise when she sees Mama holding her baby.

"Oh, my God!" the woman cries and runs over to grab her baby. Tears stream down her face as she flings her free arm around Mama. "You saved my baby's life! You did not have to help us. You did not have to help me get on. I never would have caught up to that truck if it was not for you."

The woman and Mama hug each other tight for a moment and the woman thanks Mama over and over. Finally, the woman lets go, still crying and clutching her baby tight.

"I am so happy you got on the truck," Mama tells her. "But

even if you had not, I would have taken care of this baby as if it were my own."

"Thank you," the woman says. "My baby and this one in my belly are all that I have left. My husband was killed at checkpoint at Duport Gate Road. We were passing through and they took him. And he fought so hard, I could hear him yelling all the way from where I was."

"Duport Gate Road Checkpoint?" Mama says. Everyone in our group goes silent because that is the checkpoint where Mama was taken. And we all remember the man who fought so hard he distracted the rebels, allowing Mama and Kulubah to slip away.

"Your husband," Mama says. "I know he must have loved you very much." I can see tears form in Mama's eyes.

"He did. I know that he fought to get back to us. He fought so hard that I saw other rebels come and call for help, saying that he had broken away. But I could not get to him. I was pushed through the checkpoint and I knew better than to try to go to the killing fields. They killed him, I know. And getting on that truck was the last hope I had for getting out of Fender Camp. I had to get me and my baby on that truck. I can't have my husband die for nothing. He would want us to live."

"He didn't die for nothing. I know this because. . ." Mama grabs the woman's hand. "I think. . . I think your husband saved my life."

"What?" The woman looks confused.

"I was taken at the checkpoint at Duport Gate Road as well." Mama is talking slowly, as if her own brain is trying catch up with her words. "I was taken away from my children at Duport Gate Road. I was taken to fields to be executed. They were about to kill me. But there was a man. He was. . . " Mama pauses and looks at the woman's eager eyes. "He was fighting to get back to his pregnant wife and baby."

"Oh, my God," the woman stumbles backwards. Aunt Ginger steadies her. "What? What happened?"

"He fought so much, he was like a wild man," Mama says.

"He refused to go. He broke away and even those who were there could not hold him. The girl who was supposed to kill me decided to go help restrain him. And in that moment, she let me go, while the other rebels were distracted. I was able to get away and reunite with my children."

The woman stares at Mama with shock and disbelief. No one speaks.

"My husband. He saved you." The woman lets out a deep breath. "And then you came to Fender and you saved my child. So, if it wasn't for you being there on that truck, my baby would have fallen and I would have been left behind, and we both could have been trampled to death."

Mama stares at the woman as the realization settles on her and everyone who is listening. Everyone is holding their breath as they process the story.

"I cannot believe this," Aunt Gormah says. "I just cannot believe this."

The woman looks at Mama with fresh tears. "He did not die for nothing. He wanted to save us and he did, by saving you."

Mama cries and she wraps her arms around the woman. Aunt Ginger and Aunt Gormah are crying too. It is a miracle inside a miracle. As our group binds together, in disbelief and gratitude, I can tell there is much love between Mama and this woman. They are total strangers, but they have a bond that is stronger than words could explain. When Dr. Gwenigale returns with a care package of water and snacks, Mama takes it and gives it to the woman. She explains to Dr. Gwenigale that the woman has nothing and that we are fine because we're just a few miles from Ma Etta's house.

My eyes fall on the pregnant woman who is still hugging and kissing her baby. I look at her swollen belly and I know that she will give birth soon. Suddenly, I am sorry for the unborn one, and wonder what kind of life it will have in a world like this. No father, no government, no food, and no hope. If anything happens to the woman in Mama's arms, these two will be orphans among the thousands already created by this war. I think about the killing fields and I wonder what has happened to all the children of those dead. I wonder what will become of them in this new world.

I hear Mama ask Dr. Gwenigale to do her personal a favor and look after the woman and her child for as long as he possibly can. He agrees to this a favor and swears that he will look after the woman and her baby as if they were his own. After many hugs and blessings, we finally leave her in Dr. Gwenigale's care. We go our way.

As we leave the grounds of Phebe Hospital, there is so much joy and excitement in our entire group. Ma Etta is so surprised and grateful we are all alive, she keeps hugging and kissing us while we walk. And she gives the best news of all. She says that Aunt Garmen, Uncle Thomas, and Kormah made it to Guinea, where Grandpa and most of Papa's brothers and sisters went. Aunt Garmen left him with Aunt Cecilia and Grandpa, away from the war, while she continued toward Mama's home village in Mahyah. Uncle Thomas even stayed behind to help look after Kormah. Ma Etta also tells us all that the moment she heard we were coming from Fender, she sent word to the village for Uncle Thomas to bring Kormah to Sugar Hill to meet us. When Mama hears this, she stops dead in her tracks and hugs Ma Etta for a very long time. For the first time in a long time, Aunt Ginger is genuinely smiling. Her smile matches the feeling in my soul. I feel as if a special angel is looking out for us.

I can remember all the times I have seen Mama pray. All our lives, she has been known for praying over her family every night and devoting herself to helping people. As far as I know, Mama has never turned her back on anyone who needed help in our community. Now, I feel that God is rewarding her with miracle after miracle on our journey through this war. In my mind, we have gone around the entire world in a few months, only to safely return to Sugar Hill. I remember when we first started out, in the bus head to Monrovia. I remember Gaye Town Church, where I hoped for all this to end and to finally come home. As we head toward Ma Etta's house, I say my own prayer, thanking God that we are one step closer to home.

Soon, we come to Ma Etta's village. It is like a family reunion with everyone gathered at Ma Etta's house, happy to see us alive and well. There are many big hugs, tears, kisses, and thanks to God that we have made it home. Everyone is in disbelief that our whole group has made it all the way back from Monrovia in one piece. As soon as Ma Etta gets a moment, she comments on our thin frames, and sets down rice for us all. I can't remember when I've been so happy. Ma Etta's house is filled with love and joy tonight.

I am so grateful to Mama for fighting to bring us all here. She has worked so hard and I know that she is the best mother in all of Liberia. In all the world. Tonight, it does not feel like we are in the middle of a war, but on a regular visit to Gharmue. Tonight, we do not worry about the world around us, we only eat and rest. And tomorrow, we will go home to Sugar Hill.

32

Five Teaspoons of Salt

Early September 1990

The next day, I wake up at Ma Etta's, realizing I had fallen asleep right on the floor next to my cousins Gerpili and Tinawoo. We had stayed up all night playing games and laughing. I sit up and look at all the other kids still asleep. I see Nyempu sleeping soundly nearby. She looks so peaceful—more peaceful than I have seen her in longer than I can remember. I've seen so much stress on her kind face over the past few months. She is so skinny now, and she seems older too. We both do. I smile inside knowing that today, her heart is happy and her tummy is full too. We have made it back to our home county.

I lie back down, slipping my hands beneath my head and staring up at the ceiling. I know the war is still raging, but somehow it seems far away, and I feel at peace. I cannot believe that we have made it back. After the first ambush, I thought we would never see home again. Now by some miracle, we are back in the arms of our loving family. We are fed and soon we will be on our way back to Sugar Hill.

The sound of the door cracking open catches my attention. I look up to see Mama poking her head in the door. As soon as she sees me, she smiles. "Quanei." Her eyes hold mine for a moment. "Why are you always such a busy body, my boy? Always up looking about while everybody else is sleeping." I sit up and shrug my shoulders. Mama looks around the room and seems satisfied. "Want to help Mama make food for everybody?"

I am up before she even finishes her question. I love helping Mama, and after everything that has happened, I want to help her now more than ever. It will be just like when we are at home or at the pharmacy in Sugar Hill. I help Mama in the kitchen until Aunt Gormah comes. I am glad to let her take over. She is bigger and quicker than me so that means that the food will be ready faster. Mama has me wash the rice. They are making dry rice with sardines. Aunt Gormah is opening the can. I peer over at her and say, "Oh Auntie, please can I lick the can? Please, Auntie?"

"Okay, Quanei, but be careful not to cut yourself on the sharp edge. Okay?"

"Okay!" I say and grab the top of the can. I am tickled at getting special treatment while all the other kids are asleep. Now, I know what the grownups mean when they say that the early bird gets the worm.

That morning there is so much noise in Ma Etta's house as everyone wakes up and gathers in the kitchen to eat. The talking, laughing, and eating all make me feel like I will float right out of my seat. As good as things are, they are only going to get better because soon we will be going home. That is what Nyempu and I talk about the most, what we are going to do when we get home. Nyempu says she is going to go straight to her room, grab her favorite dolls from the closet and put them right on her dresser.

"I'm going to go and put on my favorite yellow shirt," I say, slipping a handful of rice in my mouth. "And then I am going to jump on my bed!"

"Oh, me too!" Kulubah grins at both of us. "I am going to jump and jump and jump!"

"But you cannot out jump me!" I tease her.

"Oh, yes I can!" Kulubah smiles back.

"Fine," I say to her. "When we get home, we will have a contest."

We all grin at the thought of being home again and jumping on our beds. I can't wait to show Kulubah that I am the big brother once and for all.

We spend one more day at Ma Etta's house and the next morning everyone at the house gives us a big send off. There is much hugging and kissing and quick prayers as we gather in the yard. Mama and Aunt Gormah ask Ma Etta to send word to Mama's sibling in their home village that we are on our way back to Sugar Hill. Ma Etta happily agrees and slips Mama some money and a few other things for our journey home. Then she makes us promise to send her word when we have made it back.

Sugar Hill is nearly fifteen miles from Phebe Hospital, but as we set out for the main road again, I feel as if I am floating. Mama seems much happier and more at peace than I have seen her in a very, very long time. She, Aunt Gormah, and Aunt Ginger talk quickly and laugh freely. On this walk, we are not looking over our shoulders or starving or running for our lives. We are simply making a trip we have made many times before. The morning air is crisp and welcoming. I breathe in as much as my lungs can hold. The only thing that could make our homecoming better is having Papa waiting on us when we arrive.

I think about Papa as we walk. I wonder how he is and where he is. Mama has told us that Papa was staying with his cousin in New York and I wonder if he is still there. I hope so. I wonder how Papa must feel. He doesn't know if we are dead or alive. I try to think about how much time has passed since I have last saw Papa or even heard his voice. I am taller now, and I hope Papa recognizes me when I see him again. Though it is impossible for me to know when that will be. Our entire country is on lockdown. The rebels have taken over the borders and no one except rebels can get in or out. The only way to escape would be by ocean. At this point I am not sure which is more dangerous, trying to cross into a neighboring country or trying to swim away into the

Atlantic Ocean. I personally think that jumping in the ocean is the better choice. I am a good swimmer. I could swim to one of the   big American ships I heard about. But then I remembered the rest of the news: these ships bring guns and money to the rebels. Any ship helping rebels probably won't help me get to Papa. Plus I'm still the man of the family: I can't leave Mama and the rest. I can't leave Mama.

We still have not told anyone that Papa is in America. We only say that he left to get supplies and never returned, which is true. The rebels view anyone trying to leave the country as a traitor to the freedom-fighting cause and the country. They will immediately kill anyone even suspected of trying to leave the country. If anyone learns that we have ties to the outside, they will think that we will try to leave and slaughter us all. I shake these thoughts from my mind and listen to Nyempu chatter on about home and her friends and how she can't wait to do this and that.

The roads begin fill with people and even they look carefree, as if maybe they are just on a trip to see their families too. They do not look furtive or tired like those we've seen on other roads. Soon, I forget about the war again.

After some time, I see that we are approaching a checkpoint. I grab Mama's hand. We all grow quiet as draw near. I can hear my heart pounding in my ears. This is the first time we have had to walk through a check point since Mama was taken and nearly killed. My heart beats harder and I want to run away. A terrible feeling in my gut rises up and I feel my knees begin to shake. But I know I cannot do anything to draw attention to myself and my family. Mama can tell we are scared. She quickly reaches down for Kulubah's hand. "Don't worry, my loves," Mama says. "We are back home now, and we will be fine."

I want to believe Mama. I keep hold of her hand and lock my eyes on the small crowd ahead at the checkpoint. No matter what the rebels do or say or threaten, I am not letting go of Mama's hand today. Even if they point their guns at me and throw me to the ground. I will fight as hard as I can for us all to stay together.

As we get closer, I notice that this checkpoint seems much more relaxed than any others I have seen. The people passing through are doing just that—passing through like they are not even afraid. It looks like the rebels have even allowed the locals to set up some sort of marketplace. There is no hollering or crying or pleading or interrogations. Just people moving through the big iron gate into the city. The rebels are watching, but only seem to be stopping the people in cars.

Then sun is high and seems to shine a giant spotlight right on our group. When we reach the gate, the rebels simply look over us and let us through. I try not to show my shock or fear as I obediently follow the rest of my family. I hold my breath and try not to move too much, although I want to run to make sure they don't call us back. I know that once we cross the gate, we will officially be back home in Gbarnga City.

As soon as we pass the rebels, joy and freedom return to our clan like a bolt of lightning. We are truly home. I cannot believe that we have made it through that easily. As quickly as it came, our joy and excitement dissipates, turning to disbelief as we discover that Gbarnga City is nothing like it was before.

Gbarnga City looks exactly like the war-torn cities, streets, and villages we have passed through on our way back here. It looks destroyed. The homes and buildings that once lined the streets have been burned to the ground. Grass and weeds sprout where they can. The palm trees that brought us shade and beauty have been burned or cut down. Burned cars sit abandoned among trash, and I smell the decaying bodies before I see them. The happiness that carried us from Phebe Hospital has been erased, and my heart sinks further as we walk. The city now belongs to the rebel army. This is not our city. It is theirs.

"I never thought it would be this bad," Mama says in disbelief. "I knew it would not be the same but, this is not the home I know."

"This is not the world any of us knows," Aunt Gormah says.

"All of this just confirms that our entire world, our entire way of life, is destroyed. If we do not find a way out of this country, we may die." Aunt Gormah lets out a heavy breath. "Everything we knew of life in Liberia, Neyor, is over."

"This is all turned upside down," says Auntie Ginger. "This place used to be so nice to walk through, only few months ago. I can't believe this."

I start to worry about what Sugar Hill will be like. I tell myself that Sugar Hill must be okay because it is in the best part of the city—with the light poles, the pharmacy, and paved roads Mama and Papa worked so hard to bring. Even if it is not exactly the same, I still cannot wait to get back home.

I am holding Mama's hand as we walk through our city. At some point, Mama and Aunt Gormah announce that we need to go to the marketplace before going the rest of the way, so we all head in that direction. I can tell that we are just a mile or so from home and I start to feel a little better. As we head toward the marketplace, I begin to recognize the surroundings of the St. Martin's school campus.

"The school!" I shout to Nyempu. "We are almost there!"

Mama lets us run ahead a little as the massive St. Martin's campus comes into view. Nyempu and I are so excited to see our school again that we hold hands as we run. Suddenly Nyempu stops, jolting me mid-step.

"Stop, Quanei!" she says. I look at her with a frown, then follow her eyes to a body hanging from a tree just inside St. Martin's gates. My heart leaps at the sight amid the deserted shambles of what used to be the most prestigious school in Liberia.

"Let's go," Nyempu says. "I don't want Mama coming this way and seeing this. Let's just go, Quanei. Now!"

At the marketplace, I try to put the sight at St. Martin's out of my mind. Seeing people buying and selling makes me feel a little better, as if things are at least a little normal. Mama and Aunt Gormah go from stall to stall looking things over and deciding what to purchase. Aunt Ginger keeps watch over us kids while Mama and Aunt Gormah select yams, cassava pieces, one cup of red oil, and onions. And salt! I watch the market woman count five teaspoons of salt into a little plastic bag. My mouth waters as I see the salt, which is rare now. They have bought enough food for Mama to make a nice meal when we get home.

Home. At this point, I just hope that there is a home for us to go to.

33

A Broken Mirror, a Yellow Sweater, and a Smelly Mattress

We get back on the road with our purchases and soon I can tell that we are just a few blocks from home. Everything on the streets is just as bleak as the rest of the city. I brace myself for the worst.

"We are here," Mama announces as we round the corner into our neighborhood. We all stop, trying to take in the sight in front of us.

"No, Neyor," Aunt Ginger mumbles staring straight ahead. "I think you may be confused. This cannot be Sugar Hill."

Seeing Sugar Hill is like looking into a broken mirror—like when you expect your own reflection but all you see are the jagged shards. I struggle to take in everything that used to be home. Our entire community is in complete shambles. The homes that housed our friendly neighbors are burned to the ground. Trash and debris fill the main road and the stench of decaying bodies fills the air. Wild grass and weeds have grown up everywhere. As I stand gaping in shock, I imagine the rebels running wildly throughout Sugar Hill, terrorizing everyone I grew up with and burning down their homes. I have seen so much while we were gone, but I never expected to see it here. The smell of mangos and Ms. Mary's milk candy has been replaced with the stench of burnt clay and human flesh.

"Well," Mama lets out a deep breath and gives Nyempu's shoulder a rub. "We have made it this far, we must at least go and see what is left."

"Yes," Aunt Gormah says. "And if nothing else, we can eat and rest and thank God that we still have life."

We don't even make it a few yards before I see two dead bodies next to a burned house. I stop, my heart racing. I can tell that the bodies have been there for a while, as there isn't much of them left. I know this house, I know the family that used to live there, and I pray to God they are not the one's lying dead, but in my heart, I know it must be. I feel my body shaking as I walk past. This much death so close to home is frightening; my heart breaks with every step. The sun has started to go down, and with it all of our joy. I can see Mama is upset at the ruin of the dream village she and Papa worked so hard to build.

"How can this be?" Mama mutters, as she steps over a pile of broken glass. "What would be the point? What would be the point of destroying it all?"

"I am so sorry, Neyor," Auntie Gormah says. "I am sorry."

"All of my brother's hard work has been destroyed in just a matter of months," Aunt Ginger says bitterly.

We are still at the bottom of the community and our home is not yet in sight. Mama strains her neck and I know she is trying to see what we all desperately need to know: if our home is still standing on the top of the hill.

"Mrs. Karmue!"

I turn around to see our neighbor, Mr. Mullbah, waving and running toward us with a grin on his face. "I can't believe it!" he yells as he runs.

"Mr. Mullbah!" I call out to him.

"Oh, thank God!" Mama says, wrapping her arms around him.

"I cannot believe that you are alive!" he says, looking quickly at all of us. Then, with concern: "Your big boys?" and his voice trails off.

Mama smiles and nods, and Mr Mullah understands this to mean they are okay. "All of you? Alive! This is a miracle. Oh, my God." He reaches over and hugs Mama again.

"We are very grateful to God," Mama says, smiling "So much has happened, but we are all alive and that is what matters."

"Mrs. Karmue, you are right. So much has happened. Many, many people were killed. And even here, many sold out their neighbors to the rebels. It has become terrible here, but you and your husband are good people and I know this is why God has spared you and your family."

While Mama is talking to Mr. Mullbah, I walk forward a little, and to my delight I catch my first glimpse of our compound sitting atop the hill.

"Mama, it's okay!" I say, interrupting her conversation. "I see the house!"

Nyempu runs and looks. "I see it too!"

I let out a breath of relief. Our compound is still there, one of the few remaining houses in Sugar Hill. Seeing it in tact gives me a little ray of hope. Mama walks up to where I am, then smiles at Aunt Gormah and Aunt Ginger. "It's there," she says. It's the first time I have seen Mama smile since we crossed over in Gbarnga City.

"Go now," Mr. Mullbah says. "Go on to your home, while you can. You have had a long journey and I am just glad to see someone I know alive."

After we bid Mr. Mullbah farewell, Mama slips an arm around Nyempu's shoulder. "Come on, my babies. Let's go home."

As we make our way up the hill, the next person we see is Mr. Paye, Boye's father. I quickly wave at him, looking around for Boye, but Mr Paye doesn't move. He just stares at us approaching, as if we are ghosts.

Mama waves and call out to him. "Joseph!"

He stares with his mouth open. "Mrs. . . . Karmue?" He takes a step forward, his eyes wide. "It is you!"

"Yes," Mama says with a laugh. "It is good to see you too."

"Neyor! I cannot believe it! I . . . I thought we would never see you again." He calls his wife outside and with her comes Boye and his brother and sister. Boye has almost the same reaction as his father. He runs out of the house and then slows to a walk when he sees me. He just stares at me. And I stare back at him, completely shocked to see that he is wearing my favorite yellow sweater. I say nothing, but I look up at Mama to see if she notices.

"Oh, my goodness!" Mrs. Paye says, running out of the house. "It is the Karmue family! Oh, my God!"

"Yes," Mama says. "We are here, by God's grace. So, good to see all of you. I can't believe you are still here? When the rebels came and did all this, did you not have to leave?"

"We had no other place to go," Mr. Paye said. "Neyor, you are not going to believe what has happened here. Just look around!"

"I can see," Mama says. "It looks like. . . " She pauses. "A lot has changed."

"Even more than that," Mr. Paye says. "The day after you left, government soldiers came to Sugar Hill. They marched straight up to your house and came looking for people who escaped from Nimba County: your sister and brother-in- law. They were going to kill them. They suspected them of being part of the rebellion."

"What?" Mama says. "The next day?"

"The next day," Mr. Paye says. "They rolled up in Sugar Hill on a killing mission and it is only by the grace of God that you left when you did. If not, they would have surely killed all of you on suspicion of supporting the rebels."

"That is not true about my brother and sister. They are not rebels," Aunt Gormah says. "Just because people are from Nimba County does not mean they are all rebels. My sister came here running from the rebels who tore apart their neighborhood."

"Well, you know the reputation of Nimba County," Mr. Paye says, slipping his hands in his pockets. "The soldiers who were here tore apart your house looking for them. They were so angry and so mad that they found nothing, they came and questioned almost everyone. They thought that someone tipped you off that they were coming."

"The only person who gave us a tip was God," Mama says. "I just had a feeling that we needed to leave."

"Well, you left just in time," Boye's mother says.

Boye has still not said a word to me or Nyempu. Nyempu is staring right at him and he won't meet her eye.

"And there is something else," Boye's father says. "The soldiers, ah. . ." He shifts his weight and looks around quickly. "They took a few things. From your house."

Mama tilts her head to the side a little and frowns. "They did?"

"Yes," he says. "They took a lot of things."

Aunt Gormah cradles her youngest daughter on her hip. "What things?"

"All sorts of things," he replies. "Just look around! This whole town is destroyed."

"Oh! Alfred and Sister Neyor had the best of stuff in that house," Aunt Ginger says. "And now you are saying it is all gone?"

"Well, we will just have to make use of what is left." Her eyes fall on Boye and my bright yellow sweater. She looks back at Boye's father. "Thank you for the warm welcome back. We must be on our way."

"Best of luck," Mr. Paye says as we walk away.

I turn to look at Boye. He sees me but ducks inside. I think about all the work Mama and Papa put into making Sugar Hill into one of the best communities in our city, how long it takes to build entire city and country. Now all of it has been completely destroyed. I wonder how long it would take to rebuild, or if it is even possible. Who will do it? The rebels? They are the ones who tearing everything apart. President Doe? He is killing his own citizens to protect himself.

I know our country is tied to America, and all the adults say that maybe they will send help. I am sure they have been watching our war on the news. I wonder what they think when they see us on TV. Do they think this is something that we have chosen? Do they

know that Liberia was once a paradise, rich in beauty and prog-
ress? Will they think that we are just poor savages? Maybe having
our country at war is better for American businesses—this is what
grownups say about Firestone.

I think of Papa and how worried he must be about us,
especially if all this is on TV over there. Maybe Papa can talk to the
American people about helping Liberia, helping rebuild Sugar Hill.
Surely Papa can do that. I think about how hard Papa worked to
convince our neighbors to get electricity, even using his own money
to put hope in the minds of everyone on the hill. Now, the entire
country is torn to pieces and nearly wiped out. I have no idea how
we can recover. I wonder how Liberia will get back to its glory.

It turns out that the scene at our home is worse than Boye's father
described. We open the door to an empty living room and kitchen.
I lean against the door to catch my breath. Our house has been
completely ransacked. Everything is gone. What's left is destruc-
tion. The house is filthy, as if wild animals have been running ram-
pant inside. It smells of must and urine and death. I stand with my
mouth open. Mama, Aunt Gormah, and Aunt Ginger have not
moved either. I know Mama must be devastated to see our home
like this.

Nyempu walks right in, looking around wildly as if she is in a
dream. She immediately runs toward her room and I feel my heart
sink because I know that my sister will not find the bed and favorite
doll that she is looking for. I know without seeing the rest of the
house that there is nothing left. We finally step inside to see that
our couch, tables, chairs, beds, clothes, blankets, cups, bowls are
gone. Mama flips a light switch, forgetting that the whole country
is in darkness. I look up to see that all the electrical wiring has been
ripped from the ceiling and the walls.

"They even stole the electrical wires?" Mama gasps.

"Neyor, look at the windows. The bars are gone too!" Aunt
Gormah exclaims.

In our despair, I realize that not only has this war destroyed life
as we once knew it, it has propelled us back into darkness.

That night, Mama has to borrow a single pot from Mr. Mullbah just to cook over the fire. When Mr. Mullbah brings the pot, he pulls Mama to the side and tells her that it was not just the soldiers who took most of our things—it was Boye's family, along with some other neighbors who have left.

"Your children should not have to sleep on the concrete floor," he tells Mama. "The Payes have all the mattress that belong to your family. I saw them come right up here and take them out of your home. And now you are back with no place to sleep. You should make them give them back."

Mama only thanks Mr. Mullbah for the pot and finishes her cooking.

We sleep that night on the cold hard floor, using our knapsacks for pillows. I don't get much sleep and my back hurts the next day.

But this is also the day that Uncle Thomas and Uncle George show up with Kormah. Just as Ma Etta promised, as soon as they received word that we were back in Sugar Hill, our uncles immediately left to bring Kormah to us. I am so glad to see Kormah that I forget all about my yellow sweater and my sore back. We all run over to him and hug him so tight. We all hug him and walk him to Mama who gives him a million kisses all at once.

Kormah is happy to see us too, but I can tell he is shocked at the condition of our house.

"Our room is empty, Quanei! Where do we sleep?" he asks. He goes from room to room, just as Nyempu did, looking at all the damage with his mouth hanging wide open.

Once things settle down, Kormah can't wait to tell us all of his stories and everything that he saw on his journey with Aunt Garmen. Nyempu and I have less to say despite the horrors of the journey from Monrovia back home to Sugar Hill. For some reason, none of us tell Kormah about what happened at the Dupot Road Checkpoint. I wanted to tell him but as soon as I tried, the pain of became too much to put in words. I don't think I could ever tell that story again. Nyempu must feel the same way, because she doesn't utter a word about it, either.

Uncle George and Uncle Thomas get right to work helping Mama, Aunt Gormah, and Aunt Ginger clean up our house. They have even brought a few things with them, like pots and a couple of chairs, so we at least have something to sit on. Although I am glad to see the chairs, I am still a little worried because we still do not have anything to sleep on. I know that our things are at Boye's house now and I think we deserve to have them back. We shouldn't have to live like this when our belongings are just a couple houses away.

When I hear Mama announce that she is leaving, I hop up. "I am going with you." I run out the door ahead of her, before she has time to protest. I have learned that this is the best way to get things done with Mama. She can't tell me no if I am already on the way.

"So where are we going?" I ask.

"I am going to ask the Payes for a favor," Mama says.

"You mean you are going to ask them for our stuff back," I say matter-of-factly. "I am going to get all of my things back from Boye that he took. I can't believe Boye took my sweater!"

"Quanei, don't look at it that way. It is better that our friends have our things than the rebels, right? Plus, I am sure they thought we were not coming back here."

"Or that we were dead," I add.

Mama stops and gives me a look I do not understand. We approach Boye's house and Mr. Paye comes out before we can even knock on the door.

"Neyor," he says, putting his hands on his hips. He does not seem as enthusiastic to see us this time. His wife comes out a few feet behind him.

"Hello," Mama says kindly. "We are getting settled back in up at the compound."

"Good," he responds. "Glad to see that."

"Yes, but we do not have many things left. All of our things have been taken and me and my children have nothing left to sleep on."

Mr. and Mrs. Paye say nothing.

"I have heard. . . I have heard that some of our things may be here? If they are, it's okay. But the cement floor at our house is so hard. If you could please spare just one of the mattresses it would be greatly appreciated, and we can make do with that."

Mr. Paye crosses his arms. "What we have in our house is ours, Neyor. This war has been hard on all of us."

My mouth drops wide open and I stare at Mr. Paye in shock.

"Mr. Paye. You did not have to leave your home. Your home is still intact, and you have everything that you had before, yes? Well, me and my children have nothing. I don't even need it all back. We just need something to rest on."

"The answer is no," Boye's mother says and marches back inside.

Mama is silent for a moment. "Mr. Paye, surely you will not turn us away?"

I feel like I am in a very bad dream. What is wrong with the Payes? Why won't they return our things? I am glaring with my arms crossed at the spot Mrs. Paye left, and now I look up at Mama. I want to say something but I know better than to interrupt. I am about to burst with all the things that I want to scream at them. But, for every bit of rage that I feel, I notice that Mama is all the more silent. Although there is so much that I want her to say, she is not cross with Mr. Paye yet.

"I can't help you, Neyor. I am looking out for my own family now, and whatever we have belongs to me and my family."

"So, you will not help us?"

"The stuff is ours." And with that, he turns and walks away.

Mama and I stand in silence watching him go. As soon as Mr. Paye closes his door, I open my mouth.

"Mama, why didn't you demand our things back? We have nothing! Those are our things!"

"Come on," Mama says and starts to walk away.

"No! Go and get our things, Mama! Go and get the other neighbors! They will stand with you and make mean old Mr. Paye and his stupid wife give us our things back! They already have everything else and it's not fair!" I don't know what is happening to me. I am near tears and cannot control myself. I am shouting at Mama. "Go and get our things! They are ours!"

"Quanei! What good are things if you have a bad attitude, son?"

"Mama," I say slowly as I am trying to help her understand. "How can the Payes treat us this way? How can you let them take our things? We have already lost everything, and you won't even get back what is ours? Why would you let them do this?" I drop down on the ground. "It's not right! It's not fair!" I am yelling now. "I wish Papa was here, so all of this crazy stuff can just stop happening to us and I just want our things back!"

To my surprise, Mama does not scold me. Instead, she sits right down on the ground next to me. "Believe me son, there are days when I want to lie down and scream too, but you must calm yourself because we have not lost everything."

"Mama, I think you must be blind. Unless you just got here five minutes ago. How can you say that? Just look around!"

Mama lets out a chuckle and rubs my head. "No, but I know that we have not lost everything because we still have each other. No one can take who you are. Now, if you sit here calling people stupid and lose the very essence of who Quanei is, you have lost everything. Do you understand?"

I cross my arms and look away instead of answering. I don't feel like agreeing with Mama right now. We have traveled all this way to come home only to have Boye and his family take what belong to us. And Mr. Paye and his wife were so mean. They don't deserve to have anyone be nice to them, especially Mama.

Mama lets out a deep breath. "Son, we have the most important things. We have our family, and unlike so many people in Sugar Hill, our house is still standing. We have Kormah back and our entire family is waiting for us up the hill. Life is too precious to not enjoy what you have because you're worried about what someone else has done to you. Do you think that I care about those mattresses more than I care about our lives and our health and strength?"

"No, but I know that if things were different you would give the Payes anything they needed. Yet, they are so mean to us, over something as silly as one mattress."

"Yes," Mama agrees. "I would give to them and so would your Papa. But just because that is the kind of people we are, does not mean that the Payes are the same way."

"But I thought the Payes were our friends! And they sold us out over a silly mattress that belongs to us!"

"Yes, they did."

"Mama, it is stupid to care more about a mattress than your friends," I declare when I finally decide to sit up and look at her.

"Why do you think I did not argue with them, Quanei?" Mama gives me a quick nudge. "If material things make you happier than friendships, then you are in a terrible way already. Because things can come and go. If your happiness and pride are tied to what you own, then when those things leave, so does your happiness. But if you know who you are, and what you are, material things do not change that. I do not care about those mattresses. Those mattresses do not hold my happiness or my hope."

"Okay, but what will we sleep on?"

"Whatever God provides. But until then, we can snuggle with each other really tight."

That night, as my family all gathers together to sleep, the cold cement floor doesn't feel quite as hard, and I actually sleep through the night.

The next day, after we wake up rubbing our backs, Mama goes to the Payes house to try to reason with them again. They do not return our mattresses, but instead give Mama what used to be the top of a child's mattress. It is a flimsy piece of urine-stained cotton that smells horrible, but Mama graciously thanks them and brings it back to our house. Uncle George and Uncle Thomas scrub the smelly mattress with soap for a really long time. Then they wash and rinse it over and over again to get the smell out. They spread it out in the sun to dry. Finally, we have something to sleep on.

34

New Neighbors and Rough Roommates

Late September 1990

A month goes by in our new existence at Sugar Hill. Each day we find a way to make the most of what we have while Mama, Aunt Gormah, Aunt Ginger, Uncle Thomas, Uncle George, and another uncle, Uncle Chris, steadily find ways to add more. Mama instructs Aunt Gormah to make cassava and gravy to sell. Uncle George and Uncle Thomas climb up in the trees and get palm nuts. Then, by some magic, Mama turns it into palm oil, which she sells whenever she and Aunt Gormah go to the market.

Little by little, things get better. But as far as I am concerned, I am still not home. Sugar Hill still looks and feels nothing like before. I have realized that the home I knew was destroyed. Our community is gone. What is left is a sad and scary shell of a town. There are still dead bodies in some homes. Even though we have found our way back into our house, we are still very much living in a war zone. At night, any bump or noise causes us to jump up and look around wildly. Mama gets up several times in the middle of the night to check on everyone. And we've heard no word of Papa.

Mama's pharmacy has been raided and there is nothing left. Not even the shelves. But now she has started a palm oil business.

Mama is able to get some supplies that help her make palm oil even better and faster than before. The only thing is, not many people in Gbarnga City have money to buy palm oil. Half the city is still starving as the rebels continue to control the area. Sometimes I hear Mama and some grown folks talk about how long we can last, even here in Sugar Hill. They talk about how, at any point, rebels can come through and kill us all. None of the grownups seem to think that anyone in Liberia will live to see the end of this war and that the only hope for anyone is to find a way out of this wretched country. In addition to everything else that has changed, I don't play outside with Boye anymore. I barely see him, and when I do, we don't even wave at each other. We just go our separate ways.

One day, I am in the kitchen helping Mama make palm oil when Aunt Gormah comes tearing into the house.

"Neyor!" she calls frantically. "Neyor!"

Mama and I both drop whatever we are holding and run to the living room. Aunt Gormah drops her bags. She is breathing hard, as if she has just run ten miles. She looks as if she has just seen a ghost. "You are not going to believe this."

"What is it?" Uncle Thomas comes in from the back. "I saw you running up the hill. Is everyone okay?"

Aunt Gormah looks at everyone. "I just heard and saw it with my own ears and eyes."

"Heard and saw what!" Mama demands.

"Charles Taylor is moving into this neighborhood."

"Charles Taylor?" Mama asks. "What?"

"Are you sure, Gormah?" Aunt Ginger pipes in.

"What? No." Uncle Thomas says. "It cannot be true. That is crazy!"

"That is why things have been so busy in the city!" Mama says. "Oh no!"

"I saw him and a truckload of men putting things into the house just down the block. That beautiful home down the hill.

A few of your neighbors were even out there helping. I saw Charles Taylor in Sugar Hill."

Uncle Thomas goes to the window and peers outside. "How in the world can this be true?" He turns to Aunt Gormah. "So, you saw him? You actually saw Charles Taylor? The Charles Taylor, here in Gbarnga City?"

"Well, now I'm not so sure," Aunt Gormah says. "There is so much going on, I don't know which one would be him. I mean, I have seen him on the news, but I can't tell, Neyor. He is definitely here though. Some of his rebels are going through the community, picking houses to set up to, I don't know, to serve and protect him or something."

Mama looks perplexed.

"Oh, my goodness, this is great news!" Aunt Ginger clasps her hands and runs to the window. I look at Aunt Ginger as if she has lost mind. "If it really is Charles Taylor, maybe this will make the community safe. I mean, he will have a lot of body guards and once they see we are natives, they can protect all of us. As long we don't make any problems for them."

"I don't think so, Ginger!" Uncle Thomas rolls his eyes in disbelief.

"Ma Neyor!" Mr. Mullbah is suddenly outside banging on the front door. "Mrs. Karmue!"

"Let him in," Mama tells Uncle Thomas.

Mr. Mullbah comes inside with the same look as Aunt Gormah. He speaks quickly, "Hello, Mrs. Karmue. Everyone. You all are never going to believe this! Guess what I just saw? I think Charles Taylor is moving in down the hill in the Bishop's house. I think he's taking the house over for one of his wives."

"See? I told you!" Auntie Gormah says. "Charles Taylor is moving in. He has soldiers everywhere and they are bringing things in!"

"She is telling the truth," Mr. Mullbah says. "It is true. Charles Taylor is here in this very community."

Mama goes over to the main window. "Are you sure it is him?" She spins around and looks at everyone. "The real Charles Taylor is here in Gbarnga City? In Sugar Hill?"

"Yes, he is," Mr. Mullbah says. "I can't believe it either!"

"Why would he come here?" Mama asks. "What does he want?"

"Well," Mr. Mullbah says. "Is Gbarnga City his home? Charles Taylor is from Bong County. I think he is here because Gbarnga is between Nimba County and the big set up they have in Phebe, near Suakoko. It is the largest foothold the rebels have all the way up to Monrovia and he is placing himself straight in the middle of it."

"But why set up shop here on Sugar Hill?" Mama asks, her eyes wide.

Mr. Mullbah gives Mama a strange look. "Surely you know that over the years, your husband and you have made Sugar Hill one of the best communities around. You even managed to get lights, a paved road, a pharmacy, and a community car. Even among all this chaos, if he is going to be in Gbarnga City, there is no better place for him to set up shop than here."

"This is what I was thinking too. We're in a rebel zone. I think they have to at least protect us if they will move into our neighborhood, right?" Aunt Ginger adds.

"I'm not sure if I should be encouraged by that," Mama says, shaking her head. She walks over to the window and stares outside again. "This cannot be happening. I never thought in a million years this would happen." Everyone is at the window now. "Never in a million years."

"I think maybe you ladies should stay home today and not try to go to the market for a while – at least a couple of days," Mr. Mullbah says.

"I agree," Mama says. "If Charles Taylor really is moving into this neighborhood, there is no way in the world anyone in this house is going outside."

Everyone spends the rest of the day looking down the road as cars come and go. Like Mama, I would never in a million years have imagined that Charles Taylor would be living next to us on the hill, that the entire Liberian civil war would be right at our doorsteps.

"I don't think this can be safe for all of us here much longer," I hear Mama tell Aunt Gormah and Aunt Ginger later that day.

"I don't know," Aunt Gormah says. "If Charles Taylor is here, God knows that in a matter of time, this place will be overrun with his. . . his freedom fighters. Or whatever they call themselves. And what if he brings Doe's army right to us! The entire town will be destroyed, and we will all be dead, Neyor!"

Mama stands up and begins to pace the floor. "This is not safe. He could kill us all tomorrow. Maybe we should leave, now."

"But where will we go? I hear the village is not safe either."

"If they see you moving, they will kill you," Aunt Gormah says. "It is too risky."

"Charles Taylor is living here. On our little hill." Mama crosses her arms and looks out the window. "He is one of the most dangerous men in the world. And with him, come even more rebels to protect him. It is as if our entire world is being turned upside down."

"Oh," Aunt Gormah sighs. "Our entire world has been upside for a long time. But this certainly is something."

The news of Charles Taylor moving in hits what is left of our community like a tidal wave. News spreads that he has chosen Bishop Neville's house just down the hill. His leaders have sent word that Charles Taylor has given his rebels permission to take any house in the community as their own, so they can be close to guard him and operate their squads.

Everyone in our house is terrified, except Aunt Ginger. Some people here in Gbarnga feel a sense of pride to have the leader of the revolution making his headquarters in their town. There is so much disgust for President Doe that having the leader of the rebellion so close actually gives some people something to hold on to. As the gossip spreads, I can tell that Mama and people like us do not share in this sense of pride, but none of us dare breathe a word of our disapproval. It could cost us our lives.

The morning after Taylor's arrival, our household is awakened by a loud rumbling noise, like elephants stampeding our compound. Everyone is jolted out of their sleep and runs to the front room. The loud rumbling is joined by whoops, cursing, and yelling. When we all make it to the window, we see young men jumping off trucks, landing from the still-moving vehicles in excitement. It is the rebels. Mama quickly tells Uncle Thomas and Uncle George to take the children in the back and that we are not to make a sound.

Before I can even respond, Uncle George grabs pulls me to the back with the others.

"Not a sound," he says, looking at Kormah sharply. "Nothing."

I do as I am told, although I am so frightened I can barely get my legs to move. Even the mention of rebels terrifies me. I have seen what they can do, and now they are at our home.

Mama, Aunt Gormah, and Aunt Ginger stay to face the rebels together and the rest of us go into my old room and peer out the window, not making a sound. Through my little corner of the window, I see Mama step outside as a white SUV comes into view. More rebels jump out of trucks and begin to look around our compound. One man gets out of the SUV and calls out to Mama.

"I say, you girl! Who compound is this?" His voice is heavy and demanding; I can tell he must be the one in charge. But why is he calling Mama "a girl"? I figure he must think that Mama is a teenager since she is so skinny now.

"Good morning, Commander!" Mama calls out. Her voice is steady, but I can tell she is afraid. There is no telling what may happen to us. The rebel commander walks up to Mama looks at her.

"I say, who compound is this?"

"These are my houses," Mama's responds, as more soldiers gather around.

Immediately, the entire group of rebels break into a loud and hysterical laughter. I shift my eyes to Mama as she just stands there, saying nothing.

"So," says the commander. "You want me to believe that a little girl like you, owns all of this big property? An entire compound?" He laughs again. "Okay. That was a good one. How do a small girl like you own a big place like this?"

"My husband and I built this place after my husband left Ghanta Mission School. We do live here. We have lived in this city for years. We have five children and they are all inside. If you don't believe me, you can ask anyone in the community. They will tell you my name and my husband's name."

The commander walks closer to mama. "Ghanta Mission huh? So, what is your husband name?"

"Karmue," Mama replies. "He went to go and try to get some supplies when the war started, but we have not seen him since."

"Wait," The commander says, putting up his hand. "Fungbeh Karmue?"

"Yes," Mama says slowly. "Fungbeh Karmue."

My heart is racing, and I am even more shocked to hear this rebel utter my father's name.

"You mean, Alfred Fungbeh Karmue, from Ghanta Mission?"

At this moment, Mama also seems stunned. She looks around quickly and I can tell that she is wondering what this man is thinking and how he knows Papa.

"Old Ma, what your name?" he asks.

"My name is Neyor Lorpu Karmue."

"Well, Ma Neyor," the commander says with a sly smile. "I know your husband. He and I were both at Ghanta Mission together. Karmue was a good man."

Mama says nothing back. I think she is in shock. I am too. How in the world is someone our Papa once knew a commander in the rebel army? The rebel commander looks around. And then back at Mama.

"My name is Commander Nya Konah and I know Karmue. He was always a good man. So, Old Ma, you don't worry. I won't harm you and your family." Then he grows stern. "But I want this house to be for me, you hear? Me and my boys will be here watching over this whole area." He pauses and looks between Aunt Gormah and Mama. "You don't mind, do you?"

"No problem, Mr. Konah. You can have the house. No problem," Mama says quickly. I can tell she is relieved. "But if I may kindly ask of you one request. My five children and brothers and sisters are here with me in the house and the compound. If you move into the houses, will you please allow us to have one room for my children and me and one room for my brothers and sisters?

"Ma Neyor, for you, no problem. You and your family can stay in two rooms. You can stay with us. Me and my boys will protect you here, so don't worry."

Mama nods. I know she must be nervous. Aunt Ginger has entered our room and I hear her sigh with relief.

Konah turns to one of his soldiers. "Peter!" A skinny boy with an AK-47 around his waist runs up to the place Konah and Mama are standing. "Yes, Commander?"

"Peter, go put my name on the other house."

"Yes, sir."

The boy Peter takes a black marker to the front door of the compound's smallest house. While Uncle George isn't looking, I slip out of my room and step out our side door to watch Peter write over the doorpost, This is Commander Nya Konah's House.

I could not believe that this man was writing on our house. Papa built that house.

"Quanei!" I turn to see Mama standing in the doorway, glaring at me. "Get in your room right now!"

I run past her back into the room and close the door. Kormah looks at me.

"Tell me, Quanei," Kormah says. "What did he do?"

I slump against the door and slide down to the floor. "He wrote, This is Commander Nya Konah's House on the other house."

Kormah goes back to the window. He crosses his arms and says quietly, "I cannot wait for Papa to come home."

I also cross my arms. "Me too."

Kormah and I don't have long to be upset because soon everything is turned upside-down. Mama moves us from our room to the back room in the house. Whatever belongings we have are cleared out and we are all stuffed together. Uncle George sits with us and we are told not to move and not to come out of the room at all. Commander Konah gives his soldiers the command that Mama and her family are not to be bothered. Within moments, our house is filled with loud noise, cursing, and strange smells. Just like our city and our community, our home is now invaded by the rebels.

Later that day, Commander Konah goes down to Mama's pharmacy and marks his name on that too.

Scan this code with a QR reader or use the link below to follow selected chapters for a more purposeful Witness Experience

www.resources.witnessliberia.com

35

Prisoners in Our Own Home

Just when I thought life could not get any worse, living with the rebels takes everything to a new level of danger, fear, and desperation. We have a roof over our heads, but our house is not our own and we are mostly confined to the room in the back.

Being around rebels is like nothing that I have ever experienced. The rebels drink and smoke in the house, and when they get drunk, they fire their guns inside. As we try to sleep at night we here the ping of bullets hitting the zinc roof. They call this "target practice" and it scares all of us half to death.

Mama does not want us around the rebels at all, so every day at four o'clock, we all go to our room for the rest of the evening. Aunt Gormah and her children do the same. Aunt Ginger and her children do not care to be inside early, so sometimes she hangs around with the rebels. But at night, she still locks herself and her children in their room. Sometimes, Uncle Thomas and Uncle George sit around, sometimes talking with the rebel boys who carry guns all the time. Sometimes, the rebels tell disturbing stories about bad things they have done to people.

One evening, Mama is putting us all in the room for the night when Commander Konah knocks on the door. Mama cracks the door a little. A strong smell of God-knows-what fills our tiny space and I can hear the laughter of a woman from some place in the house.

"Commander," Mama says. "What can I do for you?"

He looks past her into the room. The smell of liquor on his breath is so strong I can smell it from right behind Mama. "Why are you always cooped up in this little room? Don't be afraid. It is safe outside you know, Old Ma? Come outside. We will protect you and your children." He is dragging his words and I can tell that he is very drunk. For a moment, I think now may be a good time for us to knock him out and make a run for a better life. Then I remember our entire compound is overrun with rebels and we wouldn't make it past the front door.

"I appreciate it, Commander," Mama says. "But now is the time that I teach the children their lesson. Just because there is not school, does not mean we cannot practice."

Commander Nyah leans up against the doorframe. "I can tell you are Karmue's wife. You are a smart woman. That is the same thing Charles Taylor says. He is going to start making all the children in his territory go to school very soon! He says even though we are at war, he wants the children of Liberia to get a good education. And look at you! Already thinking like him!" He peers past her again at us. "Enjoy your lesson chi-chi-children!"

Of course, we say nothing and soon he stumbles away. Mama quickly closes the door. "I guarantee I am not thinking like Charles Taylor," she says. "If anything, Charles Taylor is thinking like me."

"Amen to that," Aunt Gormah says, as she spreads out a blanket. "Amen to that."

The noise, the women, and the drugs are almost unbearable and at night we can barely sleep. But no matter what we feel or think, we don't dare step out of our room. Not for anything, not even to use the bathroom. I can tell Mama hates every moment of having to share this house with the rebel soldiers, but at this point we know we have no choice. If we try to leave now, the rebels here

will say we are traitors and probably kill us. Every night, when the
raucous is worst, I can tell from Mama's face that she is desperately
praying for a way to get us out of this horrible situation.

One night, I awaken to loud noises in the room next door.
I hear strange moaning and knocking against the wall closest to me.
My eyes pop open and I stare through the darkness at the ceiling
above. I am used to the rebels keeping up a commotion, but this is
something different. The noises coming out of the next room give
me a funny feeling in my stomach. I can hear the sharp cries of a
woman and the rough grunts of a man as they knock against the
wall. I have seen the rebels bring all sorts of women to the house
and whenever they do, they grab and touch them in places a man is
not supposed to touch a woman. So, I can image what is happening as I listen to the sounds. They are panting and breathing fast
and hard, as if they are running. I lie in the darkness with a pit in
my stomach. The woman sounds like the man is hurting her as she
cries out.

Suddenly, I see Mama sit up quickly, but I don't move. For
some reason, I don't want Mama to know that I am awake because
I feel bad even listening to the gasping, moaning, and cursing next
door. Mama stands up quickly and looks over all of us carefully
to make sure that we were sleeping. I pretend to be sleeping, but
I can practically feel how angry Mama is as she frantically moves
about, covering us with the thin blanket. When Mama moves by
me, I just lay there, still as a frightened deer, with my knees folded
in my chest.

The sounds are still coming from the next room, louder and
louder. I peek through one eye and see Mama pacing. The noises
get louder and I realize there is more than one man in the room
with the woman. I think I am going to vomit. Are they killing her?
I peep open my eyes again and see that Mama has stopped pacing
to sit on the floor, her hands covering her face as we are both forced
to listen. Mama stands back up and places her hand on her hip.
When she does, a sliver of moonlight from the window illuminates
her face and I can see the tears streaming down her cheeks. When

Mama looks over again, I close my eyes tight and decide not to open them again until morning. I do not want to see Mama cry.

I try to focus on sounds that used to make me sleep well at night. Like the Night-Night things that used to talk across the universe back when Boye and I were friends. But I cannot hear them tonight and I wonder where they have gone. If they have left, I do not blame them. We would all leave if we could. Especially after tonight. Finally, the sounds next door come to a stop, though I can hear mumbling voices. I am so glad it is over. I do not open my mouth to tell anyone, ever.

The next day, Commander Konah decides to teach himself how to drive and crashes his car right into the side of our house. It sounds like a bomb has dropped over our entire compound. Mama, Aunt Gormah, and Uncle Thomas rush outside to see if we are being attacked. We all try to follow her, but Uncle George and Aunt Ginger stop all of us kids from going outside.

Mama looks terrified as she rushes into the front yard. But when she sees Commander Konah in the car, her back stiffens and I can tell she is angry. I am too afraid to be angry, but I am shocked that this man has crashed a car into the side of our house. As I stare at the pitiful scene, Commander Konah steps out, kicks the car with his shoe, and says a bad word. He then walks over and looks at the damage he has done to this side of the house and the porch. When he sees Mama and Aunt Gormah standing by the front door, he waves at them and shrugs.

"The car was ugly anyway," he calls out. And then he and his mini troop of soldiers all explode into laughter. Mama does not look amused and she opens her mouth to speak, but Aunt Gormah grabs her hand.

Commander Konah stumbles up to where Mama is standing. "Anyways," he says, grinning at Mama. "This is my house. I can fix it! That is what a man does! He fixes his house. It's not anything to build this porch. I will take care of what is mine."

"Are you okay, Commander?" Mama asks, trying not to give away that she is upset.

"Yes!" he replies. He turns back and looks at the car. "It is ugly anyway. Especially now that we wrote on it."

Mama looks past Commander Konah and squints at the car. I can read very well, and I can see that the car has Bloody Face written all over in red and black. Mama looks at Commander Konah. "Bloody Face. What does that mean? Why is Bloody Face written all over your car?"

Commander Konah smiles at Mama and Aunt Gormah. "Because it is a bloody car, Mrs. Karmue. The man that owned this car was a rich man with a bad attitude. But today, me and my boys show him who the boss. We killed his whole family and took the car. When we left him in the street. His face was bloody. So that is what I named my car."

The rebel soldiers are standing around laughing and nodding, as Commander Konah tells Mama all about how he went from room to room with his machete, slicing the rich man's family to pieces. I know that we are not supposed to listen to such things as this—that we should cover our ears or go to our room, but all of us are too afraid to move. I am afraid that if I even breathe wrong, he will slice me up too.

Mama does not say anything when the Commander is done with his story. She looks too shocked to speak. But Aunt Gormah speaks up. "Oh," she says. "We see now, Commander. We understand."

Commander Konah turns back and looks at the car. "You see the red, Ma Neyor? That is the old rich man's blood."

When I hear this, I'm struck with so much fear I think I might pass out. I stare helplessly at Mama and Aunt Gormah, outside all alone with the murderous rebels, who are still enjoying the rush of their last kill.

Commander Konah looks at Mama and he can tell she is disturbed. "Listen. I am not a bad man. It's just war. You know what I mean? We have to take what we need to fight the war, Mrs. Karmue."

Mama nods at him. "War is war," she says.

"Exactly!" he says raising his fist. "Now boys, let's get this car moved!"

As soon as the rebels turn their attention back to the car, Mama and Aunt Gormah quickly come back into the house. "Let's go to back to the room right now. They won't be distracted long," Mama says, as she scoops up Fungbeh and grabs Kulubah by the arm. "To the back, quickly!" she tells the rest of us.

In seconds, she, Aunt Gormah, and Aunt Ginger gather all us kids in the room and Uncle Thomas and Uncle George follow. As soon as Uncle George pushes the door closed, Mama speaks. "That is enough. These people are crazy and I can't keep my children here any longer. We have got to get out of here."

"Sister Neyor, how can we go?" Aunt Ginger says. "We cannot just get up and walk out of here! Didn't you just hear what he did to that man?"

Aunt Gormah is practically shaking as she holds her daughter on her hip. "He will kill us next! It's only a matter of time before he decides to take one of our children to add to the rest of the boys following him. Aunt Gormah looks at Aunt Ginger. "And how long do you think he will be okay with three single women living with all these wild men! I have seen the way they look at us!"

Mama looks at her two brothers, Uncle Thomas and Uncle George, "And on top of that, how long do you think he will put up with two grown men who are not his soldiers living in his house? Look at my sons and Gormah's sons. You've seen what these rebels do to growing boys. At any point, they can take our children and turn them into those little rebel monsters. I will not risk it."

"I agree," Uncle Thomas speaks up. "We need to go home. We need to get to the village, where we all will be safer."

"But he will kill us if we try to leave!" Uncle George says. "There are fourteen of us, including the children. Do you think he is not going to notice us leaving?"

"You all may be leaving, but I am not," Aunt Ginger says. No one is really surprised when she says this. "Ever since we left Gaye

Town, you have been running from rebels that have been nothing but nice to us. It is safer for me and my children to have a rebel like Konah protect us. If I feel like it is unsafe, then I will make my way to Papa's village, but until then, we are staying right here. We'll be close to Charles Taylor and the protection of his rebel commander."

"Fine, Ginger, you do that if you want," Aunt Gormah says. "Everyone must do whatever they feel they need to do.

Mama looks like she wants to say something but instead walks over and peers out the back window. "Listen, they have moved the car to the back. We don't have much longer to discuss. Go back outside and act like everything is normal, everyone." She looks at Uncle George. "Just get ready to leave tomorrow and don't worry. I have a plan."

Early the next morning, Mama quietly rounds us up to head to the village. We take nothing but our clothes and whatever Mama can stuff into a small bag. Mama sends Uncle Thomas and Uncle George back to get a wheelbarrow that Mr. Mullbah gave us. She knocks on Aunt Gormah's door and tells her and her children to go outside first. Mama has already explained her plan to us, and we all know to follow along. But as we step out of our room that morning, I am still terrified. If our plan does not work, the rebels will kill us for sure.

Most of the rebels are still passed out in the living room from the night before. As we walk past them, I try not to breathe or wake anyone. I can hear Commander Konah somewhere in the back, and it takes all I can not to run at the sound of his voice. We all make it out the front door without being noticed, but as soon as Uncle George and Uncle Thomas meet us with the wheelbarrow, Commander Konah comes barreling out front. "Neyor Karmue!" he calls. I freeze in my steps. My heart begins to race, and I do not dare turn around for fear that my face will give away that we are up to something.

Mama turns to give Command Konah a pleasant smile. "Good morning, Commander," Mama calls.

"Where are you going with the children?" He asks, wiping his mouth.

Oh, my God, I think. We have been caught.

"We're going to the market for more supplies to make gravy and palm oil for me to sell. We need more food and supplies for the house."

Konah looks all of us over. "But why are you taking all of the children? You can leave them here."

At this, I turn around and look at Nyempu, who gives me and Kormah the slightest shake of the head, telling us to stay calm and stay put.

"No, Commander Konah. Do you see all of these children? We would not put that burden on you—to make you our babysitter. My children are my business and responsibility and you have important business to be about for yourself and your men. And most importantly, to protect all of us. It will be better for them to be with me at the marketplace. But do not worry, we will be back soon."

Commander Konah does not looked convinced and takes another step, staring at us. I can see on his face that he is trying to figure something out.

"My brothers are going to carry the children for me in the wheelbarrow," Mama says when she sees his eyes fall on Uncle Thomas and Uncle George. "See?" Mama says, pointing at Nyempu's bare feet. "No shoes."

"Then let me give you a ride in Bloody Face," Commander says. As soon as he utters the words, I shiver.

"You are so kind, Commander, but we have many stops to make along the way. Is it right for a civilian woman to make a rebel Commander her personal chauffer? I don't think so."

"I suppose," he says, still looking at us.

"Do you need me to bring you anything from the marketplace?" Mama asks, blinking at him innocently. "We can put almost anything in these wheelbarrows. There will be plenty of room if you need me to bring you something back."

Commander Konah is staring hard at Mama when Aunt Ginger emerges from the front door. "Neyor, please bring me a teaspoon of salt if you can manage," she calls out.

Commander Konah turns around to look at her and I realize in that moment that Aunt Ginger's decision to stay behind is actually working for our benefit. There is no way we could all be leaving if she is still there, waiting on us to bring her some salt. I'm shocked that Aunt Ginger is trying to help us.

"Ah!" Commander Konah says, turning back around. "Do not worry about us, Mrs. Karmue. You are always so kind. Save your money and bring back what you can for your sister." He locks eyes with Mama. "I will see you and your family when you get back."

"Okay, Commander. Have a good day."

Mama turns around and grabs my hand and the entire group starts down the hill. I can't believe that Mama's plan has worked. It seems as if we are safe for now. As we make our way down the hill. Mama holds my hand tight. She is shaking like a leaf.

Part Four

Desperate. Abandoned. Faith. Freedom.

Art credited to Liberian children, survivors of war now living at
Christ's Children Orphanage Home on Sugar Hill, Liberia-Oct, 2018
WITNESS: IN PARTNERSHIP WITH SAVE MORE KIDS, INC

36

Finding Higher Ground

Our group walks at a very quick and steady pace as we leave our home behind. Although I am a little sad that we must leave, I am excited to get away from the rebels. We don't get a chance to say goodbye to our remaining neighbors and friends, but that is the least of our worries now. For now, we need to put as much distance as we can between us and home, before Commander Konah realizes that he has been duped.

We stop at the local marketplace to pick up a few supplies and then we are back on the road again. When we leave the marketplace, we pass by our old school, but this time I don't even bother to look.

We walk all the way back to Phebe Hospital to find Dr. Gwenigale. When we get there, we are questioned by the rebels guarding the area around the building. We are told to wait while the rebels send one of their own inside.

"Do you think he is still here?" Aunt Gormah asks.

"He should be," Mama says. "I don't care how reckless these rebels are, even they know that they need a doctor to patch them up and run the only hospital."

"Do you think maybe it would be better if we go back to Ma Etta's house?" Aunt Gormah asks.

"Ma Etta has given us so much already. I don't want to take more from her. She has her own family to feed. Besides Dr. Gwenigale told us to come back any time. I'm sure he has more than enough."

Finally, I spot Dr. Gwengale's white coat in the distance and I pull on Mama's arm.

"There he is!" I tell her. "He is coming this way."

"Oh, thank God," Mama replies.

Dr. Gwenigale waves at us as he approaches the gate with two rebels at his side.

"Oh, my goodness, Sister Karmue!" he says with a laugh. "You are back!"

She embraces him and smiles. "For a night, yes, if you can have us," Mama responds quietly, as the rebels are still eyeing us and stick close to the doctor.

"Of course. All of you, please come in."

I look up at the rebel soldiers who apparently will be accompanying us back to the hospital. Dr. Gwenigale who seems to be unbothered by their presence. I try to act the same. He leads us into the main hospital lobby, which is practically empty, even of furniture. The hospital is nothing like it used to be. The electricity flickers on and off and the lobby clearly hasn't been cleaned in months.

"Have a seat, all of you," he says although there are hardly any chairs. "I will go get some water and something for you to eat and then we can catch up."

"Is there anything I can do to help?" Mama asks. "I know my way around here pretty well."

"Oh, you are kind to offer but it is not safe for you to wander around here alone now. Just make yourself comfortable. I will be right back."

When Dr. Gwenigale returns, he shows us into an old examination room with a few hospital beds. "There is enough space for all of you. Really, Neyor, you can stay as long as you like."

"I appreciate your help, my friend. But we won't be in here for long. We are just passing through on our way to my home village. Once we get some rest tonight, we will make the rest of the journey tomorrow."

"Sister Neyor, I wish you would consider staying here. The rebels won't bother you. Your family will be safe and have food and all that you need. I know that you want to go to the village, but Liberia is almost completely shut down. Those in the countryside do not have access to running water and it's so far out of the way that if anyone gets ill, there is no chance of getting to a doctor. It may be better for you to just stay here, where at least you have clean water and access to medical attention if you need it."

"I appreciate it, Doctor. But we have just left a place that is run by the rebels and it is not an environment I can have my family in. Not to mention that the rebels aren't the only concern. What if Doe decides to strike now that Charles Taylor is near? I think my children will be safer and more comfortable in the village—out of the way of all of this."

"You could be right." Dr. Gwenigale looks down, his face serious as he slips his hands into the pockets of his white lab coat. "But I hope that you at least think about it overnight."

Despite Dr. Gwenigale's plea, Mama sticks with her plan to leave Phebe and head to the village. The next morning, we pack up. Dr. Gwenigale gives Mama a big bag of rice.

"Please know that you can come back here if you need to."

Mama thanks him again for his kindness. I know Mama has no plans to return.

I am so elated to be out of the rebels's sight and in Mama's home village that I can barely contain myself. When the outskirts of the village come into view, all of us kids burst into a full run the rest of the way. I can't wait to see my grandma and all of my aunts, uncles, and cousins, and everyone else we know. I am most happy to see that, unlike the rest of the world, this place remains unbothered by the terrors of war, at least on the outside. Being so far away from the urban centers has protected the village from the ferocity of war tearing through the rest of the country.

"Oh, my goodness!" Grandma Yeayea spots us and runs outside with a towel in her hands. I wonder why she is back in the village. Maybe she did not like it at the Firestone plant.

"Grandma Yeayea!" We run to our grandmother and she scoops as many of us into her arms as she can manage. Next, she showers us all with kisses. The noise draws out the rest of our aunts and uncles, who emerge from the house with delight and astonishment on their faces, relieved to see us alive. Everyone at the village is excited to see us when we arrive. Mama's sisters run out to greet her and Auntie Gormah and to help them with their things. Within moments, I feel like I am being bathed in more love, warmth, and happiness than I can handle.

That night, everyone gathers at Grandma Yeayea's hut. There is so much happiness in the air, I feel like floating away. Here there is no fear, no cursing, no bad smells, and no sounds of gunfire in the distance. There is no one peering out of windows in fear. There is just fun, love, and happiness. It is like old times, with everyone around me speaking our native Kpelle tongue. We have successfully shut out the rest of the world. The only thing missing is Papa. I wish there was some way I could let Papa know that we are all safe and happy tonight.

Mama stays up all night talking with her brothers and sisters. I don't have to eavesdrop to know that she is telling them all about our travels and everything that has happened to us along the way. Mama's side of the family, Grandma Yeayea, Uncle Paye Banta, Aunt Nowah, Uncle Chris, Aunt Massah, Aunt Younger, and all of Mama's sisters, brothers, and cousins are living in this village now. Cousin Annie and her husband, Alfred, have come over to visit too and now we are having one giant reunion next to a big blazing fire.

Most of the children have passed out, but I am still up, lying with Fungbeh, who is having trouble settling down.

"I still can't believe you made it all this way, after all you have told us," Grandma Yeayea says. "Every time I breathe, I say a prayer of thanks to God that my babies are alive. I was so worried about all of you each time we heard news of how things were deteriorating."

"These rebels have taken away everything that our country holds dear," Cousin Annie says.

"This is why I am ashamed to even know any of these rebels," her husband, Cousin Alfred, says. "I cannot believe that people that I know are a part of this!"

"People you know?" Uncle Flomo Banta says. "Alfred, you were practically childhood friends with the VP Commander, Charles Taylor's number two in command! Didn't you grow up in the same town?"

"Well, I didn't know he was going to grow to be that!" Alfred says. "I could have never imagined that Enoch would grow up to be who is he is now. Let alone that he would recruit all of Nimba County and my people from the Gio and Mano tribes to join the war too. I guess Charles Taylor and his messages of freedom and a better government can sway even the most sensible people."

"Well," Mama says crossing her legs. "Your childhood friend is the number two scariest man in the whole world, and the number one scariest man is now living in my neighborhood."

At that, all the grownups burst out laughing. "Oh, my God. It's like you have to laugh to keep from crying!" Mama says, holding her sides. "Charles Taylor lives down the street and his VP Commander is Alfred's childhood best friend!"

Everyone laughs even harder until they are all holding their sides. I'm not so sure what is so funny, but I figure it must be a grownup thing.

"I don't care how powerful Enoch is now," Alfred says. "This is why our entire friendship has fallen to pieces. I do not support this rebel movement. And if I saw him I would tell him so."

Uncle Flomo leans in. "You know he'd kill you, Alfred."

"No," Alfred slips his hands behind his head. "He still owes me from that time he wet the bed and I told his mother it was me."

Everyone burst out louder this time, and even I giggle a bit. It makes me so happy to see Mama having fun, talking and laughing with her family again. If anyone deserves to be happy, it is Mama.

"I hear you and Gormah have been successful selling oil in the city," Grandma Yeayea says, in Kpelle. "That is very smart of you, Neyor. Oil, spices, and salt are so rare here now. They are like gold if you can get your hands on them. People can barely get food, let alone spices and palm oils! If people in Liberia had more money, you and your sister would be rich."

"I agree," Mama says, looking around. "But I am all out of oil now, and since the economy is so bad, we did not make as much money as I'd hoped. I need to sell a lot more than a few jars here and there if I am going to have enough money to—" Mama cuts off her words quickly and looks around. ". . . to live."

"You don't need a whole lot of money to live in the village, just a little," Grandma Yeayea says. "We have farmland here. We grow our vegetables and we fish. We have enough to survive."

"Yes, but what about fresh water? What if one of the children get hurt? Or what if we need to get a ride somewhere?" Aunt Gormah asks. "Neyor is right. You need a lot more money for those things."

"Exactly," Mama says. She looks at her brothers and sisters. "This is why I need help to make more oil."

"What kind of help?" Uncle Flomo asks.

"I need help chopping down palm nuts and gathering enough to make oil to sell in the city."

"Neyor, you don't need to be going in the city," Grandma Yeayea protests. "It is not safe to risk."

"She can go with Alfred and me when we go," Annie says. "We go in the city to do business sometimes. She can go with us. Neyor, if you can make the oil to sell, we will help you, won't we Alfred?"

"Yes, I think it's a good idea. We sell goods all the time and we even know a man who takes us to different checkpoints to sell at the different market days. Neyor can make plenty of money that way."

Mama seems instantly perk up. "You know a man who can carry you back and forth through checkpoints?"

Alfred nods. "Yes, but like you said, that costs lots of money per person and it can be very dangerous sometimes."

"Well, right now I need the money," Mama says. As I listen to the edge in Mama's voice, I wonder why she is so eager to start traveling through the country again. I don't need to be told everything to know that Mama is up to something bigger than just selling oil. "As a matter of fact, everyone here can benefit from having more money at their disposal, right? Especially here in the village."

Everyone around the fire seems to agree.

"So, how about you all help me to gather everything I need for the oil? I will make the oil and sell it in the city and I can pay you back for the work you put in. All of you."

I turn around to see the other grownups thinking it over.

"We are in," Annie says. "We will make plenty of money that way!"

Suddenly everyone seems to love the idea and all the grownups begin to discuss ways they can help Mama with her oil business. I get excited listening to them. That night, Fungbeh and I fall asleep next to the fire surrounded by the warm voices of our family.

Over the next few days, Mama's brothers and some of their friends from the village come together to cut palm nuts from the bush for Mama. As I watch the grownups working together, I see it as more evidence that Mama is still the smartest woman in the world. It seems no matter where she goes she can start a business, even in the middle of the Liberian war.

Every day we go with Grandma and the other villagers even deeper into the bush. A few miles into the forest, we arrive at the farmland. I am delighted to see the land is still just as lush and beautiful as I remember. I think of how all the destroyed farms we passed around Monrovia that used to supply rice to the region and beyond. Grandma Yeayea and other villagers have been busy growing vegetables and rice while the rest of the country is in a panic. Seeing the fields green and fruitful makes me feel like I'm in another world.

During the day, we run around happily and help the grown-ups farm. Sometimes we go to the nearby lake and fish. We are in our own farmland paradise. We are all safer this way too. If somehow the rebels do get to the village and start sniffing around, they will find nothing, not knowing we are hidden deep in the bush. In the evenings, everyone returns to the village and the grownups cook and show us how much oil they have made that day.

Soon, Mama and the neighbors make enough palm oil to sell in the city. When I learn that, I get worried. We have just escaped from Gbarnga City, now made even more dangerous by Charles Taylor's arrival. But every morning, Mama, Annie, and Alfred head out to the city to sell their oil, while the rest of us go deep into the bush to spend the day farming. Every day while we are apart, I say a prayer for Mama. I pray that she will be safe and that no rebels will bother her. I pray that she comes back to me. Living here has surely tucked us away from the daily terrors of the war, but I know at any moment that can change. Plus I can tell that Mama's mind always seems to be on other things; I can just feel it.

One night, as we sit around a fire a few weeks into selling oil in the city, Mama says to the family, "I have some news. I've been talking it over with Annie and Alfred and we have decided that we can make even more money if we sell the palm oil on the road leading up to Ivory Coast."

Everyone is struck silent. We stare at Mama as if she has sprouted a second head.

"Neyor, are you crazy?" Uncle Flomo says. "It is dangerous enough going every day into Gbarnga! Now you want to risk actually traveling through Liberia? And to the Ivory Coast, no less? Do you know what happens up there when people try to leave the country?"

Kormah, Nyempu, Kulubah, and I have stopped eating and are staring at Mama for answers.

"Neyor, this is too much!" Grandma Yeayea exclaims. "It is out of the question! It is not safe traveling in this country anywhere, let alone trying to cross the border with goods."

"But we see people at the market do this every day!" Alfred says. "We have seen many trucks going up the coast. There is much more money to be made up there. There is no war in the neighboring countries. Their economy is just fine. Plus, Ivory Coast has a big demand for oil since the war. Most of their oil used to come from Liberia, but now that we are at war, the price of red oil has almost tripled in Ivory Coast. That is what we have been told. We have plenty of palm oil and we can make a fortune!"

"I don't care if you can make a million dollars!" Grandma Yeayea says. "Is it worth your life?"

"Mama Yeayea, we have it all worked out. It is something that I need to do." Mama glances quickly over at us kids.

"Mama," I say, going to her. "You're going to go away?" Nyempu is behind me.

Mama looks at both of us. "Yes, but don't you worry. Go and finish your food and we will discuss all this later."

Later, Mama comes into the room where we have all been sleeping and gathers us all together.

"Listen to me," she says. "All of you."

"Just tell us if you are going away," Kormah spouts. "Just tell us if you are leaving us!"

"Kormah, calm down. And watch your tone."

Kormah crosses his arms and I can tell that he is acting more out of fear than his usual temper.

"I need to go on a trip to the Ivory Coast to sell oil, so we can have enough money to leave from here one day. Liberia is not safe for anyone. And I need to go and make money in case we need to leave."

"Mama, no!" I blurt out. I can barely cope with Mama going back into Gharnga City each day. I cannot bear the thought of her traveling through the country. "What if you don't come back again? What if you get captured by those bad rebels again? I don't want you to go!"

"Mama, why can't we all just stay here and be safe in the bush every day?" Nyempu asks. "We don't have to leave. We can just stay out of the way of the rebels and out of the way for the war! And then you don't have to go anywhere, Mama."

"Yeah," I agree. "You can just stay."

"Children, rebels can still find us out here, even in the bush. And if anything happens here, we are much too far away from anyone to get help. Not to mention, you children need school to learn and live a good life. You can't do that here in Liberia. This is not a life I am willing to accept for you. Out here, hiding from rebels for the rest of your life with no place to call home, no education, and no running water? No. This is not a life that your Papa and I want for you."

"Then take us with you!" Kormah pleads. "We can stay together. We can all go."

"Kormah, you know that I cannot take all of you through those checkpoints. I would never make it through. But I can go with my Cousin Annie and Cousin Alfred. With them I can sell oil to make enough money to buy you children shoes and clothes and maybe find a way for us to escape the country."

Escaping the country sounds unimaginable. I know how dangerous this would be.

"But Mama, why do you have to go all the way to the Ivory Coast?" Nyempu asks.

"Because there is no war in the Ivory Coast, Nyempu," Mama says. "Life is normal over there. People have plenty of money. I can sell the oil for so much more money. I will have enough for whatever we need—including enough for us to leave the country. This is something that I must do. I must do this for you."

My heart breaks to hear Mama explain all of this. I am terrified that I may never see Mama again. I can't imagine her traveling checkpoint by checkpoint all the way to the Ivory Coast.

"We can go to school here," Kormah offers. "When I was with Aunt Garmen, I heard talk that Charles Taylor is going to make all the kids here go to school! He says we still need an education. So, he is making people set up schools all over to teach children."

"There is no way in the world my children are going to anything set up by that Charles Taylor," Mama snaps. "Not even if I am dead will you ever set foot in anything under that man's rule. That is why I am going to find a way to get us all out of this country." She pauses and pulls us close. "I am leaving tomorrow with Annie and Alfred. We will go to Gbarnga City and find a truck that will take us safely to the Ivory Coast, just like one that brought us from Fender. We will be safer that way. When I get to the Ivory Coast, I will sell all my oil and come back with lots of money and goodies for all of you."

"How long will you be gone?" I ask.

"I don't know," Mama says. "But I do know that you children will be safe here with Grandma and your aunts and uncles. It makes my life so much easier to know that you are safe, tucked away here in the village. So please, tell me that you will enjoy yourself while I am away. Run and play and swim and fish with Grandma Yeayea all you want, until Mama comes back."

"I'll look after them, Mama," Nyempu says. She is holding Fungbeh and she gives him a little squeeze. "Until you get back. But you have to promise you are coming back."

"Yeah, promise," I tell her.

"Promise," Kormah adds.

Mama smiles at us and looks at Kulubah, "I assume you want me to promise too?" When Kulubah nods, Mama kisses her on the forehead. "I promise."

That night, we all snuggle together, each of us trying to stay as close to Mama as we can. I cry a little in the night, but I turn my head to the wall so that no one can see. As I lay in the darkness, I feel my heart breaking. This time, Mama isn't just going into the city. She is going on a dangerous mission that could take her away from me forever.

The next morning, we all gathers at Grandma's house to help Mama, Annie, and Alfred get ready for their trip. Uncle Flomo brings over a wagon he built for them to carry the gallons of oil. He ties everything down under a tarp.

In the yard, Mama hugs us tight and gives us a million kisses. Then she tells us to be good for everyone. She advises us to catch lots of fish for her and to grow as many vegetables as we can to show her when she gets back. I hold on to Mama as tight as I can and squeeze my eyes tight to keep the tears from coming out.

As I watch her walk away, I feel Mama taking my heart with her. I try not to think about what it will be like for Mama to be out there again—going from city to city out in the war. I send up a prayer for her that God will protect her and keep her safe, but the truth is, I really don't know if I will ever see Mama again.

Mama Neyor's Palm oil

Scan the QR-Code and navigate to Ch. 36 for a chance to get a unique souvenir: Mama Neyor's Palm Oil from Mama Neyor's Farm in Garmue.

www.resources.witnessliberia.com

37

The Guinea Kpelle Man and the White Man Help the No Sex Beggars

I try to believe Mama's promise to us, but every day that Mama is away, feels like a year. I do everything I do to prevent my mind from imagining her as the victim of the horrors we saw on our travels from Gaye Church. We are setting up lunch around the fire. I feel like crying. I cannot eat today.

"How many days has it been, Nyempu?" I ask her this every day, sometimes many times a day.

"It has been twenty-seven days," Grandma replies.

"She's not coming back, baby! I told her not to go!" Kormah says. "And stop asking that all the time." He gives me a little shove and I almost drop my food. I go to hit him back and Nyempu runs to him, too, with her arm raised to punch him. "Stop!" she yells. Grandma is yelling the same thing.

Aunt Gormah comes and sends them both off to do something. She hugs me. "She will be back soon. She promised."

Auntie's hug gives me courage. I know that sometimes she must be thinking the same things I am thinking. She was there, too. She saw all that I saw. I see her and grandma sit together and whisper sometimes. I bet they are whispering about Mama, and Auntie Annie, and Uncle Alfred. She leans on her mother like I wish I could lean on mine.

Aunt Gormah takes me with her to the bush but Aunt Garmen has other plans for us. We are going hunting: just Aunt Garmen, Kormah, and the other boys. Uncle Thomas is coming, too. Nyempu does not get to come. She has to stay and help with the little ones.

We head away from Aunt Garmen to check on our traps and to set new ones. I know how to set my own traps now. I run to see if I caught anything and i have a squirrel! I take it to show Aunt Garmen. On her trap is a possum. We bend to take it from the trap and reset it. The other boys are not yet back.

"This possum is not starving like the rest of us," says Aunt Garmen. "It is a good size."

As we bend, we hear a rustle. Someone or something is coming through the bush, right off the path we just left but in the opposite direction from where Kormah and the other boys are. For now we are hidden. I move backwards deeper into the bush, but Aunt Garmen does not appear to be afraid. She holds a stick and is ready to pounce if need be.

It is an older man with three boys. The one that is around Kormah's age has a red cloth wrapped around his head like he is a rebel. My heart stops but then I remember: we are in rebel territory now. It is okay to be a rebel, and he is probably just playing. There are no other boys dressed like him with them. We step out, leaving the possum and squirrel near our trap.

"Catuwa. Ku munnie?" *Hello. How you doing?* says the man.

"Hello, Uncle!" Like Aunt Garmen, I note that their basket is empty. "You going to town?" she asks.

"Yes, I just came from Gbounoi. Bad things happening there. Rebels came there and *tabey* some people. Mulba would not give his chickens."

"Mulba? Mulba Tokpah?" The man nods his head. "I know him! Him and his chicken business. He will die for them one day!"

"Well, they beat him good and left him tied up tight, laying right there. Arms up like a grasshopper. Neighbors found him in the morning." The man chuckled. "They kill all his chickens in front of him and cook them right there. Then they went next door to Ma Musu kitchen to get some rice. The poor lady begged them to let her keep her last bit of rice, but took it by force. Those boys, I tell you, not playing with nobody. They cook and eat Mulba's three chickens right before him! Beat him for keeping food from them. 'Freedom fighters' they call themselves . They are coming in the country parts now, too, and you have to be careful, ooh." He looks at me. "Be careful, young boy. They could come here next. Don't keep your food in town. Ok?"

I think of Grandma Yeayea's farm: now I understand why the farm is so far away from the village.

"Thank you for the news, Uncle," says Auntie Garmen. "We will try to keep out of the way and hope that they run Doe out soon."

"Yes, ooh. We pray for that. God is good and will end this war soon. I hear the rebels are right upon them and pushing them out of their last spot of Monrovia. Doe will be gone soon!"

The boys don't speak to me and I say nothing to them. I am happy that they leave quickly. We waved and go back to set our traps. It is odd. I see that I am hoping the rebels win. But the rebels are bad. I saw that. I wish Mama was here. I just want Mama back.

Two days later, we are all having supper with Grandma Yeayea when Mama, Cousin Annie, and Cousin Alfred surprise us all and walk into the house.

"Mama!" I drop my spoon and leap from the ground to meet her, as does everyone else. Her arrival is so sudden that it takes a moment for my brain to catch up to the fact that Mama is standing right in front of us. There's lots of kissing and hugging and Mama holds on to each for a really long time. She even cries a little as everyone welcomes them back.

We gather to see all the wonderful things they have brought from the Ivory Coast. Nyempu, Kormah, Kulubah, Fungbeh and me are practically glued to Mama's side the entire night. I breathe in her smells, the sound of her voice, and the warmth of her laugh. Later, when everything has settled down, Mama gathers us together in her room.

"Listen," she says. "I have something to tell you."

Nyempu sits up. "What is it Mama? Are you leaving again?"

"Yes and no," Mama says. "We are all leaving Liberia tomorrow."

Kormah shoots up from where is laying. "What?"

"Shhh," Mama says. "Keep your voice down. Your Grandma is already very upset by this, but I have discussed it with her and it is settled."

"Mama, how on earth are all of us going to make it all the way to the Ivory Coast?" Nyempu asks. "You said before you left that it was impossible."

"Not anymore," Mama says. "I have papers for all of us, and now that I have money, I can pay a rebel driver to drive us straight though."

"But they will never do that if they think we are leaving the country," Nyempu says.

"You let me worry about all of that," Mama says. "Tonight, we get rest and tomorrow, my children, I am getting you out of here."

Before we are finished asking Mama a million questions, she tucks us in and tells us to have sweet dreams. It has been much easier living in the country the last three months. I don't have as many nightmares, and I almost always sleep through the night. But this night, after Mama tucks us in, I lie awake thinking of what it will be like to leave. I have never been outside Liberia, and though it is plagued by war, it is still my home. Things have moved quickly ever since Mama got back. One minute we were enjoying another lazy day in the village, and the next we are planning a major escape. I guess I should be used to that by now, given our lives since the war started. I am worried about leaving the peaceful happiness of Grandma Yeayea's village behind, but I have learned that when Mama says it's time to go, it's time to go.

My stomach gets butterflies just thinking about it. I cannot sleep. I see Mama slip away when she thinks we are all asleep and decide tonight would be a great night to play spy. I haven't done this for a while, but if we are leaving tomorrow, I need to know more.

The adults are sitting around the fire and I hear Uncle Alfred laughing as he talks. The other grownups are laughing so hard they are gasping. "Tell us again, Alfred – tell us about these No Sex Beggars!"

"I know forever I can trust the honor of my wife! We tried for days to get out of Gbanga. No one would give us a ride. No one! We had fifteen dollars only and they wanted thirty-five dollars apiece. We were there a whole week and I was thinking we would have to give up and come back, but Neyor, she would not let us turn back. We were there a second week, and I was saying, 'this is no good – we must go back' but Neyor would not leave. That day I was going to insist but I heard a man speaking Kpelle and he had a truck! In those weeks I had never seen a civilian operating a truck on the roads. Maybe if he was from Nimbo County or from the Gio or Mano tribe, but him? I was shocked!

"I said to a rebel 'who is dat man? He not Gio or Mano man,' and the rebel says 'he Guinea Kpelle man who pays us good money to let him do business here. He goes back and forth through Bong County and everybody lets him through. He gives us what we want, so we don't bother him too much. He negotiates well, we get a lot from him, so we let him go through.'

"Well this Guinea Kpelle man was just as shocked as me when I told him I was travelling with two Kpelle women. We didn't have the money, but he gave us a ride because he knew no one else would. He figured it could help because I was Gio, so if we had trouble, I could do some talking for him. So we went with him as far as we could. We were at a checkpoint and nothing we said was working! I thought they were going to kill this man!"

"Yes!" chimes in Auntie Annie. "We got through so many checkpoints but this one looked like the end. We were in Ghanta City. Almost half way to Ivory Coast. And each time, when we got trouble with the rebel, Alfred would speak and they would hear he was Mano and they would let us through. But not this one! They got on the truck like it was theirs and we were so sure we were going to lose all the palm oil. We were worried for this Guinea Kpelle man. But then, Sis Neyor, oh my God – Sis Neyor and her craziness!"

Mama tries to interrupt, but Auntie Annie wants to tell this part of the story. "Alfred stayed with the Guinea Kpelle man and he was trying to keep them from killing us. We went off to sell some palm oil – we hoped we could sell enough to bribe the rebels. Then, if you can believe it, we saw a white man! A white man in the middle of this war? He looked wealthy – he had to be to pay all the bribes to stay alive. We figured we must get help so we went to him."

Auntie Annie and Uncle Alfred are giggling and I don't know why. Auntie Annie tries to talk, but keeps getting into fits of giggles so Mama takes over: "So I ask him what he is doing here? And he says back to me 'what are you doing here?' He thinks I must be rebel and I whisper – 'I was a nurse at Phebe Hospital and my husband worked at BCADP before all of this. We even built a pharmacy in our community. I know that it could get me killed to say it, but, Mr. Hassan, I am not a part of the rebels and this war. God willing, if I can get my children out of this country, we never will. I have come all the way from Gbarnga City and we just need help to make it the rest of the way.

"'Wait,' he said. 'Gbarnga? How long were you there? At that checkpoint?'

"I told him that we'd been there a few weeks. We couldn't get a ride because—' and he interrupted me and said very loudly, 'Because you wouldn't sleep with the rebels! You and your cousin! You are the No Sex Beggars!' He was pointing at us and laughing so hard that everyone turned and looked at us. He said 'I have heard all about you! You and your cousin have made quite a reputation

for yourselves. You are the no sex beggar women! Everyone knows
about you! I will help you.' And he went and paid the bribes the
rebels wanted and made them take our oil and put it in his truck.
Then we let the Kpelle man go back to Gbanga City. Without Hassan, we would all have been dead right now!"

"Well, the back of that truck was disgusting. It smelled so
bad and when he closed the doors on us, we could not see our
hands in front of our faces! We could hardly breathe. And every checkpoint we had to get out. I would say: 'My husband left
months ago, and I have not seen him since. I'm now stuck with
five children that I must take care of all by myself, you know what
I mean? I say, my people, the children have nothing on them—
not even shoes on their naked feet! I just want to go sell my oil
tomorrow at the market day at the next town and buy some
things for my children. They have to be ready for the new schools
Charles Taylor is opening. Things have been so bad for me and
my family.'

"When I was speaking, I was trying so hard not to vomit. It was
bad, bad, bad in the back of the truck. The rebels looked at me, I was
sweaty and I must have looked as bad as I felt. One of them said 'That
true what the Old Ma is talking. The woman look like she suffering
for sure. Look how dry she looking. Let the Old Ma and her sister go.
Hassan will take care of us. Leave her oil alone. Let her get to
the market.'"

Everyone laughed again at Mama's description because she was
doing the actions and copying the accents of the rebels.

"We almost died again at the Lagatuo Checkpoint" Uncle Alfred said solemnly. "Hassan told us it would be hard. This checkpoint is the most heavily guarded in the entire country. It is through
Logatuo that Charles Taylor's rebels entered Nimba County, armed
with military supplies and extra rebels. So as soon as the truck
stopped, the doors fly open. These rebels were angry! They were angry at Hassan. And didn't even wait for us to come out. They came
in and threw us out of the truck like we were ragdolls. They yelled

at Hassan, 'Who are these people here? Why do you have them in the back of the truck? Why you trying to cross over the border? Where are your papers?' They are saying all this, and even Hassan's rebel protectors could not calm them down. I started to talk and because they could hear I am Mano, they started to listen.

"But still they are angry. Neyor told her story. She told them she is getting the kids ready for Charles Taylor's school but that didn't calm them down enough. 'What business do you have in Ivory Coast?' they kept asking this, then they pushed me against the bed of the trailer. I was sure we were done for. They took the oil and they said 'This oil now belongs to Charles Taylor.' They had their guns out and Hassan's rebels were powerless against them. In all that chaos, they had Hassan at gunpoint too! He looked afraid and then he yelled 'Wait! You will be making a terrible mistake if you do anything to hurt the VP Commander's brother!

"'What VP brother? What you talking about, Hassan?'

'Him!' he pointed at me. 'You can see right now that he is Mano. How can you treat the VP Commander's brother this way?' And then I knew right away what to do! I had them then. The rebels all stopped in their tracks and turned their eyes to me. They started to talk to me in Gio. Thank God, I know how to speak both Mano and Gio! 'What is this the man talking about?' they asked me in Gio. They started to interrogate me. All of them yelling at once! I said in Gio, "My brother is Enoch Dogolea. Why do you think I am here doing business? I told them all about Enoch: where we grew up, even about how he got the scar beneath his chin. I told them, 'I am here to do business in Ivory Coast and I am stopping by to do some business with my family on the way.' I figured they probably were guarding him too – and I knew exactly where Enoch moved his family. When they realized I knew Enoch's hideout location, their faces changed. 'Oh, God! You are really his brother!'

"One of the rebels put his arm around me and said 'It is my pleasure to escort the VP Commander's brother to do his business!' Only then did we allow ourselves to breathe. We were sure it was over until then. Then the head rebel yelled to all the other ones to stop hassling us! And he said 'We have very important guests here at Lagotuo Gate today! We must let them through. Papers or no papers. We will figure it out. Put the oil back on the truck and move them along quickly. They are very important people.'"

Uncle Alfred stopped then. And all the grownups were quiet for a moment. "And that is how we got into Ivory Coast."

Sex Trafficking Awareness

No Sex Beggars
After finishing this chapter, scan the QR-Code and navigate to Ch. 37 to bring awareness to Sex Trafficking, the world's fastest growing crime.

www.resources.witnessliberia.com

38

Silly Flip-Flop Slippers

Late November 1990

W e were so popular in the Ivory Coast market," Auntie Annie continued. "We were swarmed. We sold the oil in minutes! With all that money, it was easy to bribe a rebel to drive us all the way back. And at each checkpoint, this crazy one," she pointed at Mama, "kept talking about how excited she was about Charles Taylor's schools. And she showed them the shoes she got for the kids. She gave them all, all the rebels we passed, some salt. I thought she was nuts to give those evil men so much of her salt. But when she told me of her plan, I understood that she was even more crazy than I thought!"

Early the next morning, Mama wakes us and packs everything for our journey. "Here," she says, digging into her bag. "I promised each of you a new pair of shoes. And you each have your own color."

"Oh, yes Mama!" Nyempu says running over and peering in the bag. "Which color is mine?"

"Pink of course," Mama says.

"What about me?" I ask.

"You get green. Kormah, you get blue."

Mama hands out all of our shoes. I eagerly grab my pair. Until now, I have forgotten what it feels like to actually have on shoes. I try to think back to when I lost my mine. It was probably as I was running after that first ambush. After that, I walked so many hours in the hot sun every day without shoes. Hours on hours just moving, day after day. All day we would walk on the tarmac of the roads, over rocks, over sticks, over broken glass sometimes too, through deep puddles during the pelting rains of the rainy season. My legs just carried me like they were separate from the rest of me. I was so hungry and so tired yet my feet kept moving even when my head told me I could not go any further. Sometimes the burning of my feet would at least make me forget the cramping of my empty stomach.

By the time we got back to Sugar Hill, none of us had shoes. Once we were home, Uncle Thomas found some old tires and crafted us each a pair of sandals out of them. We did not know at that time we were not through with walking. As we walked from Sugar Hill to Grandma's farm, the heat of the road seemed to make those tire shoes almost melt; some of my sores were burns from those tire shoes. I threw them away as soon as we got here. Even with all these weeks at the farm, my feet ache and I have sores that still have not healed.

I sit down and try to slip the flip flops on and notice how the black of the tarmac has discolored the bottom of my feet; they are no longer clear and pale but instead spotted with dirt buried into my skin. My soles are almost as black as my skin.

I'm so disappointed; They do not fit. I take them off and stare at them again. I frown trying to figure out what is wrong with these shoes Mama has brought us from the Ivory Coast.

"Mama," Nyempu says, holding up her shoes. "These are the wrong shoes for each foot!"

"Yea," I say frowning. "These shoes don't go."

Kormah has somehow managed to wriggle both of his feet into the slippers, even though his shoes are also on the wrong way. "Mama, I have two rights."

"And I have two lefts!" I say.

"This looks stupid!" Kormah says flinging off his slippers. "There is no way in the world I am wearing these slippers!"

Mama stands up and looks at all of us. "I don't have time for this. Not this morning," she says sharply. "I don't care if you think your slippers are stupid or not. You will put those shoes on and you will be happy about it."

I cross my arms and stare at Mama. "I will just go barefoot then."

"Fine! Then you'll walk all the way to the Ivory Coast barefoot. I will gather our things so we can go. And I don't want to hear anything else about these slippers!"

An hour or so later, we say goodbye to the village and our family there. I can see the worry all over Grandma Yeayea's face as she hugs and kisses all over us. Everyone seems to think that Mama is making a big mistake trying to escape the country, but they know she cannot be swayed. This time, we are not a large group. Aunt Gormah and her children are staying behind. Now it is just Mama, Uncle Thomas, and the five us of us facing the rebels and the entire world alone.

We arrive at the busy Gbarnga City checkpoint and Mama instructs us all to hold hands and stay close. Mama walks right up to a rebel truck and takes a large sum of money.

"I need a ride to Ivory Coast," Mama tells the man.

"Aye, look! It is the No Sex Beggar!" the man says with a smile. "I already told you, money only," he says, mocking the line that earned Mama her nickname.

"Fine," Mama says handing him money. "Does this cover it?"

The man's eyes grow huge when he sees the money Mama hands him. He looks past Mama at all of us. "You going to sell more oil?"

"I sold the oil," Mama says.

"Where you going now?" he asks.

"Will sixty dollars apiece get us all the way to the Ivory Coast?

I have more business to attend to there and buy more things to sell and settle with some people too. Or do we need to try someone else?"

The rebel raises his hand, "Sixty apiece? Say no more, Old Ma. You and your children have a ride here. I'll pick up a few more people and we can leave in an hour."

When the time comes, we make our way to the truck, one that is very similar to the truck that we took from Fender. This truck has more room and we are all able to sit comfortably. I am glad that we finally have a chance to sit. My feet are killing me in these awful slippers Mama has brought back to us. They have started to cut into my feet on the walk to Gbarnga. I wonder bitterly if that's how they make shoes in the Ivory Coast.

I look around the busy checkpoint as the truck begins to load with a few more travelers. The rebels make conversation with each other. Most of them are holding guns and wearing the trademark red bandannas on their head or arms. They seem comfortable here in our city, running everything as if it is their own. I guess it is all theirs now, as they have managed to take control of the entire country.

Mama gets everyone settled in their seats and tells us again to be on our best behavior. She reassures us that everything is going to be fine. Soon, the truck is loaded up with the rest of the travelers and our journey to Ivory Coast begins.

My stomach is filled with butterflies as the truck rolls forward, leaving Gbarnga City. Everyone in the truck seems to be in their own world, with a lot on their minds. I can tell from some of the people's faces that they are weary. In the village, we ate decent food most of the time and built up our strength, but I can tell these people have not been so lucky. When we start to approach another checkpoint, I feel the usual fear rising. I look at Mama and notice that she does not seem nervous, so I try not to be either. As expected, the rebels approach the truck and order us all out. We comply and the soldiers begin their usual round of questioning all the travelers. When it's our turn, one of them looks right at Mama.

"Old Ma, what you doing coming back this way?" he asks. "You just came here yesterday. Where you going now?"

My heart leaps right into my throat and I look up at Mama to see what her answer is.

"Oh," Mama says plainly. "You are not going to believe this! I have to go back to the marketplace in the next town. I bought the shoes I showed you for my children, but look!" Mama points down at our feet, which are barely inside the ill-fitting shoes. "The woman at the market, she took my money, ripped me off, and gave me these crazy shoes for my children!"

The rebel soldier looks at our feet and bursts into laughter. "Oh, my goodness! Look at these stupid-looking slippers!"

I am already mad at having to wear the stupid-looking slippers and I get even more upset when the rebels start making fun of us.

"Oh, and look there at the little man sour face!" another says. "I would be vex too if it was me." All the soldiers erupt into laughter. They clearly remember Mama and are very comfortable talking and laughing around her.

"You see!" Mama says. "I am so vexed right now! I cannot have my children looking like this! They will be the laughing stock of the entire school. I cannot do this to them. I tell you, that woman at the market, she ripped me off! How can she do this to me? That is why I am going back to try on new shoes and get the right ones for the children. I need to go and deal with her today. It won't be easy in the market today. My children can't walk around like this!"

"Oh, Old Ma, you too nice. You don't deserve this," the first rebel soldier says. "You did well to bring us salt when you come through the other day. You a nice lady, Old Ma. You work too hard to get these for your children! You need to go back there and get this straightened out. Go ahead. You and your children get back on the truck. You are fine. And if that market woman give you hard time, come tell us. We will deal with her."

I let out a small sigh of a relief when I hear this. Somehow these rebels are really sweet on Mama.

"Thank you," Mama says, pushing us back toward the truck. "I cannot wait to get this fixed."

"Good luck, mismatched kids!" the other soldier calls out with a laugh.

We get back on the truck and we are still frowning at being made fun of for our shoes. Soon, the truck lurches forward again, and we are on our way. At each checkpoint, the same scene repeats. We get off the truck, the rebels remember Mama, she shows them our slippers, they make fun of us, then let us pass right on through to the next town. After getting through three cities this way, I sit staring down at my feet as we ride. I am trying to understand how in the world someone as smart as Mama could possibly buy the wrong shoes. Then again, I guess it has worked out to our benefit because it is the only reason the rebel soldiers are so easy on us.

Then it hits me. Mama is not stupid at all. She bought the wrong slippers on purpose. As the truck bumps along, I sit back and think about all of this. Mama left the village with palm oil, telling the rebels at each checkpoint that she was just going to the next town over to sell oil to buy shoes for her children. Mama must have done this all the way up the Ivory Coast, knowing that if she gave the same story in each town, the rebels would not suspect her of trying to escape. On her trip back, she was sure to show the rebels at every checkpoint the shoes and give them a little salt. Now, Mama is using the story of the mismatched slippers to get us all to Ivory Coast again.

At our next checkpoint, I watch as Mama hops off the truck and effortlessly runs through her routine, working her magic to gain us safe passage to the next town. She has figured out how to use the rebel's greed and arrogance for our benefit. The rebels are so high on their belief that Charles Taylor is a wonderful leader, they easily give Mama a pass when she tells them her children will be going to one of his schools. They have so destroyed the country that even something salt is a treasure, and Mama uses this to her advantage as well. Now that I have figured out what Mama is doing, I relax a little, seeing the brilliance in her plan. Their own greed and arrogance are how Mama is able to slip us all through the country right under their noses.

Our truck stops at a checkpoint overnight and Mama buys a few mats for us to spread next to the truck, so that we can sleep near the checkpoint. Mama also buys us rice, pepper soup, and mango. I can only imagine how much this has cost. As we huddle together eating and resting, Mama lets us know that we are more than halfway there and that tomorrow everything will change.

In the morning, we load up and drive another four hours toward the Ivory Coast. I am nodding off when I notice everyone around perk up and move about in the truck. I look up and instantly I know that we are approaching the border. Most of the passengers who started the journey with us have gotten off. Those who remain are anxiously watching everything. The VP Checkpoint at Legato is bustling with lots of activity and commotion. There are rebel soldiers everywhere, all clad with AK-47s.

"Eyes up, children," Mama says. "Be quiet and stay close to me. We are about to cross the border."

Mama makes sure we are alert as the truck rolls to a stop. All of us are wide awake and anxious as the truck creeps forward. I scoot closer to Mama and say a quick prayer. I know how serious this moment is. Either we will be successfully cross into Ivory Coast or we will be killed. Butterflies fill my stomach as rebel soldiers approach our truck. As expected, they demand that everyone get out. We quickly shuffle out of the truck and stand under the blaze of the sun, waiting for the rebels to reach us. After what feels like an eternity, it is our turn to be interrogated.

A tall rebel soldier with bullets strapped across his chest approaches us and peers down at Mama. "What you doing here woman? What's going on? These your children? Where you going? Tell me now!"

Mama calmly tells the soldier that she needs to go the market place and explains her story about the shoes. The soldier looks down at our feet. Our mismatched slippers looked just as ridiculous as they have before, but now our feet are swollen, to add to the horrible image.

The solider frowns at the sight of our feet in the slippers and looks back at Mama with disbelief. "Someone sold you these?"

"Yes," Mama says. "Right over there at the marketplace. I come to Ivory Coast because they are supposed to have the best shoes and clothes, but the woman took my money and give me this mess here for my children to be shame everyday going to school!" Without missing a beat, Mama pulls out the Lassie Passé papers she purchased and shows them to the rebel soldiers. "Sir, you know Charles Taylor been saying all the children should go to school. My children cannot start school looking like this. I need her to fix this. It is an embarrassment!"

"Okay, I hear you," he says, looking at the papers and then back at our slippers. "Listen, woman, if you are going to be raising these children right, you really have to watch your back with these market people. If you are not careful, they will pull a fast one right in front of your face."

He hands Mama the papers. "Okay, you are fine. You and your children can get back on the truck." He waves at the rebel soldier a few feet away, signaling that everything is okay.

As soon as the rebel turns his attention to the next person, we all climb back onto the truck as fast as we can and sit still as stones, waiting for whatever is next. I have a strange feeling, like we have stolen something and are hoping not to get caught. I get more afraid when I see one of the men from our truck being pulled away. As soon as I see the rebels grab him, I turn my head, but I can still hear his pleas. I can tell that everyone still on the truck feels terrible about this, but none of us says a word or moves a muscle. Mama keeps her face calm and motionless as she squeezes Fungbeh closer to her chest. I tell myself to act like I belong right where I am so I don't look suspicious.

After what feels like forever, the rest of the travelers are allowed back on and the truck begins to move. I hold my breath as the truck inches forward. We all remain completely silent, holding our breath as we cross over the Liberian border and into the Ivory Coast.

Silly Flip-Flops Souvenir
Scan the QR-Code and navigate to Ch. 38 for
a chance to get your own pair of Mama Neyor's Silly Flip-Flops Souvenir.

www.resources.witnessliberia.com

39

A New Place Call Freedom

Late November 1990

The other side of the border is not protected by rebels, but by official government soldiers who nod and smile at us. They simply ask for our Lassie Passé papers that allow us into the Ivory Coast. Mama looks at us all squeezed tightly together. She pulls me closer and reaches for Nyempu and Kormah to lean into her arms. I glimpsed Mama's face, her eyes filled with emotion. She looks across at Uncle Thomas, and I see him smile at Mama. The tears escape her face, dripping onto my hand that rests on her lap. This is a tear of joy, so I don't mind it. I can see the happiness in Mama's eyes through her tears. "We are refugees now in the Ivory Coast, children, but we are free. We are free now."

The truck comes to a stop at the buzzing market ground, in the city of Danane. Our family eagerly jumps down, looking around at our new surroundings and taking it all in. Everyone is speaking French. As soon as the rebel driver pulls off, Mama grabs each of us and holds us tight.

"Oh, thank you, Jesus!" Mama says. "Thank you, God." More tears stream down Mama's face, as she kisses each of us. She keeps hugging us and thanking God over and over. As I lean against Mama, I understand why she is crying. Almost a year after the start of the war, Mama has somehow managed to escape the unimaginable, getting all of her children to safely to freedom. We all just stand there for a moment, huddled together right in the middle of the market place.

Once we have calmed down and Mama has wiped her tears, we take a moment and look around. Mama tells us that the first stop she is going to make is at the marketplace so we can get the right shoes. I am glad to hear this, but I am still a little stunned at the environment around me. Everyone in Ivory Coast seems to be walking and living freely without a care in the world. In Ivory Coast, the government is intact, there is no war, and they are seemingly untouched by what is going on in Liberia. As we walk through the market place, I keep looking around, halfway expecting to be stopped or moved off the road by a truck full of rebels. But that does not happen. Apparently, no one here answers to anyone but themselves. There isn't a sad or angry face in sight.

My brain is trying to understand how there is no fear here when just few miles behind us is endless terror and starvation. Cars come and go freely on the roads and children laugh and run and play. The air even smells different here and the people here seem free to breathe as much of it as they like. I am shocked at the drastic difference between this quiet and happy place and the war-torn Liberia down the road. Stepping over a single line, we have entered a whole other universe—one filled with people who have not a care in the world. I cannot believe it. Now I understand why Mama worked so hard to get us here. By doing so, she has probably saved our lives.

Just as Mama promised, we stop at the marketplace to buy new shoes. Mama explains that she is going to use her remaining money to buy us some food, and then we will go to a friend Mrs. Woto's house, where we have been invited to stay.

I am still trying to wrap my head around the fact we are doing as we please and are not running from death. Occasionally I see Mama wipe away a tear as she moves about the marketplace.

While Mama is buying supplies, the woman working the stand notices that we are Liberians and tells Mama that there is a refugee camp up the road. She also tells Mama about a nearby bank, in case Mama knows relatives who can send her money. Mama thanks the woman but does not mention that all of our family is back in Liberia, trapped, poor, and unable to help us with anything. When Mama pays the woman for our goods, I notice that Mama has some money left over and I hope it is enough to keep us afloat while we are here. We leave the marketplace and Mama tells us that we are going to head toward the refugee camp.

"Why are we going there, Mama?" Kormah asks. "I thought we were going to stay at the lady, Mrs. Woto's house."

"We are, but. . ." Mama looks down at the remaining money in her hand. "I think we need to try to make a phone call. So, we will go through the refugee camp to this Telecomm place." Mama takes a deep breath and looks at all of us. "I am going to try to call Papa."

My heart races as Mama leads us to the refugee camp, which is about a quarter mile away. My head is spinning at the idea of connecting with Papa. I find myself wiping away tears as we walk. Kormah and Nyempu are asking Mama questions, but I don't say much. Uncle Thomas is holding Kulubah's hands and walking alongside.

My mind is thinking about the past nine months. Now we are walking through a free country and the war cannot touch us. I think about how Mama sang African hymns to us during cold and depressing nights to bring us comfort during the worst times of our lives. I think about how Mama saved me at the ambush at Duport Road and how she continued to be our hero day after day, month after month. As we approach the refugee camp, I am still amazed at how Mama used something as simple as slippers and oil to help us escape to the Ivory Coast, right before the rebel's eyes. Most of all, I cannot believe that we are finally free.

The refugee camp in Ivory Coast reminds me a lot of Fender. Hundreds of tarp tents line either side of a dirt road. I see people

milling about their tents. The difference between this camp and
Fender is that these people are not afraid, though they do look
depressed and hungry.

Mama leads us to what looks like a giant, crowded picnic pavilion. A woman sits at a small school desk. Mama tells her that
she is looking for the telephone station. The woman walks us to a
booth under the pavilion, where a few wooden booths are occupied
by people talking on phones. My mind is still racing at the idea of
reaching Papa after so long. It has been almost a year since I last
heard his voice. Just thinking of calling Papa makes me tremble.
Is it even possible to call across the ocean? How does Mama know
where to reach him? Does he think we are dead? What if he has
found a way back into the country and is now running around
Liberia looking for us?

"Hello," Mama greets the woman standing at the booth. "I
need to try to make a call."

"Okay. Where are you calling?" The woman asks with a quick
smile.

"I want to call the United States," Mama responds.

"Ok. It will be twenty dollars for a fifteen-minute call."

"Okay." Mama reaches in her wallet and hands the lady a
twenty-dollar bill and the woman directs us toward the wooden
booths.

"Do you think you can reach him?" Nyempu asks. Her voice is
shaking. "Do you think you can actually reach Papa?"

"I don't know," Mama says. "All I have is this old phone number he gave me before he left. So, I am going to try, okay? We have
to at least try."

The woman leads us over to a wooden booth with a single
chair; the telephone sitting on the wooden table.

"You can make any international call you like," the woman
says. "But you only get one call or else it will be another twenty
dollars."

"Thank you," Mama says, swallowing hard.

"What is the number, Old Ma?" the lady asks.

Mama sits down slowly and fishes a tattered piece of paper from her purse. I recognize the paper with the number scribbled on it. My mind flashes back to the day Mama and I went to Telecomm near home, and I remember her jotting down a phone number while she talked to Papa. I realize that Mama has given her last dime for one chance to call a number that Papa gave her over nine months ago. My heart beats wildly in my chest as I watch Mama try to straighten out the paper and I wonder how in the world she has managed to hold on to it for so long. The paper is torn, and the ink has started to bleed. The phone number has faded quite a bit and Mama has to squint to make out the numbers.

The woman tells Mama, "The country code is zero zero. Then dial one before the area code, okay?"

"Yes, thank you," Mama says. After the woman walks away, Mama sits staring at the phone for a moment. Uncle Thomas grips my shoulder and gives it a quick squeeze. I can tell he is nervous too. Finally, Mama picks up the phone and dials. My heart is caught in my chest as we all watch Mama dial each number. None of us say a word. We all hold our breath until Mama dials the last number on the paper. We wait in silence to see what happens next. We breathe a sigh of relief when we hear the phone begin to ring. My heart skips with each ring and I pray to God that we are able to get through.

Suddenly, there is a voice on the other end. "Hello?"

"Yes, this is Neyor Karmue. Is . . ."

Mama is suddenly interrupted by a man. "Who? What?"

Mama speaks loudly now. "This is Neyor. Is Alfred Fungbeh Karmue there? This is his wife, Neyor!"

We all hover right over Mama's shoulders to hear what little we can.

"Neyor? Neyor! Karmue's Neyor?"

Before Mama can answer, there is loud shouting. We all hear it through the phone. Whoever is on the other end appears to be yelling as loud as they can, calling for someone over and over. Then there is silence and we all just wait. Then, I hear Papa's voice through the receiver.

"Lize! Lize, is that you!" My ear leaps into my throat. I can't believe it. It is Papa!

Mama drops her head and tears stream down Mama's face, as we all inch closer to her.

"Alfred," Mama says her voice breaking with emotion. "It's me."

"Oh, my God! Lize, it is you!" I hear Papa exclaim. "Oh, my God. Lize, please tell me, are you safe? Are all of my children with you? Are you safe?"

"Yes, honey," Mama says, wiping her face. "We made it out to Ivory Coast. We are all here."

"Papa!" we all cry excitedly hoping he can hear us. Tears steam down Nyempu's face and she calls his name again.

"Who is that?" Papa says. "Those are my kids?"

Mama laughs. "Yes, those are our kids, Alfred. I have them all with me. We all made it."

"Tell me," Papa says. "Nyempu is there?"

"Yes, Nyempu is here."

"Kormah and Austin, are they there, Lize? Are they safe?"

"Kormah is here, Austin is with your father. They are both safe."

Papa sounds as if he is trembling and I stand on my tiptoes just to be closer to the sound of his voice. "Quanei is there with you?" I can tell now that Papa is crying on the other end of the phone, and we are all crying now too.

"Yes, Alfred. Quanei is safe. He is right here too."

"Kulubah and Fungbeh?" Papa asks.

"Yes. And Thomas too."

"Let me speak to them," Papa says, weeping. "I want to hear all of their voices. Lize, I…"

When Papa stops talking, I somehow know that it is because he has broken down into tears. I wish so badly that I could wrap my arms around his neck and hug him.

"It's okay now, Alfred." Mama says, wiping away tears of her own. "We did it. We are all free. We are all here. We are all safe. And most importantly, we are still all together. We made it and for the first time in a very long time, our family is okay."

Be A Witness in Liberia
After finishing this chapter, scan the QR-Code and navigate to Ch. 39.
Explore the possibility of being a Witness in Liberia.

www.resources.witnessliberia.com

EPILOGUE

Troublemaker

Late Fall 1993

I t is almost three years before we are all in the same home again, together as a family, reunited with both Papa. We take a plane and leave behind the refugee camps of Ivory Coast.

"It will be cold in New York, that is where the plane will take us," Papa says.

"I know, Papa, I have heard it is cold there. Just like being near the mountain in Garmue in the rainy season, right, Papa?"

"Even colder than that, Quanei, but don't worry—we have heavier clothes for the American cold."

I wonder how it could be colder in New York than near the mountain and find out as soon as we step out of the airport. The freezing wind causes me to hold my breath; it surprises me to see the misty air coming out of my mouth like a cloud of smoke. A smiling, tall and slender Black American man, comes towards us. Papa introduces him as his friend, Mr. Williams. Mr. Williams takes us to his mini-van. "This will be like driving from Gbarnga to Monrovia," Papa announces and we take off, heading to Rhode Island.

We're all tired but excited to smell the American air. Our new home is in a large brick apartment complex with three tall stories in Providence, much larger than our home on Sugar Hill. To me, it is paradise. Papa feeds us so much big chicken legs, American mashed potatoes, and rice. He is teaching us to be American. He tells us to call him "Daddy" instead of "Papa." I prefer to say "Papa" but if I'm going to be American, I guess I have to call him "Daddy" from now on. Every morning, he makes hot chocolate with little white sponge-like things he calls "marshmallows." The drink reminds me of medicine. I don't like the way it looks. Some days, I feel tired of eating.

I am 12 years old and happy to start my new life in this new place where Papa lives. We all get to go back to school: the only school that was in the camp was so overcrowded that we all had to sit on each other laps, bunched together like sardines in a can. I am excited to see what an American school will be like. We have not done much school learning for going on five years.

In my new backpack is a case with colored pencils which I sharpened myself. It includes notebooks in which I carefully wrote my name, the whole thing, "Quanuquanei Alfred Karmue," right on the cover. Papa does not yet have a car of his own in America so he borrows one from our neighbor, Aunty Wonica, to take us to school the first day. Once there, he walks us to a building with over 1000 students in it. My jaw drops when I see how high and wide it is.

There are only about 40 kids in the classroom I am taken to. I note that all the students have their own desks; they are not sitting on the ground on each other laps. I glimpse across the room. I see many children that look just like me; they are my color, perhaps they are Black Americans or could they come from Africa, too? I am shocked to see that some black boys have their hair braided and they have earrings in one ear. I also notice a few white kids. They are not many. The others are all the shades in between. Most of the kids look heavier than me. I'm still a little slender and my face and body are not as full as my classmates'. I am eager to get back to a proper school in America.

The teacher greets me at the door as I walk into the classroom. "Hello, young man, you must be the new student. Call me Mrs. Williams."

I smile and nod gracefully without saying a word.

"Class, attention to me." The kids continue to chatter as she walks to the front of the chalkboard. "Class! Dray! Norman! Stephanie! Turn around! I'm talking!" Mrs. Williams says louder.

"Whatever, who cares," Dray murmurs. The class, chuckles. Dray is tall and dark skinned. He is turned into his seat so he is facing the back of the room. His pants appear oversized and are dragging over his red and white sneakers. We are inside but he is still wearing a heavy jacket over a navy blue oversized shirt. He leans towards a boy I later learn is Norman.

"Dray! Eyes up on me, everyone, all eyes on me now!" she is shouting. I'm in shock. It's hard for me to believe the class response. This would never happen in any school I've been to—not even with our oversize class in the refugee school. "We have a new student," she yells.

I'm still standing near the door. I can feel the fabric of my sweatshirt crawling up my neck as a chill creeps up me like a gecko. Everyone is now looking directly at me. Mrs. Williams motions me to stand with her in the front. Dray and Norman are staring me down.

"Please introduce yourself to the class," Ms. Williams directs.

"My name is Quanuquanei Alfred Karmue" I blurt out.

"What? QuawuQua?" Dray, interrupts.

"Qua-nu-Qua-nei" I repeat.

"Whatever, Kunta Kinte, you ugly African." The class laughs.

I'm confused and don't know how to reply. I look at Ms. Williams.

"Class, Dray, straighten up and cut it out," Ms. Williams shouts. "Welcome to Room 12. Quawu …"

I lean in and whisper, "Call me Quanei."

"Thank you, that's better" she replies as she directs me to my new seat right next to a beautiful white girl with the blue eyes. The girl leans over. "My name is Inez but you can call me I.I.," she whispers. I feel a sense of relief but also a new sense of pressure is building up. I feel the heat of Dray and Norman's eyes boring into my back—they are directly behind me.

My eagerness is erased within weeks by the ridicule of my classmates. They laugh at my clothes, at my shoes, at my accent. They laugh because I was born in Africa. At home, Papa is always at work or telling us to be quiet as he needs to sleep. Mama is busy and when she asks "how was school today?" I say "fine." But it is not. I become lost in a large unfriendly place, clouded by memories of the war and enraged by the taunts of my classmates.

I am now 13. I slide myself into the chair attached to the desk, taking my usual spot. I am avoiding all eye contact. I'm in Mrs. Williams homeroom class. I have been away for three days, my second suspension this year. I hear snickers around me, Jamila whispering something to Alisha. I know it's about me. I feel, rather than see, Dray slip into the seat behind me.

"Good morning, Mr. Karmue. Nice to see you back," says the teacher, Mrs. Williams. The class is now full and when the bell rings, the students take their places and the national anthem comes on. I put my hand on my heart as we all recite the Pledge of Allegiance. Afterward, Mrs. Williams hands back our tests, making comments about the results as she licks a finger to separate each test from the other and places it on the recipient's desk. I get mine back and I am relieved to see it is a B.

This B won't be good enough for Papa, who now looks at me with worried eyes. "I used to only worry about Kormah, now you too, Quanei?" he said when I had to admit to him I had been suspended. "I will not have this! If you continue in this stupidity, I will come to the school and give you my belt in front of your class." I got it real good at home and I went to school today with all intentions of staying out of trouble. I planned to make sure any future beatings continued to take place at home.

Papa does not understand what it was like to deal with the white-boy gang led by Norman. Now Dray and his friends have wedged their way in to become my number one tormentors. All the teachers look at me with suspicion, with mouths pressed tightly and anger in their eyes. They think I am a troublemaker. Nyempu acts like she is my mother. She tells me to stop stressing Papa. "You have a responsibility after all Papa did to get us here. You have to remember you are a child of God, not an American thug. Just walk away when they bother you, Quanei."

And just then, with the teacher's back toward me, I feel it in the back of my neck. The sudden cold of a spitball. Disgusting. I jump up and wipe my neck and turn to face Dray. Where am I to walk away to, I wonder? Where are all these wise advice-givers when this boy is tormenting me like this?

Everyone giggles, and looks at me, waiting for a reaction. But I do nothing. I do not look at them. I turn my head back to the front of the class. I see Mrs. Williams is looking at me with an eyebrow up. I look straight ahead and pretend I do not see her.

How are these teachers so dumb they don't see what Dray does? I don't want to get in trouble again. Not because of him or his dumb side-kick, Conrad. I get blamed when I am only defending myself. I feel my cheeks warm and beads of sweat form despite the cold of the classroom temperature. My stomach is in knots. I think of my father and his threat. I know he would probably do it, he too would torment me in this very room, and then I could never come back to school.

I feel the cold ping of another spitball and I jump up out of my seat. Mrs. Williams looks at me with a worried look in her eyes and I sit down. Then I feel it again and jump up, only to sit down as if pushed back by Mrs. Williams' stare. The spitballs are coming with greater frequency. I look to the left and the right and know the witnesses would pretend they saw nothing. Now they are grinning, looking from me to Dray, from me to Conrad, from me to their cohorts. They are full of glee, waiting for something more interesting to break out, something more dynamic than Mrs. Williams' soliloquy about Charles Dickens and his importance as an American icon.

Dray kicks my chair and I jolt up, almost knocking my desk over. "African booty scratcher," he sneers just loud enough for me and those sitting nearby to hear. My eyes narrow and I move closer to him. I am pleased to see he still has a bruise on his cheek from where I got him a few days ago. Now I take a step closer and I feel—I know—I could kill him. I feel I have the power of ten rebels in me when he whispers again, "African booty scratcher."

"Quanei," Mrs. Williams is standing too, the tension in the room can be seen like smoke. "Quanei, take your seat. Return to your seat right now, Quanei."

"African booty scratcher," Dray taunts.

My whole body is a taut muscle. My next action surprises even me. Instead of killing him, which I know he deserves, I walk to my teacher's desk. I feel like I am about to explode. I walk to her and stand in silence for a few seconds. It feels like ages before I can talk.

"I can't take it," I say and I tell her what is happening.

Mrs. Williams hugs me. Like a mother, she hugs me. I feel like crying, but I won't. Not here in front of them. She hugs me and tells me she is proud of me; she tells me how important today is. She tells me that by controlling myself I am changing my future. She hugs me. She shows me that strangers care.

After she hugged me, Mrs. Williams took me from class to class and told the other teachers what I did. They all said, "Great job! Great job, Quanei." The teachers who once saw me as a troublemaker smiled when they saw me in the halls. From that day onward, I don't want to disappoint anyone anymore.

I become fascinated with art class. One day our art teacher plays a video of a cartoon. I am awestruck when I learn that each image in the animation is drawn by hand. She projects an image of Tweety Bird on a screen and gives us all paper. "Draw Tweety Bird and imagine how many times they had to draw and redraw him to show what looks like smooth movement."

I focus on creating Tweety Bird and block everything else out. When I finish, my drawing turns out exactly like the one on the screen. Everyone circles around me, amazed. People who had picked on me asked me to draw their pictures. It stuns, Norman, one of my worst enemies. He becomes my best friend. It turns out he lives near our building, so we start walking home together each day.

As soon as I reach our building, I race to our apartment and show my drawings to Papa. He buys me paper and I draw the ghetto I see out of the window. I draw whatever I see: the streets, my closet, my shoes, myself in the mirror. Drawing takes my mind to a safe place and is how I find peace in America. My belief that school is the devil changes. I graduate from Oliver Hazard Perry with straight As. I even receive a scholarship to Bancroft Prep School, a prestigious private school. And Mama goes back to school to get her American nursing degree because she does not have any documents from Liberia to prove her qualifications.

Then one day, President Bush announces that the war in Liberia is over. To our amazement, Mama packs her bags. Mama never forgot her promise to God, the promise that saved her as she crouched naked with her eyes closed in prayer in that killing field of bloated, stinking bodies and flies. She had vowed then that if she were spared, she would become a mother to the children whose innocence had been stolen, children like the one who had stood pointing a gun at her head that day, the weapon so large compared to her tiny, child's frame.

The day after President Bush's announcement, Mama steps on a plane without us. Not even Papa goes with her on that first trip. Mama travels back Liberia, to Sugar Hill, to fulfill her promise to God and to make our old home a paradise on Earth once again.

About the Author

Quanuquanei A. Karmue, better known as Q, is a survivor of the Liberian Civil War. He is an artist, activist, and Executive Director and Co-Founder of Save More Kids, Inc. Save More Kids is a non-profit organization dedicated to empowering young people in Liberia to ultimately help in rebuilding a once beautiful country left in devastation due to the war.

Q wrote *Witness*, to take readers through his childhood experience as a boy confronted with the bloodshed and chaos of war-torn Liberia. After escaping to the US through the strength and fortitude of his mother, Q adapted to American life, completed an undergraduate degree from Savannah College of Art & Design (SCAD) and a Masters of Fine Arts Degree at East Tennessee State University (ETSU).

As an adult, Q returned to his native Liberia to help his mother fulfill her promise to God of adopting orphaned children. Renewed with a sense of purpose and a mission greater than himself, Q and his wife, Wendy, formed Save More Kids to provide resources and create opportunities for the forgotten children of post-war Liberia.

WWW.WITNESSLIBERIA.COM

Become a Witness Experience (WE) Ambassador

Now that you have become a Witness, here's an opportunity to take the experience to another level. Click on the QR Code and navigate to the WE button to learn how you can become a WE Ambassador and make your journey even more impactful.

www.resources.witnessliberia.com